PHILOSOPHY THROUGH FILM

PHILOSOPHY THROUGH FILM

Mary M. Litch

Routledge
New York   London

Published in 2002 by

Routledge
270 Madison Avenue
New York, NY 10016

Published in Great Britain by
Routledge
2 Park Square, Milton Park
Abingdon, Oxon, OX14 4RN

Routledge is an imprint of the Taylor & Francis Group.

Printed on acid-free, 250-year-life paper.
Manufactured in the United States of America.
10   9   8

"Meditiation One" from René Descartes, *The Philosophical Works of Descartes, Vol. 1*, trans.
Elizabeth S. Haldane and G. R. T. Ross, is reprinted with permission of Cambridge University Press.

Library of Congress Cataloging-in-Publication Data

Litch, Mary M., 1963-
        Philosophy through film / Mary M. Litch
            p. cm.
        Includes bibliographical references.
        ISBN 0-415-93875-9— ISBN 0-415-93876-7 (pbk.)
        1. Motion pictures—Philosophy. I. Title.

PN1995 .L535 2002
791.43'684—dc21   2002069660

Contents

Preface

Philosophy through Film grows out of my experience teaching a course of the same name at the University of Alabama at Birmingham. It is geared for use as the primary textbook in a first course in philosophy and covers the same topics as a standard introductory text. However, the novel avenues for philosophic exploration opened up by the use of film make *Philosophy through Film* appropriate for an upper-level course in some contexts. The movie enthusiast interested in a deeper understanding and appreciation of films may also find the book engaging and informative.

Some feature films can be interpreted as attempts to provide answers to classic questions within philosophy. This is an underlying assumption of *Philosophy through Film*. Each chapter examines one such question in an approachable yet philosophically rigorous manner, using one or two focus films as a source for the standard positions and arguments associated with that question. The discussion of the films in question is fully integrated into the discussion of the philosophical issue: the films are not mere "add-ons" to an otherwise straightforward introductory philosophy text. One consequence is that the bulk of each chapter is most fruitfully read *after* viewing the relevant films. Each chapter begins with a brief introduction (to the topic and to the films) to be read first; however, the remainder of each chapter assumes that the reader has already seen the one or two films associated with that chapter and has them freshly in mind.

The focus films associated with each chapter run the gamut in styles and genres. The main requirement for inclusion was philosophical relevance: does the movie "cover the topic" in a way that will be familiar to philosophers? A second requirement for inclusion is that the title is readily available for rent through the major national video rental chains (e.g., Blockbuster, Hollywood Video). In deciding whether or not a movie satisfied this second criterion, I used the "Blockbuster Test," noting if a particular film was available at my local Blockbuster store. All of the focus films used in *Philosophy through Film* passed.[1]

Many people have contributed to the writing of this book. In earlier drafts, the students in my course Philosophy through Film offered criticisms and suggestions for improving the book. Jennifer McKitrick drew the artwork in chapter 2. In addition, several of my colleagues at UAB, Jennifer McKitrick (again), James Rachels, and Mary Whall, read draft chapters and offered many helpful comments. As always, responsibility for any leftover errors remains my own.

Introduction

What Is Philosophy?

While it is hard to give a one-sentence definition of the term *philosophy*, it is relatively easy to describe the field by reviewing some of the classic questions philosophers study. Here are some examples. What are the limits of human knowledge? (Can I, for example, *know* that an external world exists?) What is the ultimate nature of reality? Does it make sense to talk about the way the world is apart from our conceptualization of it? What makes me *me*? What does it mean to have a mind? What distinguishes morally right from morally wrong action? Under what circumstances can I be held morally responsible for my actions? Does God exist? If so, is that God worthy of praise and adoration? Does life have meaning? If so, is God a necessary prerequisite to making sense of life's meaning? At first glance, nothing seems to tie these diverse questions together, leaving the impression that they are all considered "philosophical" questions only because of some historical accident in the development of the Western intellectual tradition. On closer examination, however, the questions are seen to share at least one attribute in common—they are all basic questions. By basic, I mean that each of these questions must be among the first questions asked when building a framework for thinking about and acting in the world.

The usual method employed by philosophers in examining one of these questions is to describe and then argue for a particular answer to it. An **argument** is nothing but a set of reasons that are given to back up or justify some statement. For example, the skeptic argues for the view that we cannot know that an external world exists by giving us reasons to believe that we cannot have such knowledge.

What Is Philosophy through Film?

Formal argumentation is not the only way to approach these questions. A work of fiction can sometimes function like an argument: it presents a position (e.g., an answer to one of the above questions) in a way that makes the reader say, "Yes, I see that this is a plausible position." Indeed, it is not uncommon to see philosophy taught at the college level with the aid of fiction. While there are important differences between novels and films, they share in common the ability to address the above questions in a philosophically respectable and interesting way. This book proposes to use feature films to introduce and discuss some of the most enduring questions within philosophy.

Film, like other forms of fiction, can even make the transition to philosophical thinking easier. I mentioned above that one of the classic questions within philosophy is, "Can I know that an external (mind-independent) world exists?" At first glance, this may strike you as an absolutely preposterous question. "Of course, I can!" you answer. Indeed, the original question may strike you as so preposterous that it doesn't deserve serious thought. A movie can be an effective tool for introducing a philosophical topic, because it allows the viewer to drop many preconceived notions. We are all used to suspending our commonsense views about how the world works in the context of fiction. This suspension can be used to the philosopher's advantage. Consider the film *Total Recall*. It first draws the viewer into the fictional world created by the film, pointing out that the protagonist cannot know that *his* experiences represent an external world or that *his* memories correspond to experiences he had in the past. It is only once the viewer has accepted this that the film's subtext becomes clear: *the viewer* is in exactly the same position as the character. This realization can produce an "Aha!" experience—a sense of sudden understanding—that skepticism (the thesis that we cannot know that an external world exists) is not so preposterous after all!

Other films can have the same force. Indeed, my main criterion for using films in the book is that they do just that—that they present and defend an answer to one of philosophy's classic questions. Whether the writer or director responsible for a film had the intention of doing philosophy is beside the point. Each film we will be discussing deals with one or more of the questions posed in the first paragraph of this chapter. As already noted, *Total Recall* offers us a defense of skepticism, as does *The Matrix*. *Hilary and Jackie* can be interpreted as presenting arguments for relativism—the view that the truth of all statements can only be judged relative to a conceptual scheme and other background assumptions. *Being John Malkovich* and *Memento* consider what makes a person who she is: Is it my body, my mind, or my immaterial soul that identifies me at birth as the same person I am now? *AI: Artificial Intelligence* poses questions at the intersection of philosophy and artificial intelligence: What does it mean to have a mind? What does it mean to be a person (in the sense of someone who has moral rights)? Woody Allen's *Crimes and Misdemeanors* examines the nature of morality: which ethical theory is correct? *Memento*, along with *Gattaca*, considers the question of whether human beings are free? Do I have free will, or are all of my actions pre-determined by the laws of nature governing the universe? The next two films, *The Seventh Seal* and *The Rapture,* consider the problem of evil: God couldn't possibly exist, because, if God did, there wouldn't be so much suffering in the world. Even if we assume that God exists, a God that allows so much suffering is not worthy of our praise and adoration. Thus, religion is discredited, not because there is no God, but because God's worship (the primary activity of the religious life) is unwarranted. How does the theist respond to this charge? *The Seventh Seal* is also a useful source for discussion of the role that God plays in making human existence meaningful. *Crimes and Misdemeanors* also raises this topic at several points. Finally, *Leaving Las Vegas* addresses the existentialist question outside of a religious framework: Does life have meaning?

The Layout of the Book

Even though philosophy through film is an unorthodox approach to teaching philosophy, the topics have been chosen to cover roughly the same material as a standard introductory textbook. Each chapter corresponds to one of the classic questions within philosophy. The structure within all of the chapters follows the same pattern. The first two or three sections serve as a general introduction to the topic and are intended to be read *before* that chapter's focus film or films are screened. Sections thereafter will make repeated reference to the film(s), so they are best read only *afterward*. I will be referring to individual scenes in the focus films by their minute marks—the amount of time that has elapsed since the opening credits began. The appendix contains plot summaries by elapsed time (through minute marks) for all eleven focus films. It may be useful to refer to these at various points, either while watching the film or while reading the latter sections in each chapter.

PART I

Knowledge and Truth

1

Skepticism

Total Recall (1990) and *The Matrix* (1999)

Melina: I can't believe it, it's like a dream. What's wrong?
Quaid: I just had a terrible thought. What if it *is* a dream?
Melina: Then kiss me before you wake up.

——closing scene in *Total Recall*

Morpheus: You have the look of a man who accepts what he sees, because
he is expecting to wake up. Ironically, this is not far from the truth.

——from *The Matrix*

We are all used to thinking that our senses reveal a world that exists independently of
our minds. But is this belief justified? What can I know about this external world?
Can I be sure that what my senses report to me is accurate? Maybe my senses are giving me radically misleading information about what is going on in the world outside
of my mind. Can I even know that an external world exists? Philosophers have been
examining these questions for centuries. Some philosophers hold a position called
skepticism, according to which genuine knowledge in such matters is unattainable.
As we shall see, the science-fiction virtual-reality genre is ideal for introducing this
topic, and the movies *Total Recall* and *The Matrix* are both excellent sources for the
standard arguments supporting skepticism and for hints at how modern philosophers
have reacted to these arguments. My advice is to read up to and including section 1.3,
then to watch the movies before resuming reading the rest of the chapter. The first
two sections introduce the topic of skepticism in very general terms; having it under
your belt *before* viewing *Total Recall* and *The Matrix* will help you extract more of the
philosophical content out of the movies. Indeed, I predict that, if you read the material on skepticism carefully, you will be surprised by how closely the plots and dialogue
of the two movies stick to their philosophical script. The material beginning in section 1.4 makes constant reference to the movies, so it would be most profitably read
after viewing the movies.

1.1 What Is Skepticism?

In everyday discourse, to call someone *skeptical* is to say that that person is prone to disbelieve what others say. It is commonplace to show distrust or disbelief in what a politician is promising by stating, "I'm skeptical." The term *skepticism* as it is used within philosophy has a slightly different, albeit related meaning. Someone who is skeptical about X in the *philosophical* sense is someone who claims that it is impossible to know whether X is true or false. To see this more clearly, consider the following statements:

S1: George Washington was the twenty-first president of the United States.
S2: 2,356,717 is a prime number.
S3: I am not dreaming right now.

Suppose I were to ask you, for each of *S1*, *S2*, and *S3*, whether you *know* with absolute certainty that that statement is true. What would your response be? If you are like me, your answers were:

S1': I know that *S1* is definitely false.
S2': I don't know about *S2*, maybe it's true, maybe it's false. If I were a math whiz or someone with some time to kill, I could probably figure out, though, whether *S2* is true or false.
S3': I'm not quite sure what to make of *S3*. I tend to *believe* that I'm not dreaming right now, but I can remember times in the past when I thought I wasn't dreaming, only to wake up a few minutes later when my alarm went off. The more I think about *S3*, the weirder *S3* seems. At least if asked whether *S2* was true or false, I could think of a way to figure it out. But *S3* is qualitatively different. I can't think of a calculation I can carry out or a test I can perform that would give me conclusive evidence either way. I guess the correct thing to say in this case is that *I can't know with absolute certainty whether S3 is true or false.*

The response given in *S3'* above captures exactly what philosophers mean by skepticism: skepticism is the view that knowledge is not attainable. Note the difference between skepticism in its everyday usage and its philosophical usage. According to the former, skeptics are deniers. According to the latter, skeptics are doubters.

It is possible for someone to be skeptical about some domains but not about others. Thus, a *moral* skeptic claims it is not possible to know whether moral statements are true or false; however, this moral skeptic may think knowledge is attainable in other areas. Such circumscribed versions of skepticism will not be discussed further. The version of skepticism that this chapter deals with is all-encompassing. Sometimes the term *epistemological skepticism* is used to distinguish this all-encompassing version of skepticism from versions that involve more limited claims. (*Epistemology* is the name of the subarea of philosophy that studies what knowledge is and how knowledge claims are justified.)

Skepticism has a long history, which predates the advent of virtual reality movies by some 2300 years. The first skeptics lived in ancient Greece in the third and fourth centuries B.C.E. in the generation after the influential Greek philosopher Aristotle. While none of the writings from these very early skeptics survived, we are familiar with their views based on the writings of later skeptics who had had access to those original documents. Among the latter group, Sextus Empiricus (175–225 C.E.) has been the most influential in defining ancient skepticism. According to the ancient skeptics, all one's claims to knowledge are to be rejected, except for the knowledge of one's current perceptual state. Thus, I can know that I am having a visual impression of redness right now (a current perceptual state), but I cannot know that that impression of redness is caused by, or represents, or has anything whatsoever to do with goings-on outside of my own mind. Notice that these ancient skeptics are not claiming that my current impression of redness is not caused by something outside of my mind (remember, skeptics are *doubters*, not deniers). They are "merely" claiming that I have insufficient evidence to know whether my current impression of redness is thus caused by an *external* object (that is, an object that is mind-independent, that exists external to the mind). The ancient skeptic, just like his modern counterpart, would say that active *dis*belief in the existence of an external world is just as unfounded as active belief in such a world. Strange as it may sound, the ancient skeptics held that the natural psychological response to adopting skepticism would be a blissful detachment from the world. Whether the ancient skeptics were blissfully detached is anyone's guess; the modern response to skepticism has been repugnance. (Watch for the responses offered by characters in *Total Recall* and *The Matrix* when the skeptical hypothesis enters the picture—do they become blissfully detached?) Philosophers are like other people in finding something profoundly unsettling about skepticism. Indeed, much of the epistemology done in the modern era can be interpreted as an attempt to refute skepticism. So deep is the disdain for skepticism among some philosophers (e.g., George Berkeley, whom we shall meet in section 1.6) that they will reject any assumption, solely on the grounds that it will lead to skepticism.

The strain of skepticism that began in ancient Greece died out during the Early Middle Ages and had no or only very few adherents in Europe for over a thousand years. It wasn't until the religious and scientific revolutions of the fifteenth and sixteenth centuries that interest in skepticism reemerged. This reemergence was further spurred by the republication of the writings of Sextus Empiricus in the middle of the sixteenth century. The time was ripe for philosophers to grapple once again with doubt. By far the most influential writer on the topic of skepticism during this time was the French philosopher René Descartes (1596–1650). In retrospect, historians of philosophy have marked his emergence as the beginning of philosophy in the modern period.[1] Descartes laid out skepticism in the form that it has retained to this day. Because of his influence, I have allocated all of section 1.2 to a discussion of his views. Skepticism remained on philosophy's front burner for the rest of the seventeenth and most of the eighteenth centuries. Another highly influential philosopher of this period, David Hume (1711–1776), refined the arguments for skepticism still further, showing just what would be required to justify a claim to know that an external world exists, and showing how this requirement could not be satisfied—not even in theory. We shall discuss some of these arguments in Sections 1.4 and 1.5.

While skepticism has been relegated to philosophy's back burner in the nineteenth and twentieth centuries, it has certainly not disappeared all together. The reading list at the end of the chapter offers suggestions for those interested in pursuing what some present-day philosophers have to say about skepticism.

1.2 Descartes's Formulation

The most influential work ever written on skepticism is the first essay in *Meditations on First Philosophy*, originally published by **René Descartes** in 1641.[2] In this essay, Descartes lays the framework for modern skepticism and sets the standard according to which any presumed refutation of skepticism must pass muster. In the remaining five essays that make up the *Meditations*, Descartes sets forth what he believes to be a refutation of skepticism. While philosophers greatly admire the thoroughness and ingenuity of the arguments Descartes offers in favor of skepticism, most philosophers believe Descartes's "solution" to the problem of skepticism presented in the second through sixth essays doesn't work. Thus, Descartes's *Meditations* have become the classic source for skepticism, rather than the refutation of skepticism that Descartes had intended the work to be.

The complete first essay from Descartes's *Meditations on First Philosophy* is reproduced below. In this essay, Descartes sets about trying to find a belief whose truth he cannot possibly doubt. He notes that his senses have deceived him in the past; so, any belief based on the report of his senses can be doubted. (Recall the distinction emphasized above between doubting the truth of a statement and believing it to be false.) Furthermore, he recalls having experiences while dreaming that were indistinguishable at the time from experiences while awake. Thus, while close and careful examination of an object in good light is normally sufficient to dispel concerns that his senses are deceiving him, close and careful examination in good light is wholly insufficient for distinguishing "real" reality from the "virtual" reality created within a dream. He decides that he is looking for indubitability in the wrong place. If he has any indubitable beliefs, they are more likely to be found within the domain of pure mathemat-

ics (for example, arithmetic statements such as "2 + 3 = 5"). On further consideration, however, he decides that, even here, doubt is possible. Descartes believes that an
all-powerful God exists—a God who created him and would not allow him to be massively deceived. He admits, though, that his belief in the existence of God can be
doubted. Perhaps the truth is that, instead of God, an all-powerful and evil demon
exists; this demon has created Descartes so that he constantly falls into error, even
when he performs simple calculations such as adding 2 and 3. He cannot know for
sure that this is not the case. If such an evil demon exists, then even beliefs based solely
on his powers of reason are called into doubt. Descartes decides to adopt the hypothesis that just such an evil demon exists, not because this hypothesis is well founded
(quite the contrary, Descartes would say), but because such a hypothesis will steel
Descartes in his resolve not to allow in any belief as indubitable if that belief has the
slightest shred of grounds for doubt. It is on this note of abject skepticism that his first
meditation ends.

As mentioned above, Descartes believed he had refuted skepticism in the later
essays. While most of the remainder of the *Meditations on First Philosophy* lie outside the
scope of this chapter, there is one item from the beginning of the second meditation
that bears remarking upon. In his search for a belief whose truth he could not possibly
doubt, Descartes settles upon the statement "I exist." He bases the indubitability of
this statement on the reasoning that even if the evil demon exists and is constantly
causing him to fall into error, Descartes could not possibly be mistaken in believing he
exists as a thing that thinks—as a thing that doubts. This is because he would at least
have to exist as a thing that was being deceived. Thus, Descartes formulates the argument "I think; therefore, I exist" (in its original Latin, *cogito, ergo sum*) as showing
beyond a shadow of a doubt that he exists. Now, the first essay from Descartes's *Meditations on First Philosophy*.

MEDITATION ONE—ON WHAT CAN BE CALLED INTO DOUBT [3]
René Descartes

It is now some years since I detected how many were the false beliefs that I had from
my earliest youth admitted as true, and how doubtful was everything I had since
constructed on this basis; and from that time I was convinced that I must once for
all seriously undertake to rid myself of all the opinions which I had formerly
accepted, and commence to build anew from the foundation, if I wanted to establish
any firm and permanent structure in the sciences. But as this enterprise appeared to
be a very great one, I waited until I had attained an age so mature that I could not
hope that at any later date I should be better fitted to execute my design. This reason caused me to delay so long that I should feel that I was doing wrong were I to
occupy in deliberation the time that yet remains to me for action. Today, then, since

very opportunely for the plan I have in view I have delivered my mind from every care [and am happily agitated by no passions] and since I have procured for myself an assured leisure in a peaceable retirement, I shall at last seriously and freely address myself to the general upheaval of all my former opinions.

Now for this object it is not necessary that I should show that all of these are false—I shall perhaps never arrive at this end. But inasmuch as reason already persuades me that I ought no less carefully to withhold my assent from matters which are not entirely certain and indubitable than from those which appear to me manifestly to be false, if I am able to find in each one some reason to doubt, this will suffice to justify my rejecting the whole. And for that end it will not be requisite that I should examine each in particular, which would be an endless undertaking; for owing to the fact that the destruction of the foundations of necessity brings with it the downfall of the rest of the edifice, I shall only in the first place attack those principles upon which all my former opinions rested.

All that up to the present time I have accepted as most true and certain I have learned either from the senses or through the senses; but it is sometimes proved to me that these senses are deceptive, and it is wiser not to trust entirely to anything by which we have once been deceived.

But it may be that although the senses sometimes deceive us concerning things which are hardly perceptible, or very far away, there are yet many others to be met with as to which we cannot reasonably have any doubt, although we recognise them by their means. For example, there is the fact that I am here, seated by the fire, attired in a dressing gown, having this paper in my hands and other similar matters. And how could I deny that these hands and this body are mine, were it not perhaps that I compare myself to certain persons, devoid of sense, whose cerebella are so troubled and clouded by the violent vapours of black bile, that they constantly assure us that they think they are kings when they are really quite poor, or that they are clothed in purple when they are really without covering, or who imagine that they have an earthenware head or are nothing but pumpkins or are made of glass. But they are mad, and I should not be any the less insane were I to follow examples so extravagant.

At the same time I must remember that I am a man, and that consequently I am in the habit of sleeping, and in my dreams representing to myself the same things or sometimes even less probable things, than do those who are insane in their waking moments. How often has it happened to me that in the night I dreamt that I found myself in this particular place, that I was dressed and seated near the fire, whilst in reality I was lying undressed in bed! At this moment it does indeed seem to me that it is with eyes awake that I am looking at this paper; that this head which I move is not asleep, [I put my hand out consciously and deliberately; I feel the paper and see it]; what happens in sleep does not appear so clear nor so distinct as does all this. But in thinking over this I remind myself that on many occasions I have in sleep been deceived by similar illusions, and in dwelling carefully on this reflection I see so manifestly that there are no certain indications by which we may clearly distinguish wakefulness from sleep that I am lost in astonishment. And my astonishment is such that it is almost capable of persuading me that I now dream.

Now let us assume that we are asleep and that all these particulars, e.g. that we open our eyes, shake our head, extend our hands, and so on, are but false delusions; and let us reflect that possibly neither our hands nor our whole body are such as they appear to us to be. At the same time we must at least confess that the things which are represented to us in sleep are like painted representations which can only have been formed as the counterparts of something real and true, and that in this way those general things at least, i.e. eyes, a head, hands, and a whole body, are not imaginary things, but things really existent. For, as a matter of fact, painters, even when they study with the greatest skill to represent sirens and satyrs by forms the most strange and extraordinary, cannot give them natures which are entirely new, but merely make a certain medley of the members of different animals; or if their imagination is extravagant enough to invent something so novel that nothing similar has ever before been seen, and that then their work represents a thing purely fictitious and absolutely false, it is certain all the same that the colours of which this is composed are necessarily real. And for the same reason, although these general things, to with, [a body], eyes, a head, hands, and such like, may be imaginary, we are bound at the same time to confess that there are at least some other objects yet more simple and more universal, which are real and true; and of these just in the same way as with certain real colours, all these images of things which dwell in our thoughts, whether true and real or false and fantastic, are formed.

To such a class of things pertains corporeal nature in general, and its extension, the figure of extended things, their quantity or magnitude and number, as also the place in which they are, the time which measures their duration, and so on.

That is possibly why our reasoning is not unjust when we conclude from this that Physics, Astronomy, Medicine and all other sciences which have as their end the consideration of composite things, are very dubious and uncertain; but that Arithmetic, Geometry and other sciences of that kind which only treat of things that are very simple and very general, without taking great trouble to ascertain whether they are actually existent or not, contain some measure of certainty and an element of the indubitable. For whether I am awake or asleep, two and three together always form five, and the square can never have more than four sides, and it does not seem possible that truths so clear and apparent can be suspected of any falsity [or uncertainty].

Nevertheless I have long had fixed in my mind the belief that an all-powerful God existed by whom I have been created such as I am. But how do I know that He has not brought it to pass that there is no earth, no heaven, no extended body, no magnitude, no place, and that nevertheless [I possess the perceptions of all these things and that] they seem to me to exist just exactly as I now see them? And, besides, as I sometimes imagine that others deceive themselves in the things which they think they know best, how do I know that I am not deceived every time that I add two and three, or count the sides of a square, or judge of things yet simpler, if anything simpler can be imagined? But possibly God has not desired that I should be thus deceived, for He is said to be supremely good. If, however, it is contrary to His goodness to have made me such that I constantly deceive myself, it would also appear to be contrary to His goodness to permit me to be sometimes deceived, and nevertheless I cannot doubt that He does permit this.

There may indeed be those who would prefer to deny the existence of a God so powerful, rather than believe that all other things are uncertain. But let us not oppose them for the present, and grant that all that is here said of a God is a fable; nevertheless in whatever way they suppose that I have arrived at the state of being that I have reached—whether they attribute it to fate or to accident, or make out that it is by a continual succession of antecedents, or by some other method—since to err and deceive oneself is a defect, it is clear that the greater will be the probability of my being so imperfect as to deceive myself ever, as is the Author to whom they assign my origin the less powerful. To these reasons I have certainly nothing to reply, but at the end I feel constrained to confess that there is nothing in all that I formerly believed to be true, of which I cannot in some measure doubt, and that not merely through want of thought or through levity, but for reasons which are very powerful and maturely considered; so that henceforth I ought not the less carefully to refrain from giving credence to these opinions than to that which is manifestly false, if I desire to arrive at any certainty [in the sciences].

But it is not sufficient to have made these remarks, we must also be careful to keep them in mind. For these ancient and commonly held opinions still revert frequently to my mind, long and familiar custom having given them the right to occupy my mind against my inclination and rendered them almost masters of my belief; nor will I ever lose the habit of deferring to them or of placing my confidence in them, so long as I consider them as they really are, i.e. opinions in some measure doubtful, as I have just shown, and at the same time highly probable, so that there is much more reason to believe in than to deny them. That is why I consider that I shall not be acting amiss, if, taking of set purpose a contrary belief, I allow myself to be deceived, and for a certain time pretend that all these opinions are entirely false and imaginary, until at last, having thus balanced my former prejudices with my latter [so that they cannot divert my opinions more to one side than to the other], my judgment will no longer be dominated by bad usage or turned away from the right knowledge of the truth. For I am assured that there can be neither peril nor error in this course, and that I cannot at present yield too much to distrust, since I am not considering the question of action, but only of knowledge.

I shall then suppose, not that God who is supremely good and the fountain of truth, but some evil genius not less powerful than deceitful, has employed his whole energies in deceiving me; I shall consider that the heavens, the earth, colours, figures, sound, and all other external things are nought but the illusions and dreams of which this genius has availed himself in order to lay traps for my credulity; I shall consider myself as having no hands, no eyes, no flesh, no blood, nor any senses, yet falsely believing myself to possess all these things; I shall remain obstinately attached to this idea, and if by this means it is not in my power to arrive at the knowledge of any truth, I may at least do what is in my power [i.e. suspend my judgment], and with firm purpose avoid giving credence to any false thing, or being imposed upon by this arch deceiver, however powerful and deceptive he may be. But this task is a laborious one, and insensibly a certain lassitude leads me into the course of my ordinary life. And just as a captive who in sleep enjoys an imaginary liberty, when he begins to suspect that his liberty is but a dream, fears to awaken, and conspires with these agreeable illusions that the deception may be prolonged, so insensibly of my own accord I fall back into my former opinions, and I dread awakening from this slumber, lest the laborious wakefulness which would follow the tranquillity of this repose should have to be spent not in daylight, but in the excessive darkness of the difficulties which have just been discussed.

1.3 An Overview of the Movies

TOTAL RECALL (1990). DIRECTED BY PAUL VERHOEVEN.
STARRING ARNOLD SCHWARZENEGGER, RACHEL TICOTIN, SHARON STONE.

Arnold Schwarzenegger stars as Douglas Quaid, a twenty-first-century earthling who visits a firm called Rekall to receive a memory implant of a trip to Mars. Nothing seems out of the ordinary (relative to the movie's futuristic setting, of course) until something starts to go wrong during the implant procedure. As a result of this mishap, Quaid learns (or does he?) that his entire life — or, more correctly, the entire set of "memories" that comprise his life — is an illusion, produced when agents working for the government implanted a memory chip in his brain. He learns that, in his *real* life, he was a secret agent named Hauser who had turned traitor to the government. The second half of the movie follows Quaid/Hauser as he attempts to learn more about his true identity. This latter part of the movie consists of a narrative whose truthfulness we are never quite sure of: are these things really happening to Quaid/Hauser, or is this all part of the package of fake memories Quaid has bought from Rekall?

THE MATRIX (1999). DIRECTED BY ANDY AND LARRY WACHOWSKI.
STARRING KEANU REEVES, LAURENCE FISHBURNE, CARRIE-ANNE MOSS.

The Matrix is the most recent blockbuster to ask the question, "How would you know the difference between [a] dream world and a real one?"[4] Like *Total Recall*, it is set in the future, when scarcely imaginable technological advances allow for the creation of a perfect virtual world. While fancy computers are not, strictly speaking, necessary for a discussion of skepticism (after all, Descartes managed to do just fine back in the seventeenth century making reference only to the virtual world created in normal, human dreams), bringing technology into the picture makes skepticism an easier sell. Neo, the main character in *The Matrix*, cannot tell when he is experiencing a real world and when he is experiencing a virtual one.

In some ways, *The Matrix* is not as good a film as *Total Recall* when it comes to introducing the topic of skepticism, for the viewer is left with the impression that all the philosophical doubts concerning what is real and what is not are cleared up in the end (Hollywood sequel-writers notwithstanding). Since the thrust of skepticism is *not* that the world revealed by the senses is unreal, but rather that we can never know whether it is or not, a film that ties up all the loose ends knowledge-wise is not a film about skepticism. However, *The Matrix* is useful for introducing how one very important philosopher, George Berkeley (1685–1753), responded to Hume's and Descartes's skepticism. It is for that reason that *The Matrix* is included here.

If you are following my advice given at the beginning of the chapter, now is the time to watch *Total Recall* and *The Matrix*. The appendix entries for these two films give plot summaries and corresponding minute marks (the total amount of time that has elapsed since the opening credits began) for the major scenes.

1.4 *Quaid and Neo as Embodiments of Descartes's Problem*

So, you just finished watching *Total Recall*. What happened in the movie? Who were the main characters? What did they do? Suppose, instead of asking you these questions after having watched *Total Recall* to the end, I had asked you the same set of questions at various points during the movie. Would your responses have built gradually on one another as you slowly accumulated information about the characters' lives, or would your responses have changed radically depending on when in the movie I asked the questions? Let me be more specific. Suppose I had asked you who Quaid and Hauser were seventeen and a half minutes into the movie. (This is the scene in which Quaid is visiting Rekall. He has already picked out the ego trip he wants implanted and has identified the woman he wants to be a part of that ego trip, but the implantation procedure has not begun.) What would your answer be? What if I had asked the same questions— Who is Quaid? Who is Hauser?—one hundred minutes into the movie? (This is the scene that takes place at the reactor, as Cohaagen is trying to prevent Quaid/Hauser from starting it up.) Would your response have changed radically from what you said at the 17:30 minute mark? Now, compare both of your responses with the way you now answer the questions after having watched the entire movie. Did your response change radically yet again? Here are my responses to the questions during each of these scenes:

1 (17:30 minute mark—part way through visit to Rekall) Quaid is a construction worker. I don't know who Hauser is.
2 (100 minute mark—at the reactor with Cohaagen) Quaid is made up. Hauser
   is real. Hauser's body is currently inhabited by the fictional personality and
   set of memories that constitute Quaid.
3 (at end of movie) The viewer is not provided with conclusive evidence, but
   various hints dropped along the way imply that Quaid is real and Hauser is
   made up.

This sort of nonlinear progression in preferred interpretation is not uncommon in
movies. (After all, people go to movies for something out of the ordinary. If someone
wants to experience linear progression in interpretation, they can watch real life.)
What is uncommon in *Total Recall* is the use made of these jumps in preferred interpretation. Under the second interpretation, the narrative being offered in the film
(except the dream sequence during the first three minutes) is from the point of view
of a quasi-omniscient observer (that is, an observer who sees the action unfolding
from a ideal vantage point, not from the limited vantage point of any particular character). Those agency men are real, they are not phantoms in Quaid/Hauser's mind.
The treacherous taxi driver also exists independently of Quaid/Hauser's mind, as does
the reactor. Indeed, the use of the quasi-omniscient observer perspective makes it
hard to interpret the film, up to this point, in any other way on first viewing. But, the
hints that this is *not* the overall most coherent interpretation accumulate throughout
the film, so that, by the end, the third interpretation mentioned above seems to make
the most sense. Everything that Quaid/Hauser has experienced since the visit to Rekall
fits in with the undercover secret agent ego trip he picked out. In case the casual
viewer doesn't pick up on this, the scene at the 60 minute mark with Quaid/Hauser
and Dr. Edgemar reviews the relevant facts.

> **Dr. Edgemar:** You're not really standing here right now. . . . You're not here, and
> neither am I. You're strapped into the implant chair at Rekall. . . . Think about
> it. Your dream started in the middle of the implant procedure. Everything after
> that . . . are all elements of your Rekall secret agent ego trip. You paid to be a
> secret agent. . . . And what about the girl? Brunette, athletic, sleazy, and demure.
> Is she coincidence?

But even with this prodding, Quaid/Hauser persists in believing that his current perceptions are genuine. It is not until the final scene, after the reactor has created a martian
atmosphere (and a blue sky, just as the technician at Rekall had promised before putting
Quaid under[5]) that Quaid/Hauser seriously entertains the possibility that his perceptions
are not genuine (Quaid: "I just had a terrible thought. What if it *is* a dream?").

There is one problem with the third interpretation, though. Who or what in this case is generating the narrative? Under this interpretation, everything we see onscreen from the 17:30 minute mark on is part of Quaid's purchased ego trip.[6] So, are the sounds and images we as viewers of the movie are receiving the same perceptions that Quaid is having as his purchased memories are being implanted? (We're not told how this implantation technology works. Maybe Rekall gives memories by "loading them in" via the client's current stream of consciousness, in the same way as "real" memories are uploaded.) Or maybe these sights and sounds that we as viewers are experiencing are Quaid's postimplant reminiscing about his adventure as a secret agent. Neither of these explanations works perfectly, because much of the narrative after MM 17:30 includes information Quaid would not have access to (for example, conversations between two characters when Quaid is not present). So, even though there are many hints that the third interpretation is the preferred one, those hints taken together cannot be considered conclusive. We shall come back to the issue of how to decide between two competing interpretations after considering *The Matrix*, for we shall see the same sorts of issues arising in the context of that movie.

The Matrix offers us the same sort of nonlinear progression in interpretation as was offered in *Total Recall*. We discover at MM 12:00 that everything that has happened up to that point (for example, the strange messages Neo is receiving on his computer) was a dream. Similarly, when Neo awakes *again* at MM 21:30, we discover that the events between MM 12:00 and MM 21:30 were a dream, and that, therefore, the first twelve minutes was a dream within a dream. After this second awakening, major events happen very quickly. Neo meets Morpheus. Morpheus begins to explain what "the matrix" is. Neo chooses to learn more, even though the truth may be very upsetting. This sequence culminates with the "real" Neo waking up in his vat, being released and flushed out into the "real" world, and being greeted by the "real" Morpheus. From this point on in the movie, the interpretation that Neo has entered the "real" world is never questioned. Thus, except for the times when he reenters the matrix to fight the (virtual) bad guys, all of his perceptions are genuine.

But what does it mean to say that Neo's postrelease perceptions are *genuine,* whereas his prerelease perceptions are not? Similarly, what does it mean to say that, under the third interpretation, all of Quaid's perceptions after MM 17:30 are *not genuine*? What both of these movies do so well is highlight the starting point of skepticism: both movies make it clear that *when we perceive, we are not immediately aware of external objects.* Our perceptions exist only in our minds, they are not themselves external objects. It is only by distinguishing between perceptions and external objects that sense can be made of (1) the virtual reality created by the matrix, (2) Quaid's experiences under the third interpretation, and (3) the virtual reality found in normal, human dreams. But once it is granted that perceptions are not themselves external objects, what then? Descartes recognized this as an important question. In the third essay of his *Meditations on First Philosophy,* he develops a theory that I shall call the **theory of representative perceptions**. According to this theory, a perception is genuine if it is caused by and accurately represents the external object(s) that give rise to it. Thus, the visual perception of a telephone I am having right now is genuine if there really is a telephone that exists "out there" in the mind-independent world of material objects, and that telephone is causally responsible for producing the perception I am experiencing right now. Furthermore, my perception must accurately depict that telephone: it must offer accurate information about the telephone's size and shape, as well as its location relative to other objects I am also perceiving at present. If these conditions are all satisfied by a perception, then that perception is said to be *genuine.* It is clear that many of the perceptions that Quaid and Neo have are not genuine according to these conditions. All matrix-generated perceptions (whether in Neo or any other character hooked into the system) fail the accuracy-of-representation requirement. Thus, even though the perceptions are caused by an external source (the physical computer that is running the matrix program), they are not caused by the external objects they purport to represent. The same goes for Quaid's perceptions under the third interpretation. To take a particular example, there is no material object that causes and resembles the visual and auditory sensations Quaid has when he (seems to) interact with Melina.

Descartes is not alone among philosophers in believing that the theory of representative perceptions (or something very much like it) is the only way to make sense of the possibility of illusion; although, he was alone among the great philosophers of the seventeenth and eighteenth centuries in arguing that this theory did not inexorably lead to skepticism. **Descartes's problem** is explaining how a perceiver could get evidence that a current perception is caused by and accurately represents an external object. Consider how Quaid and Neo respond to this challenge. During the conversation with Dr. Edgemar (MM 60:00), on being told by Edgemar that he is really strapped into the implant chair at Rekall, Quaid reaches out and touches Edgemar and remarks (ironically), "That's amazing." Similarly, Neo's response on being plugged into not the matrix but a computer construct (MM 39:15) is to reach out and touch a sofa and ask, in amazement, "This isn't real?" In both cases, the characters respond to the challenge of Descartes's problem by seeking tactile confirmation that, indeed, they are not experiencing a visual illusion. In his first meditation, Descartes himself describes a similar search for tactile confirmation as his initial response to the challenge. "I put my hand out consciously and deliberately; I feel the paper and see it." But further consideration convinces all three individuals that tactile sensations are just more perceptions—they do not provide unmediated information about the characteristics of, or even the existence of, external objects. While tactile sensations are qualitatively insufficient to meet the challenge of Descartes's problem, there is a reason why this is Neo's, Quaid's, and Descartes's initial response. It is commonplace that our visual sensations deceive us. Even in a waking state, we have all experienced optical illusions; so, the average person is willing to occasionally distrust the visual system. Similarly, auditory illusions are relatively common, as is the corresponding willingness to distrust our hearing. The sense of touch is much less susceptible to waking illusion; it seems the natural choice in testing the genuineness of our visual and auditory reports. But, as both *Total Recall* and *The Matrix* demonstrate, tactile sensations cannot provide the evidence necessary to distinguish between genuine and nongenuine perceptions.

Skepticism has its source in the fact that all we directly experience are our own sensations, not the external things themselves. Neither you nor I have ever, in our entire lives, had contact with an external object where that contact was not mediated by the senses. We cannot, therefore, justify our belief in external objects with reference to our *direct* contact with them.

Are *we* any different in this regard than Neo and Quaid? Admittedly, we haven't gone to an establishment like Rekall, for such establishments do not exist—we *presume*. Furthermore, we are living in the first decade of the twenty-first century, not the year 2199, as did Neo. But, hold on a minute. This line of reasoning will get us nowhere. What generates skepticism is the recognition that all we are ever directly aware of are our own perceptions, not mind-independent objects in some material world. We assume such a world exists and is causally responsible for the perceptions we have, but we have no way of peeking around our perceptions to view these mind-independent objects to check the assumption. There is, though, one important difference between us on the one hand, and Quaid and Neo on the other: they have been given a reason to actively suspect the genuineness of many of their perceptions, we have not.

Consider again the scene from *Total Recall* in which Quaid is visited by Dr. Edgemar. Quaid is reminded of his trip to Rekall and the near-perfect fit between events of the past few days and the secret agent ego trip he had selected. At this point, Quaid needs to decide which of two competing theories is the best one when it comes to explaining his current perceptions. One theory (this is the one that corresponds to the third interpretation above) is that his perceptions are not genuine; rather, they are caused by the physical device that is carrying out the implant procedure. What evidence is there in favor of this theory? First, many of his recent experiences have been highly atypical (even Melina has remarked, on hearing Quaid/Hauser tell of his switched identity: "This is too weird"). Second, there is a near-perfect match between his experiences and the selected ego trip. And third, he can remember going to a firm that specializes in providing nongenuine perceptions. The other theory (this is the one that corresponds to the second interpretation above) is that his current perceptions are caused by and accurately represent external objects. What evidence is there in favor of this theory? Not much. Admittedly, Quaid has a natural inclination to trust in the genuineness of his perceptions, but that by itself is not evidence one way or the other. In stating the case this way, it is clear that the most coherent theory is the first one (the one corresponding to the third interpretation)—it does the best job of explaining the close fit between his perceptions and the ego trip, which remains a massive coincidence according to the second theory.

Can a similar analysis be given for *The Matrix*? Let's consider the two theories contending for explanation of Neo's perceptions between MM 21:30 and MM 32:00. (This is roughly the period of time between Neo waking up for the second time and the "real" Neo waking up in his vat.) According to one theory, Neo's perceptions are the result of a computer stimulating his nervous system in a way indistinguishable from the way in which his nervous system would be stimulated were he actually interacting with material objects. Thus, according to this theory, all of his perceptions during this time period are nongenuine. What evidence is there in favor of this? First, he has the equivalent of a "waking up" experience at MM 32:30 which, at the very least, calls into question the genuineness of the preceding perceptions. Second, many of his experiences during this time period were highly atypical. And third, Neo has experiences throughout the rest of the film that flesh out the hows and whys of the matrix. According to another theory, Neo's perceptions during this time period are genuine. There's not much to say in favor of this theory, with the possible exception that Neo's experiences, while admittedly atypical during this time period (judged relative to those of the average human), are no more atypical than the things that he experienced both before and after this portion of the movie. Unlike in *Total Recall*, there is a third theory that has some plausibility: maybe Neo is still dreaming; maybe everything that happens throughout the entire movie is a dream. After all, we're already allowing for the possibility of a dream-within-a-dream. (Recall, that is what is going on during the first twelve minutes.) This alternative has one major point to recommend it: Neo has sequences of highly atypical experiences sprinkled throughout the movie—they are not just confined to the first thirty-two minutes.

This latter interpretation of *The Matrix* brings up a question originally posed by Descartes in his first meditation: Are there any reliable signs distinguishing sleeping from waking? By the end of his *Meditations*, Descartes believes he has found just such a reliable sign, noting that "the events in dreams are not linked by memory to the rest of my life like those that happen while I am awake."[7] Thus, for Descartes, there is nothing in the perception itself that would allow someone to say that this is certainly a genuine perception. Rather, this judgment of genuineness can only be made in the context of the individual's *other* perceptions—past, present, and future. Other philosophers in the modern era claim that Descartes got it wrong—they hold that there *is* an intrinsic (noncontextual) difference between genuine and nongenuine perceptions. One of these dissenting philosophers is George Berkeley, who held that genuine perceptions are more intrinsically vivid than their nongenuine counterparts.[8] Berkeley held that there are three criteria that distinguish genuine perceptions from nongenuine ones: (1) the vividness of the perception, (2) its degree of independence from our will, and (3) its connectedness to previous and future perceptions.

Does the evidence of nongenuineness in some of Quaid's and Neo's perceptions tend to support Descartes or Berkeley? A few pages ago, we isolated several attributes that led us as viewers, as well as Quaid and Neo, to interpret some of their perceptions as genuine and others as nongenuine. For *Total Recall*, these attributes were: (1) the atypicalness of some of Quaid's perceptions, (2) the near-perfect match between his experiences and the selected ego trip, and (3) his memory of having gone to a firm that specializes in providing nongenuine perceptions. Are these attributes of isolated perceptions or attributes of perceptions relative to other perceptions that the individual has? Clearly, (2) and (3) are a function not of current perceptions considered in isolation, but of the relationship between a current perception and some past or future perceptions—they are strictly contextual. Even the first attribute (atypicalness) is judged relative to the entire set of perceptions that an individual experiences during a lifetime. So it, like the others, tends to support Descartes's contention that the only way to tell whether a perception is genuine is to consider that perception in the context of the individual's other perceptions.

The attributes isolated in *The Matrix* likewise support Descartes over Berkeley. Recall the three attributes mentioned as clues that certain of Neo's perceptions were nongenuine: (1) Neo's "waking up" experience at MM 32:00, which, at the very least, calls into question the genuineness of the preceding perceptions; (2) the atypicalness of some of Neo's perceptions; and (3) Neo's experiences throughout the latter part of the movie that flesh out the hows and whys of the matrix. According to the first and third attributes, earlier perceptions are judged nongenuine because of something that happens later. The second attribute is one we have already met in the discussion of *Total Recall*. Here, as there, atypicalness is a contextual attribute.

The upshot from the preceding few paragraphs reinforces the claim that Berkeley got it wrong: there may be nothing about a nongenuine perception that marks it off as nongenuine—its nongenuineness may only be ascertained by considering the perceptions that went before and after it in an individual's stream of consciousness. This explains why it is difficult for humans to distinguish perceptions in dreams as nongenuine *while those perceptions are being experienced*. After the fact, when the abrupt discontinuity in perception occurs at waking up, the individual has no problem at all identifying the previous perceptions as nongenuine.

Skepticism is not concerned so much with individual perceptions as it is with our entire mental lives. How can I know that I am not massively deluded about the existence of an external world? The preceding discussion provides us with a new way of describing skepticism: How can I know that I will not have perceptions in the future (for example, the typical abrupt discontinuity in perception that corresponds to waking up) that will invalidate my current perceptions and all my perceptions that have come before? The response that the skeptic would give to both ways of posing the question is the same: I can't know.

Before we leave this section, there is an important disanalogy between *Total Recall* and *The Matrix* on the one hand and skepticism on the other that bears mentioning: neither movie considers the possibility that there are *no* material objects whatsoever. *Total Recall* never questions the existence of Quaid's physical body. Further, the movie presupposes that at least some other people exist, as do the fancy pieces of equipment responsible for either Hauser's new identity as Quaid (the second interpretation) or Quaid's ego trip (the third interpretation). Similarly, under all the interpretations of *The Matrix* mentioned earlier, none denied that Neo exists in some physical form or other. The consistent skeptic would say that you cannot be justified in claiming to know that any physical body exists anywhere. It is possible that *you* are nothing but a bunch of perceptions, it is possible that there is no physical body that corresponds to you. Recall that this is the quandary in which Descartes found himself at the end of his first meditation. He can doubt the existence of all material objects; he can even doubt the existence of his own body; but he cannot doubt his existence as a thing that thinks.

1.5 Quaid and Hume's Radical Skepticism

Was Descartes overstepping the evidence when he pronounced his famous, "I think; therefore, I exist"? Some philosophers who came after Descartes thought even this limited claim to knowledge was unjustified. In this section, we shall consider the views of **David Hume** (1711–1776) who argued that not only can the existence of an external world be doubted, but even the existence of a centralized and continuous self can be doubted. Hume's skepticism goes even deeper, for he argued that memory could not be trusted to provide us with certain information about our previous perceptions.

What is the *I* in Descartes's "I think; therefore, I exist"? Descartes assumed that he could perceive an unchanging self that was the entity doing the perceiving, thinking, and so on. But did Descartes really have such a perception? Do you ever have a perception of yourself as a continuous, unchanging self? I'm not speaking here of a perception such as that of seeing yourself in a mirror over an extended period of time, we are not dealing here with issues of your bodily existence. Rather, I am asking whether you can discern some unchanging thing (your *self*) in the flux of thoughts and perceptions that occur. At this point, this is probably striking you as an even stranger question than "Have you ever perceived an external object?" But, if you consider it, you may well find agreement with Hume, who argued that "when I enter most intimately into what I call *myself*, I always stumble on some particular perception or other, . . . [however], I never can catch *myself* at any time without a perception, and never can observe any thing but the perception. . . . The mind is a kind of theatre, where several perceptions successively make their appearance; pass, re-pass, glide away, and mingle in an infinite variety of postures and situations. There is properly no *simplicity* in it at one time, nor *identity* . . . whatever natural propension we may have to imagine that simplicity and identity. The comparison of the theatre must not mislead us. They are the successive perceptions only, that constitute the mind."[9] According to Hume, we have no evidence that an unchanging self exists, since all we are ever aware of are fleeting thoughts and perceptions. To the extent that a self exists at all, it is nothing but a bundle of thoughts and perceptions. Hume would say that, in pronouncing "*I* think; therefore, *I* exist," Descartes never considered the possibility that there is no *I*; really, all Descartes could know with certainty was that *thoughts* and *perceptions* exist. It was an unjustified leap on Descartes's part from "thoughts exist" to "I exist."

But, things get even weirder than that. Consider memories. What are the conditions for a memory's being *genuine*? In some ways, the conditions are less stringent than the conditions for genuineness of a perception: there is no requirement that an external object exists. Thus, I can have a *genuine* memory of a perception I had during my dream last night. In order for one of my memories to be genuine: (1) a previous perception must have occurred, (2) that previous perception must be causally responsible for the current memory, and (3) the current memory must accurately represent the previous perception. These conditions should look familiar, for they are the same conditions used for genuineness of a perception, with the phrase "previous perception" substituted for "external object."

Quaid is faced with the question, "How can I distinguish genuine from nongenuine memories?" at MM 26:00. At this point in the movie, his wife Lori tells him that his lifetime worth of "memories" as Quaid the construction worker are nongenuine; the only genuine ones of the bunch are the memories of events that he has accumulated over the past six weeks, during which time he has been living the life of Quaid. So, for example, his "memory" of their wedding, while indistinguishable in its qualitative feel from his memory of eating breakfast that morning, is nevertheless bogus: it refers back to a set of perceptions (Quaid's perceptions of the wedding ceremony) that never occurred. Is there any way Quaid can discover whether Lori is telling the truth?

Contrast Quaid's situation with that of Neo at MM 68:00. Neo has reentered the matrix and is (virtually) traveling in a car with Morpheus and the others through his old neighborhood. Reminiscing, he asks Morpheus, "All these memories never happened?" In this case, Neo is not questioning the *memories'* genuineness, but rather the genuineness of the original perceptions. He, and we, the viewers, recognize that the original perceptions occurred; thus, the memories of those perceptions are genuine. It's just that the original perceptions were of a virtual world, not the real one. *The Matrix*, unlike *Total Recall*, never toys with the most radical form of skepticism, called **solipsism of the present moment**—the claim that all that can be known with certainty is the moment-by-moment perceptions and thoughts that flit by.

1.6 Responses to Skepticism

Skepticism is a rather unsettling thesis (the ancient skeptics notwithstanding). If we follow the line of reasoning that begins with the claim that we are not directly aware of objects,[10] we seem to be led inexorably to solipsism of the present moment. But, do we have to start down that path? Two important philosophers in the modern era, George Berkeley and Immanuel Kant, argued that we do not. Their ways of avoiding that path are the topics of this section.

George Berkeley (1685–1753) held the view that our perceptions give us direct experience of objects. For him, the fact that Descartes's claim (that we are not directly aware of objects) leads to skepticism is reason enough to reject the claim as obviously untrue.[11] This type of argument is called **reductio ad absurdum** (reduction to a contradiction). In this form of reasoning, one assumes that a statement is true (for example, one assumes that Descartes's theory of representative perceptions is true), then demonstrates that that assumption implies a contradiction. This shows that the original statement was false. Oftentimes, reductio arguments weaken the requirement that a *contradiction* must be implied. Instead of a contradiction, all that is required to falsify the assumed statement is to show that it implies something that is highly counterintuitive or unacceptable on some other grounds. Berkeley believed that skepticism is sufficiently unacceptable as to falsify the assumptions that give rise to it. These assumptions are: (1) the view that we are not directly aware of objects in perception, and (2) the view of genuineness that goes along with this, the theory of representative perceptions. Once Berkeley has rejected this theory, the burden is on him to say what perceptions are, if not representations of external (mind-independent) objects. In the next several paragraphs, we shall consider Berkeley's response to this challenge. Of the two movies used in this chapter, *The Matrix* has the closest affinity to the concerns and claims of Berkeley, so I shall be drawing most of my examples from it.

Berkeley held the view known as **idealism**, which claims that there are no such things as *mind-independent* objects. Rather, objects are collections of perceptions: "to be is to be perceived." As Berkeley notes, "[A]ll the . . . furniture of the earth . . . have not any subsistence without a mind . . . their being is to be perceived or known, . . . consequently, so long as they are not actually perceived by me or do not exist in my mind or that of any other created spirit, they must either have no existence at all or else subsist in the mind of some external spirit—it being perfectly unintelligible . . . to attribute to any single part of them an existence independent of a spirit."[12] On first hearing, this theory sounds outlandish. However, Berkeley makes the case that the theory, despite its initial strangeness, accords quite well with our usual way of talking about our experience of objects; hence, it is closer to common sense than the theory of objects one finds in Descartes. Indeed, Berkeley holds that the theory of representative perceptions is a philosopher's confusion, *not* the view of Joe Everyman. An additional reason in idealism's favor is that it avoids skepticism (at least in its standard form, described in terms of "skepticism regarding external objects").

According to idealism, objects are nothing but collections of perceptions. To the extent that a perception "represents" anything (as in the theory of representative perceptions), it represents this collection. The skepticism-generating gulf between what I can know (my current perceptual states) and objects disappears, all I need to do in order to know whether there is *really* a telephone in front of me is to open my eyes and—voila!—there it is. Objects are not mind-independent things "out there."

Even though Berkeley doesn't rely on accuracy of representation to distinguish between genuine and nongenuine perceptions, he *does* recognize a difference between the two. If this were not the case, Berkeley's theory would be very far from common-sense indeed. We already met the signs Berkeley uses to distinguish real from imaginary perceptions in section 1.4. Real perceptions (1) are more vivid, (2) arise independently of the will, and (3) are connected to preceding and subsequent perceptions in a way that imaginary perceptions are not. However, as our analysis of genuine versus nongenuine perceptions in *Total Recall* and *The Matrix* have made clear, these conditions do not allow Berkeley to avoid all forms of skepticism. Recall how the argument from section 1.4 went. With regard to the vividness condition, Quaid's and Neo's genuine perceptions were indistinguishable from their nongenuine ones. Also, in both cases, the two characters' perceptions arose independently of their wills: we, as quasi-omniscient spectators, observed that neither individual was producing the perceptions himself. Finally, connectedness is a property that cannot be judged until the last perception is in, for there is always the chance that some abrupt discontinuity in the stream of consciousness will occur some time in the future that will mark the preceding perceptions off as "nongenuine." So, despite the fact that idealism is seen as an antidote to skepticism, it is not up to the challenge. General skepticism is avoided, but Descartes's problem is left unsolved. Berkeley's three signs of genuineness would all be satisfied by many of the (clearly) nongenuine perceptions experienced by Quaid and Neo.

Berkeley argues that there are additional reasons in favor of idealism, above and beyond a desire to avoid skepticism. I shall consider here only one of these arguments. We can see the outline of the argument in the closing sentence of the quotation above: "it [is] perfectly unintelligible . . . to attribute to any single part of [objects] an existence independent of a spirit." Berkeley held that it is not possible to even conceive of the unperceived existence of objects, for, were I to try, I would do so by framing the idea of an unperceived object in my mind. But this idea of an unperceived object is itself a perception (perception here and throughout the rest of this chapter means not just sensory perception but also perception in thought). But now look at what I've done; I am perceiving this presumably unperceived object—a contradiction. One can imagine the following conversation between Descartes and Berkeley on our (in)ability to conceive of mind-independent objects:

Descartes: I can perfectly well think about mind-independent objects. In fact, I'm doing so right now. I'm thinking about a tree deep in an uninhabited forest.

Berkeley: So, even if no one is *looking* at this tree, at least you are *thinking* about it. Isn't that true?

Descartes: Yes, like I said, I'm thinking about this tree.

Berkeley: But the tree is supposed to be *mind-independent*.

Descartes: And it is.

Berkeley: But it is not independent of *your* mind.

Descartes: I disagree. True, I am thinking about it right now, but its existence doesn't depend on that fact.

Berkeley: But your *thinking about it* right now certainly does. How could you, or anyone for that matter, be so inconsistent to say that you can think about something that is not being thought about by anyone? Isn't the patent absurdity of this claim obvious?

Descartes: Okay, how about this? I am thinking about a tree right now that will continue to exist later, even after I have forgotten about it. Now *that* is a thought of a mind-independent tree.

Berkeley: No, that is a confusion. What's at issue here is whether this tree will be conceived by you at that point.

Descartes: At what point?

Berkeley: At the point at which you stop thinking about it.

Descartes: No, that's what it means to say "I've stopped thinking about it."

Berkeley: So, you admit, at *that* point, you won't be conceiving an idea of this unthought-about tree?

Descartes: That's correct.

Berkeley: So we agree, then—you can't conceive of a mind-independent object.

Descartes: No, we don't agree. I can't put my finger on it, but there's something fishy here.

Irrespective of whether there is something fishy here or not, you get Berkeley's point: it is not possible to conceive of a so-called mind-independent object, because, the minute you try to do so, the original description of the object (that it is not being perceived or conceived of by anyone) is no longer correct. How, Berkeley asks rhetorically, could someone build a theory around a concept, that of mind-independent objects, that no one can possibly conceive of?

Most readers probably had the following reaction while reading the above imaginary conversation between Descartes and Berkeley: "Berkeley's theory has some really weird consequences. It is strange that he thought he was capturing the commonsense notion of *object*. Fine, I'll buy that I can't think about something that's not being thought about. But I don't buy that these unperceived or unthought-about objects *don't exist* whenever they are not being thought about or perceived by someone. If *this* view were correct, then the moment I stop looking at my phone—poof!—it ceases to exist. Then, when I look at it again—poof!—it pops back into existence. I don't buy this, and neither will Joe Everyman." Berkeley himself recognized that his view seemed to be at odds with the commonsense view in this regard, so he worked up an explanation of how idealism *did* allow for the existence of unperceived objects. Hence, Berkeley's view is not committed to the "jerky" existence of objects—existent one moment and nonexistent the next. In some respects, the famous, pithy summary of Berkeley's view "to be is to be perceived" is misleading, for this way of putting it does seem to imply that unperceived objects cannot possibly exist; but Berkeley's view is more subtle than that. It turns out that Berkeley gives two (competing?) explanations of how unperceived objects exist. In some passages,[13] he states that, even if no finite mind is perceiving an object, God, who perceives everything,[14] is nevertheless perceiving it.

According to Berkeley, it is God who not only preserves the continuous existence of unperceived objects but also maintains the coherence of perceptions, both within an individual and between individuals.

Though it may sound strange to put it this way, the matrix program in *The Matrix* plays the same role in preserving intra- and interindividual coherence and access to publicly observable objects that God plays within Berkeley's theory. Let's take these one by one. Neo's experiences while in the matrix are internally coherent. He turns his head and his field of vision changes. He turns his head back. What he now sees has not changed radically from a few moments ago. He looks down and sees his hands— the same hands he has seen thousands of times over in his life. Think about this for a moment. The "real" Neo is in a vat; he is not "seeing" anything, at least not with his eyes. So, this coherence within his own perceptions is not something that results from the fact that the "real" world is not changing much from moment to moment. Rather, the matrix, in feeding electrical impulses to Neo's nervous system, is taking care to do it in such a way that coherence is not sacrificed. Take another example. Neo's brain (in the vat) sends out electrical impulses that, in a normal human, would cause the muscle contractions corresponding to walking. The matrix notices this and changes the electrical impulses feeding Neo's sensory pathways in the brain so that (1) his field of view changes appropriately, and (2) he receives tactile information, if his commanded movement would have brought him into contact with another object.

The matrix also maintains interindividual coherence and access to publicly observable objects. Although the rationale for this is never explained in the movie, the matrix program coordinates the sensory information for each of the humans in vats, so that they all are participants in the same virtual world. (Actually, this shared virtual world is never explicitly stated; however, several things in the movie strongly imply it.) So, not only are Neo-in-the-vat's perceptions coherent, his perceptions take into account the virtual actions of other humans in vats. He and other humans can interact with the same publicly observable (albeit virtual) objects.

Maybe, then, Berkeley would say that matrix-generated perceptions *are* real. Would this response be wise on his part? I think not, for several reasons. First, Berkeley took himself as supporting the commonsense view of objects against the "philosopher's confusion" view of objects that people like Descartes put forward. I don't think there can be any doubt that the commonsense response is that matrix-generated perceptions are not real, no matter how vivid and intra- and interpersonally coherent they are. Furthermore, the matrix cannot guarantee continued coherence. Even within the movie (recall the double black cat scene [MM 78:30]), small glitches or changes in the matrix produce minor, local incoherence. Berkeley's infinite God, on the other hand, guarantees *absolute* coherence.

What is posterity's final assessment of Berkelian idealism? The common view among present-day philosophers is that Berkeley's avoidance of skepticism turned out to be an illusion: while his brand of idealism does avoid skepticism in its classical form (stated in terms of our knowledge of *external* objects) it succumbs to a variant form. The idealist wants to maintain a distinction between genuine and nongenuine perceptions; yet, as we have seen, the three signs of genuine perceptions offered by Berkeley are not adequate: many nongenuine perceptions (for example, those experienced by Neo while plugged into the matrix) possess all three signs of genuineness.

Berkeley's defeat did not mean the end of the struggle to refute skepticism. In the remainder of this section, we shall consider the views of the great German philosopher, **Immanuel Kant** (1724–1804).

Kant is one of the most influential thinkers in the history of philosophy. He is also one of the most obscure and difficult-to-read writers in the history of the discipline, as even a cursory glance through his highly praised *Critique of Pure Reason* will attest. Kant believed that no one to date had successfully countered skepticism, and took the failure to refute skepticism as a major "scandal" within philosophy. As he described it, "[I]t still remains a scandal to philosophy and to human reason in general that the existence of things outside us . . . must be accepted merely on *faith*, and that if anyone thinks good to doubt their existence, we are unable to counter his doubts by any satisfactory proof."[15]

Kant agreed with Berkeley that the theory of representative perceptions leads inevitably to skepticism. Thus, in Kant's reworking of a theory of objects, the theory of representative perceptions had to go: whatever a perception represents, it cannot be an external, mind-independent object (what Kant called a "thing in itself"). But he thought Berkeley's theory had equally fatal flaws: it did not recognize the role *the active mind* plays in influencing our experience of the world. As we shall see, Kant's new way of looking at the relationship between the mind and the world had revolutionary consequences in epistemology and, indeed, had repercussions throughout much of the rest of philosophy. These repercussions will be the topic of the next chapter.

The most important item to know about Kant's philosophy is that he distinguished between the world of objects as revealed by experience (in Kant's terminology, the "phenomenal world") and the (purely conjectural) world of things in themselves (the "noumenal world"). According to Kant, knowledge was restricted to the phenomenal world. He would describe Descartes's (and Hume's) mistake as thinking that skepticism would be refuted only if we could gain knowledge of the noumenal world. For Kant, the noumenal world always had the status of an "I know not what. . . ." One may assume that the objects in the phenomenal world bore some relation to things in themselves, but even that must also remain conjecture.

Kant's way of approaching philosophy is often described as revolutionary, in that it challenged what previous philosophers took the logical order of investigation to be. The similarity between Kant's new way of looking at the world and the Copernican revolution in astronomy is sometimes remarked upon. Copernicus's major contribution to astronomy was to overturn the then-standard view of the heavens, according to which the earth is at the center of the solar system. Copernicus showed that the movement of heavenly bodies could be explained in a much simpler fashion if one reversed the then-standard view. Thus, Copernicus inferred that the sun (not the earth) was at the center of the solar system. The earth, along with several other planets, revolves around the sun. Just so, Kant reversed the order of philosophical investigation. Earlier philosophers (for example, Descartes) held a view of objects as mind-independent entities. With this assumption in place, these philosophers would ask, "How do these mind-independent objects affect the mind and how can the mind gain knowledge of them?" Thus, the Cartesian order of enquiry is that first you decide what objects are and then you ask questions about the possibility of obtaining knowledge of these objects. Kant, like Copernicus, asks, What happens if we switch the order? What happens if we assume we have knowledge of the world, then ask what the world must be like, given this knowledge? Since Descartes and Hume had so little success in defending against skepticism with the standard approach, Kant's attitude is: Let's give this new way a try and see what happens. As he writes, "We must . . . make trial whether we may not have more success in the tasks of metaphysics, if we suppose that objects must conform to our knowledge."[16]

Kant has turned the mind/world relation on its head. Previously, philosophers had viewed the mind as a passive perceiver of reality: via perception, our mind receives occasional snapshots of what is "out there." For Kant, reality isn't "out there" at all. It is "in here" and it is something that our mind constructs. Don't be misled: the use of spatial terms "out" and "in" is purely metaphorical, for space and time themselves are also "in here." Likewise, I (my phenomenal self) am also "in here," along with the other objects that make up the world of experience. A mind is like a factory. The raw materials are sense perceptions. The output is the world of experience (the phenomenal world). The rules used to forge the world out of perceptions—the cognitive machinery—are innate. Kant's method of doing philosophy is to look beyond (to "transcend") experience in order to understand the cognitive machinery creating it. Once you understand what principles the mind uses to construct the phenomenal world (the world of experience), you will know what the necessary attributes of all experience are, such that no human could have a conscious experience that deviated from these principles. One of these principles identified by Kant is that the world is made up of objects. My mind necessarily interprets perceptions as perceptions *of objects*—it cannot do otherwise. Whether other sorts of beings with a radically different kind of consciousness could use different principles is a question that Kant leaves open. At a minimum, for beings like us with a consciousness of a *coherent* world filled with *causally interacting objects*, we could not have a conscious experience that deviated from these principles.

Within Kant's framework, the skeptic's challenge can be reformulated: Can I be certain that my perceptions accurately represent objects in the world? Kant would answer: Yes, you can, because you could not have a perception that failed to accurately represent objects in the world; however, you should not misinterpret these represented objects as things in themselves.

Kant's theory can help us understand what may be happening in *Total Recall* after the 17:30 minute mark (part way through Quaid's visit to Rekall). Remember that the overall preferred interpretation is that Quaid never left Rekall: the rest of the movie is the ego trip that Quaid had purchased. There is a problem with this interpretation, however. What (or who) is producing the narrative? We can't find an answer that makes sense of the fact that the post-17:30 narrative includes scenes in which Quaid isn't present. I think Kant would say that the post-17:30 narrative is the phenomenal world being generated by Quaid's mind. Quaid is presented with some perceptions while in the implant chair. Quaid's mind uses those perceptions to construct a coherent narrative. Things aren't that much different with me. Consider an everyday example. I leave outgoing mail in the "out" box on my secretary's desk at time t_1. An hour later (time t_2) I come back in the secretary's office and note that the piece of mail I left at t_1 is now missing. Do I assume that the piece of mail has vanished into thin air? No. I "fill in the gap" by inserting a bit of narrative into the phenomenal world between t_1 and t_2 that has the secretary going to the mailbox and dropping the letter in. While I may explicitly picture to myself the secretary's doing this, I don't have to. All that is necessary in order to fill in the gap in my narrative is that the secretary's doing this becomes part of the phenomenal world my mind constructs. Similarly, just before t_2 I left my own office, to return shortly after t_2. On my return, my desk telephone was just where I left it. I fill in the gap with the phone's staying put during that interval. (By the way, my desk also stayed put during that interval.) My mind does all of this automatically. Indeed, it requires some mental exertion to even make myself aware of the fact that my mind has filled in the gaps in my perceptions in that way. Kant's great contribution was noticing that and then describing how the mind does this. So, what is the best interpretation of the post-17:30 narrative in *Total Recall*? The world of Quaid's experience, with all the gaps filled in.

As I mentioned previously, Kant's views have been widely influential in nineteenth- and twentieth-century philosophy; he is not, however, without his detractors. He, like Berkeley, cannot solve Descartes's problem. Kant recognized the distinction between genuine and nongenuine perceptions; however, his theory provides us with no means of determining at the time a particular perception occurs, whether that perception is genuine or not. Many philosophers have credited Kant as the source for the emergence of philosophical relativism within modernism and postmodernism. We shall revisit Kant's theory in chapter 2 and consider the charge some level against him: that he has refuted general skepticism, but at the cost of making all knowledge subjective (that is, relative to a single individual).

1.7 The Dangers and Lessons of Skepticism

What is an appropriate response to skepticism? The ancient skeptics thought blissful detachment from the world was the appropriate (and natural) response to our lack of knowledge about even the most basic things. Few have followed them in this regard, although Cipher's traitorous act in *The Matrix* (betraying his comrades in order to reenter the matrix as a wealthy and powerful person) shows that, at least for some, skepticism is not something to worry oneself about. For Cipher, virtual perceptions are just as good as real ones; indeed, if they are pleasant, virtual perceptions are preferable to real perceptions. Cipher's response certainly isn't shared by either Quaid or Neo. Maybe the "natural" response to skepticism is general anxiety. (Imagine one of Woody Allen's characters contemplating his total lack of knowledge.) We've seen how many philosophers in the modern era took skepticism as a view to be wrestled with and overcome — so much so that successful refutation of skepticism became the litmus test for the correctness of a theory of objects. Which of these attitudes makes the most sense? You may be surprised to find that David Hume, the greatest defender of skepticism, was also the greatest defender of the claim that skepticism is irrelevant to real life. Were someone to manage to adopt skepticism as a "lifestyle" (to put it in contemporary terms), the results would be catastrophic. As Hume has noted, "[N]o durable good can come of [adopting skepticism as a lifestyle]. . . . [Such a person] cannot expect, that his philosophy will have a constant influence on the mind: Or if it had, that its influence would be beneficial to society. On the contrary, he must acknowledge, if he will acknowledge any thing, that all human life must perish, were his principles universally and steadily to prevail. All discourse, all action would immediately cease;

and men remain in a total lethargy, till the necessities of nature, unsatisfied, put an end to their miserable existence."[17]

Hume thought that the chances of skepticism having this sort of impact were small, because he felt no one could maintain skepticism as a lifestyle. Our minds are wired to accept the report of our senses as accurate, and that is all there is to it. If anything, Hume thought, skepticism is what happens when reason runs amuck. He felt that the function of human reason was to aid in practical problem solving: I want to accomplish A; what plan should I adopt to achieve that goal? *That* sort of activity is the natural domain of our rational faculty. But sometimes, like a wayward child, reason escapes its natural bounds and gets into all sorts of mischief. Skepticism is one sort of mischief that reason, when not properly restrained, can get into.[18]

So, Hume wasn't trying to convince us to adopt skepticism as a lifestyle. What, then, was the purpose of his arguments? He, like many later philosophers, saw a lesson that skepticism could provide to both philosophers and nonphilosophers alike. Skepticism can serve as a check against dogmatism of all stripes. The skeptic's constant insistence on the question "But how do you *know* that?" can be a very useful refrain in the real world.

Skepticism can also serve as a lesson in humility. I think the great twentieth-century philosopher Bertrand Russell (1872–1970) described this best:

> The value of philosophy is, in fact, to be sought largely in its very uncertainty. The man who has no tincture of philosophy goes through life imprisoned in the prejudices derived from common sense, from the habitual beliefs of his age or his nation, and from convictions which have grown up in his mind without the co-operation or consent of his deliberate reason. To such a man the world tends to become definite, finite, obvious; common objects rouse no questions, and unfamiliar possibilities are contemptuously rejected. As soon as we begin to philosophize, on the contrary, we find . . . that even the most everyday things lead to problems to which only very incomplete answers can be given. Philosophy, though unable to tell us with certainty what is the true answer to the doubts which it raises, is able to suggest many possibilities which enlarge our thoughts and free them from the tyranny of custom.[19]

Discussion Questions

1. At the beginning of the chapter, I posed the question "Can you know with absolute certainty that you are not dreaming right now?" How did you answer the question then? Was your response adequate? How would you answer the question now?

2. What are the similarities between skepticism as found in Descartes's first meditation and as found in *Total Recall*? What are the differences?

3. What are the similarities between skepticism as found in Descartes's first meditation and as found in *The Matrix*? What are the differences?

4. There are several references in *The Matrix* to Neo's feeling that "something isn't quite right," even before MM 32:00 (when the "real" Neo is "flushed out" of his vat). Would skepticism on Neo's part have been *rational* during this time period? Would skepticism on Quaid's part after MM 18:00 have been *rational*? Would skepticism on *your* part constitute *rational* doubt?

5. What is the "natural" response to skepticism: repugnance, indifference, or contented acceptance?

6. Do you usually remember (at least part of) your dreams? If so, are you generally aware while dreaming that you are dreaming, or does this recognition only come after you wake up? In either case, explain which characteristics of your dreams allow you to recognize that they are dreams.

7. Do you think Berkeley's argument that mind-independent objects cannot be conceived of is a good one? (This is the argument summarized in the hypothetical conversation between Berkeley and Descartes.) Was your reaction the same as Descartes's ("I can't put my finger on it, but there's something fishy here")? If so, what possible criticisms are there?

Annotated List of Films Relevant to Skepticism

Thirteenth Floor (1999). Directed by Josef Rusnak. Starring Craig Bierko, Armin Mueller-Stahl, Gretchen Mol.
  As in *The Matrix*, this movie supports the skepticism-raising claim that there could be a thoroughly virtual world that is indistinguishable from our world in every detail.

Strange Days (1995). Directed by Kathryn Bigelow. Starring Ralph Fiennes, Angela Bassett, Juliette Lewis.
  This movie shares a plot element in common with *Total Recall*: the retail sale of nongenuine perceptions for recreation, this time by black market street hustlers.

eXistenZ (1999). Directed by David Cronenberg. Starring Jennifer Jason Leigh, Jude Law, Willem Dafoe.
  A future in which the latest virtual reality game plugs directly into the nervous system of its players.

Annotated List of Books Relevant to Skepticism

"CLASSICS" IN THE HISTORY OF SKEPTICISM

Sextus Empiricus
Outlines of Pyrrhonism, first published in Greek, ca. 210 C.E.

René Descartes

Meditations on First Philosophy, first published in Latin, 1641. There have been many translations of the work into English. (The first of the six *Meditations*, included in its entirety in section 1.2, is the *locus classicus* for skepticism in the modern era.) The *Meditations* are also available in their entirety online at <http://philos.wright.edu/Descartes/MedE.html> and at <http://www.utm.edu/research/iep/text/descart/des-med.htm>.

George Berkeley

A Treatise concerning the Principles of Human Knowledge, 1710. The quotations included in this chapter have been taken from a useful collection of the same name that includes both Berkeley's *Treatise* and critical essays on Berkeley's theories by leading philosophers that was published in 1970; the *Treatise* is also available in its entirety online at <http://www.utm.edu/research/iep/text/berkeley/berkprin.htm>.

Three Dialogues between Hylas and Philonous, 1713. Berkeley argues for his version of idealism in dialogue form. The quotations included in this chapter have been taken from the Hackett edition of 1979; the *Three Dialogues* are also available in their entirety online at <http://www.utm.edu/research/iep/text/berkeley/berkdial.htm>.

David Hume

A Treatise of Human Nature, 1740. Hume's magnum opus. It contains not only his famous arguments in favor of skepticism and other issues within epistemology but also his ethics and theory of human psychology. The scholarly standard for this work is the 2nd edition, put out by Oxford University Press in 1978. The *Treatise* is also available in its entirety online at <http://socserv2.socsci.mcmaster.ca/~econ/ugcm/3ll3/hume/treat.html>.

An Enquiry concerning Human Understanding, 1748. For the average reader, the *Enquiry* is a much more approachable work than the *Treatise*. It is fairly short (just over one hundred pages) and written in a quite lively and modern-sounding style. The quotations included in this chapter have been taken from the Hackett edition of 1977; <http://www.utm.edu/research/hume/wri/1enq/1enq.htm>.

Immanuel Kant

Critique of Pure Reason, first published in German, 1st edition 1781, 2nd edition 1787. Probably the most difficult book to read among the major works in the Western philosophical canon. For the very adventurous person who wishes to tackle this behemoth, the standard scholarly version of this work is the combined

1st and 2nd editions, translated by Norman Kemp Smith, published by St. Martin's Press in 1929. If you are interested primarily in reading those parts of the *Critique* dealing with skepticism, a useful commentary is *Kant's Theory of Mental Activity* by Robert Paul Wolff, published by Peter-Smith in 1973. The *Critique* is also available in its entirety online at <http://www.hkbu.edu. hk/~ppp/ cpr/toc.html> and <http://www/arts.cuhk.edu.hk/Philosophy/ Kant/cpr>.

Prolegomena to Any Future Metaphysics, first published in German, 1783. In this work, Kant attempts to boil down the theory laid out in his *Critique of Pure Reason* in a form that is more accessible than the larger work; the *Prolegomena* is also available in its entirety online at <http://www.utm.edu/research/iep/ text/kant/prolegom/prolegom.htm>.

Contemporary Works on Skepticism

Richard Popkin, *History of Skepticism* (Berkeley and Los Angeles: University of California Press, 1979).

Myles Burnyeat, ed. *The Skeptical Tradition* (Berkeley and Los Angeles: University of California Press, 1983). A collection of essays discussing the historical development of skepticism, as well as current controversies.

John Greco, *Putting Skeptics in Their Place* (Cambridge: Cambridge University Press, 2000). This book argues that skepticism is not the easily refutable position so many philosophers believe it to be; it is very readable.

Paul Kurtz, *The New Skepticism* (Buffalo, NY: Prometheus Press, 1992). This is the only book in this section that deals with skepticism in all its forms (moral, political, religious, etc.).

2

Relativism

Hilary and Jackie (1998)

> [T]he order and regularity in the appearances, which we entitle *nature*, we ourselves introduce. We could never find them in appearances, had not we ourselves, or the nature of our mind, originally set them there.
>
> —Immanuel Kant, *Critique of Pure Reason*

Although each chapter of this book is intended as a stand-alone essay on its particular topic, in several respects the material in this chapter is a continuation of the previous chapter. Here we will be examining some of the implications of Immanuel Kant's reworking of a theory of objects described in chapter 1. If the mind is an active constructor of the world of experience rather than a passive perceiver of it, what does that imply about the world and our knowledge of it? *Hilary and Jackie* is an excellent starting point for an examination of this question. The movie is a "multiple-perspective film": it retells the "same" story from several different perspectives, allowing the viewer to see how the various characters interpret their perceptions differently. Section 2.1 provides the philosophical background useful for understanding what is going on in *Hilary and Jackie*, and section 2.2 offers a brief introduction to the film that will draw your attention to things to watch for during your viewing. The material beginning with section 2.3 makes heavy reference to the movie, so it is most profitably read *after* you have finished watching it.

2.1 What Is Relativism?

It is pretty obvious that the truth value of some statements is relative. Consider the sentence, "Fifi is big." Suppose I asked you: What size does Fifi have to be in order for this sentence to be true? Your answer would depend on what Fifi is. If Fifi were a field mouse, Fifi would not have to be very big (in absolute terms) in order for the statement to be true. If Fifi were an elephant, however, Fifi's absolute size would have to be much greater in order for the statement to be true. The moral to draw from this is that the truth or falsity of the statement is dependent on various factors. One such factor is the set of other individuals against which Fifi's size is compared: The statement is not true or false *simpliciter,* but true or false only relative to Fifi's comparison class. This example of truth relativity should not strike anyone as particularly radical. **Cognitive relativism** is the view that *all* statements are like the one above, in that their truth or falsity is relative to some set of (implicit) background conditions and assumptions. A major focus of this chapter is to clarify these background conditions, according to the cognitive relativist. We shall see that, unlike the example of relativism involving Fifi, full-blown cognitive relativism is a *very* radical theory in that it smashes our commonsense view of what the world is like and what we can know.

Cognitive relativism is the most far-reaching and inclusive type of relativism. There are other, more circumscribed versions of relativism. **Aesthetic relativism** is the view that the truth of judgments of aesthetic merit (for example, whether something is beautiful) is relative. According to this view, there is no such thing as objective beauty. "Beauty is in the eye of the beholder." Many people (both lay people and philosophers) hold this version of relativism. Similarly, **moral relativism**, the view that the truth of all moral judgments is relative, has many adherents. We will be discussing moral relativism at length in chapter 5 in the context of a general treatment of ethics. What aesthetic and moral relativism have in common is that they both involve the truth relativism of judgments of value or worth, as opposed to nonvalue judgments. To see the difference, consider the two statements:

S1: Some of Hitler's actions indirectly caused the death of millions of people.
S2: Some of Hitler's actions were morally wrong.

S1 is what philosophers call a "nonvalue judgment"—it is not making any sort of evaluation of Hitler's actions. (On being confronted with *S1*, you may *infer* moral condemnation of some of Hitler's actions, but that is an inference on your part—it is not contained in the actual sentence *S1*.) *S2*, on the other hand, *is* a value judgment. It states that, judged morally, some of Hitler's actions come up wanting. Cognitive relativism is the view that the truth or falsity of all judgments (both value judgments and nonvalue judgments) is relative. As we shall see, cognitive relativism breaks up into several subtypes; what they all have in common, however, is a rejection of an objective standard against which the truth (or justifiability) of a judgment is determined.

The most straightforward entry into a discussion of relativism is to compare it with its main rival: **cognitive objectivism**, which consists of two related theses. The first is a thesis about the nature of the world, and this thesis states that there is a mind-independent world, a world made up of objects whose existence is independent of what anyone or any group of people happens to think. The second thesis that comprises cognitive objectivism is a thesis about the nature of truth; this second thesis is called the **correspondence theory of truth**. According to it, the truth of a statement is determined by whether or not that statement corresponds to one of the facts true of this mind-independent world. Denial of the first thesis yields a version of idealism. (Not Berkelian idealism, as discussed in section 1.6, but something akin to it.) Denial of the second thesis yields cognitive relativism.

Recall the discussion of skepticism in chapter 1. The problem that gives rise to skepticism is that I have no way of knowing that my perceptions accurately represent the objects "out there" in the mind-independent world; I have no way of "peeking around" my perceptions and observing these external objects directly to make sure that the perceptions got it right. Kant's way out of this quandary was to note that the mind was not the passive perceiver of the world of experience as assumed within René Descartes's theory of representative perceptions, but rather the active *constructor* of the world of experience. The mind receives sensory data. The cognitive machinery in the mind then works on this sensory stream, ultimately producing the spatiotemporal world. This is the world of everyday objects: tables, chairs, cups of coffee, telephones, and so on. This is the world that I, as an agent, operate in. When I perceive, the objects represented by my perceptions are nothing other than these objects. When I drink from my cup of coffee, I manipulate the cup in various ways, resulting in there being less liquid in the cup than when I started the action. All this is as it should be—as common sense tells us the world is.

Within Kant's world, skepticism, at least in its standard form, never arises. I can know that my perceptions accurately represent objects in the world because my mind has constructed the represented objects. The scaffolding that the mind uses to construct the world of experience are concepts. According to Kant, concepts are like rules that guide the mind in deciding which perceptions go with which other ones as being perceptions of one and the same object, or as being related as cause and effect. Without these concepts, our sensory stream would not reveal to us a coherent world. Rather, it would be, to use William James's words, a "buzzing, blooming confusion." Try for a moment to imagine what "the world" would look like if you were unable to interpret your visual sensory stream in terms of interrelated objects. There would be no regularity from one moment to the next. No objects persisting through time. For that matter, there would be no objects at all—just uninterpreted patches of color of various shades. In terms of information content received (as opposed to mere sensory stimulation received), you would be no better off than a blind person. Kant summed this up by saying that: "percepts without concepts are blind."[1]

But Kant's reinterpretation of the role of the mind in perception comes at a philosophical cost: if *we* are the ones who impose a structure on our perceptions, deciding where object boundaries are, for example, then it seems as though Kant has avoided skepticism by driving headlong into radical subjectivism. Knowledge and truth are now relative to the individual perceiver. Kant would disagree. He thought that all perceivers (or, at least, all perceivers with a consciousness like ours) had to share in common a few basic guidelines in order for our form of consciousness to arise. We must all view the world as made up of persisting objects, for example. We must also all view these objects as interacting causally with one another. This much has to be innate. The particular rules we use in carving our perceptual stream up into individual objects are presumably the result of learning. There is no objectively correct way of carving up our perceptual stream. Some methods of carving it up may be better than others based on pragmatic considerations; but, since objects are not "out there" in the mind-independent world, one cannot even make sense of the notion of "an objectively correct" way of carving up the perceptual stream into objects.[2]

Consider an example. I interpret some of the color patches in my visual field as telephones. In fact, I'm looking at the telephone on my desk right now. It is beige, with black touch-pads used for dialing. Someone who lacked the concept of a telephone may interpret that set of beige and black color patches as a part of the desk. For that matter, someone may interpret the beige and black color patches as made up of several distinct objects that do not together form a larger object. The point is, what a perceiver is given in her visual stream is just a bunch of color patches, but not information specifying what color patches belong together. The latter information is generated by us. This point is hard to grasp, since we are seldom consciously aware of what the mind is doing as it segments our sensory stream into objects. It is easier to grasp if we think for a moment about how an infant views the world. Let's assume that the infant in question is old enough to have normal vision, but young enough that it lacks the concept of a telephone. If confronted with one, the infant would not automatically interpret the color patches corresponding to a phone as belonging together. Why not? Because the infant has not yet learned to associate these color patches together under the concept "telephone."

The set of concepts a perceiver uses to interpret her perceptual stream is called a **conceptual scheme**. (Many philosophers also include the rules a perceiver uses for updating her conceptual scheme in light of new information as a part of the conceptual scheme.) Individuals with different conceptual schemes may interpret exactly the same set of raw sense data in widely disparate ways. For example, the infant and I may interpret our visual perceptions differently when looking at a telephone. Is there a guarantee that all adults will eventually adopt the same conceptual scheme? In that case, even though we still couldn't talk about the *objectively correct* conceptual scheme, we could at least know that others were interpreting their perceptions in the same way that we were. Many philosophers, psychologists, and cultural anthropologists answer this question in the negative: there is no such guarantee that all cognitively mature perceivers will ultimately adopt the same conceptual scheme; in fact, there is evidence that they do not.

Consider the evidence for divergence of conceptual schemes coming out of cultural anthropology. Cultural anthropologists have come back from the field with reports of cultures whose individuals use quite different conceptual schemes for interpreting their experience. What initially appear to be irrational beliefs on the part of the research subjects are shown to "make sense" in the context of the culture-specific conceptual scheme. The conceptual scheme an individual adopts is usually very similar to the conceptual scheme used by his peers (that is, intracultural similarity of conceptual schemes is high). At the same time, there are consistent differences between the conceptual schemes used by the members of different cultures (that is, intercultural similarity is low). This is explained, not by some sort of genetically inherited predisposition to certain conceptual schemes, but because (1) the environment in which the culture lives shapes what perceptual attributes are salient,[3] (2) the conceptual scheme an individual adopts is in large measure determined by the language an individual learns,[4] and (3) much learning is supervised.

Even though the preceding paragraph stressed the culture specificity of conceptual schemes, there is no reason why individuals within a culture *must* have identical conceptual schemes. I have on occasion run across fellow Americans who interpret much of their experience as involving the work of the devil. When asked whether they genuinely believe that the devil exists (as opposed to merely using that term metaphorically) they insist that they are being quite literal. They can even point to specific events as being caused (or, at least, partially caused) by the devil. They can explain in detail how the devil fits into the causal sequence in question. And, relative to the rest of their conceptual scheme, the explanation makes perfect sense. So, for them, the devil is not just some abstract entity that they believe in, but an entity that plays a major role in organizing their world.

It is open to debate whether someone who believes in the devil and someone who does not are members of the same culture. Clearly, cultural boundaries need not follow political boundaries. While this brings up an interesting set of issues, they lie beyond the scope of this chapter.

An issue that shall take up much of our time in later sections of this chapter is the question of whether there is any reason to say that one conceptual scheme is better than another. For example, is a conceptual scheme that includes the devil *objectively* better or worse than one that doesn't? The cognitive relativist would answer: no. Remember, step one of cognitive relativism was throwing out the idea that included among the raw sense data that our sense organs take in is the "correct" segmentation of the raw sense data into objects. It is the mind that does the segmentation, based on the conceptual scheme that the individual uses. So, at a minimum, the cognitive relativist would argue that neither the conceptual scheme with the devil nor the one without is better by virtue of being the *objectively correct* one.

Is there some other criterion that could be uniformly and universally applied to conceptual schemes to rate them in terms of their overall goodness? Here again, most cognitive relativists would answer: no.[5] The reasons cited by relativists to justify this response vary. Some argue that the only criterion other than objective truth that could be used in rating conceptual schemes is the overall rationality of the scheme; there is, however, no rational foundation for deciding between conflicting conceptual schemes. Other cognitive relativists argue that rationality itself is internal to a conceptual scheme; there is no such thing as a conceptually neutral version of rationality that could be used to compare different conceptual schemes with one another. Conceptual scheme number one would grade itself based on the notion of rationality that goes along with that conceptual scheme, and—surprise—would be shown to be quite rational. Conceptual scheme number two would grade itself on the notion of rationality that goes along with itself and, again, is found to be quite rational. This way of arguing can be summed up in four words: rationality is itself relative. We shall be examining this line of argument further in later sections of this chapter.

Before closing out this section, I would like to draw several historical parallels between cognitive relativism and skepticism. Both positions have their philosophical roots in ancient Greece. The name most closely associated with relativism in the ancient world is that of Protagoras (ca. 480–421 B.C.E.), a slightly older contemporary of Socrates. Like those of the early skeptics, the bulk of Protagoras's writings are no longer extant; however, a few tantalizing fragments have managed to survive (mostly in the context of criticisms of relativism by subsequent generations of Greek philosophers). The most famous among these is: "Man is the measure of all things: of what is, that it is; of what is not, that it is not."[6] Here we see the rejection of the correspondence theory of truth. According to Protagoras, it is not correspondence with mind-independent "facts" that distinguishes truth from falsity. Rather, "man" is the ultimate arbiter of what is true and what is false.[7]

Cognitive relativism died out at the end of the ancient period, and only reemerged in the modern period. Its initial reemergence was not the result of any belated encounter with relativism in ancient sources, but almost exclusively the result of the influence of Kant's writings on later philosophers. Even though cognitive relativism has taken a turn into postmodernism that would have unsettled Kant, I believe that postmodernist relativism also traces its source back to Kant. (We shall discuss postmodernist relativism in section 2.6.)

Another remarkable similarity between relativism and skepticism is their philosophical resilience. A leading contemporary philosopher, Alasdair MacIntyre, has, I think, put this best, noting that "relativism, like skepticism, is one of those doctrines that have by now been refuted a number of times too often. Nothing is perhaps a surer sign that a doctrine embodies some not-to-be-neglected truth than that in the course of the history of philosophy it should have been refuted again and again. Genuinely refutable doctrines only need to be refuted once."[8] Even if you ultimately reject cognitive relativism as untenable, you may find yourself in agreement with

MacIntyre that it contains a kernel—an insight—that the cognitive objectivist should not ignore.

2.2 An Overview of the Movie

HILARY AND JACKIE (1998). DIRECTED BY ANAND TUCKER.
STARRING EMILY WATSON, RACHEL GRIFFITHS, JAMES FRAIN,
DAVID MORRISSEY.

The most important thing to know about *Hilary and Jackie* for the purposes of this chapter is that it is a multiple-perspective film: telling the same story from the perspectives of several different characters. On many points, these retellings disagree with one another. The rest of this chapter will be concerned with the philosophical import of this disagreement.

While the multiple-perspective structure of film should be obvious, it is useful to have it in mind, for, right from the beginning, the film is dropping hints about when perspective changes and what to make of those changes. In the plot summary for the movie included in the appendix, I have tried to make explicit when perspective changes. It may be helpful to read the appendix entry while watching it, in order to see when the various switches in perspective occur, for, while the filmmaker has provided us with explicit labels ("Hilary and Jackie," "Hilary" and "Jackie") for the first three-quarters of the film, by the end, perspective is switching at a rather fast clip from Hilary to Jackie and back again, and, by now, no labels are provided.

Based on the book by brother and sister Hilary and Piers du Pre (originally entitled *A Genius in the Family*, later retitled *Hilary and Jackie*), the film *Hilary and Jackie* follows the lives of the two du Pre sisters from their childhood in 1950s England to sister Jackie's rise to stardom as one of the world's preeminent concert cellists. The two girls, both musicians (sister Hilary plays the flute), are originally very close, but Jackie's increasing success and celebrity tear them apart. The trajectories of their lives diverge even more as Hilary settles down, marrying her first love Kiffer Finzi, while Jackie becomes ever more isolated in the role of "musical genius," eventually marrying the gifted pianist and conductor Daniel Barenboim. Jackie's increasing isolation and unhappiness with the life she has chosen (or, from her perspective, the life she had thrust upon her) is brought to a head during a fateful visit to Hilary and Kiffer's country home. When Hilary and Piers du Pre first published the book detailing their family's lives, it caused quite an uproar among the classical music community, within which Jacqueline du Pre had been almost deified. Some suggested that Hilary's picture of Jackie was the result of envy and jealousy at her sister's musical success. The film's release only reignited the controversy. Gossip column flap aside, the charge that Hilary and Pier's portrayal of Jackie is colored by subjectivity only adds to the philosophical usefulness of the film in exploring the issue of cognitive relativism.

2.3 *What* Really *Happened?*

So, you've just finished watching *Hilary and Jackie*. What happened? What *really* happened?

Hilary and Jackie differs from most of the other films presented in this book, in that its philosophical import is not to be found in the story or in bits of dialogue, but in the structure of the film.[9] In the film's various retellings, the viewer is made aware of the markedly different interpretations each of the characters puts on the "same" set of events. Most films (and virtually all mainstream Hollywood movies) convey a story from a single omniscient or quasi-omniscient perspective: the film's narrative is not bound by the knowledge or point of view of any single character. Rather, it is as if the narrative is being generated by some disinterested spectator who can observe events taking place without regard for distance in time or place. Within this narrative convention, questions about what to make of differing interpretations never come up. However, *Hilary and Jackie* confronts us with different pictures of the world, and thereby forces us to try to make sense of these differences. What is responsible for generating the differences? What do the differences tell us about the nature of the world?

Let's begin our investigation of the film by looking at its narrative structure. The first label identifying whose perspective is being offered occurs at the 3:30 minute mark,[10] as the words "Hilary and Jackie" flash briefly on the screen. This shared perspective lasts through the two girls' childhood and teenage years, ending on the night of the Italian wedding (MM 23:20). Hilary's perspective (clearly demarcated as the name "Hilary" flashes on the screen) picks up when she awakens the next morning to find that Jackie has gone. We are then presented with events as experienced by Hilary over the next decade or so of fictional time. I will come back shortly to discuss several key events in this series; first, though, I want to lay out the rest of the film's structure. At MM 63:30, the word "Jackie" flashes on the screen and we are back in Italy the morning after the wedding as Jackie is awakened early to catch a train for her next performance. For the next twenty-seven minutes of the film, we review roughly the same time span, now from Jackie's perspective. Beginning at MM 90:00, perspective shifts back and forth from that of Jackie to that of Hilary. This time, though, we are not provided with labels to warn us of the changes in perspective. Other clues (for example, scenes in which only one sister is present) are needed. The film ends as Hilary and Piers are driving back after Jackie's death.[11]

Events recounted from Hilary's and Jackie's perspectives have much in common. A careful viewer should have little problem recognizing that many events described from

Jackie's perspective match up with those from Hilary's. However, there are three events recognizable in both Hilary's and Jackie's perspectives where there is major disagreement about what really happened. These three events are: Kiffer's first "visit" to the du Pre home; the nighttime conversation between Hilary and Jackie, when Hilary announces her engagement to Kiffer; and circumstances surrounding Kiffer and Jackie having sex. Let's start with the last event and work our way back in time. (In the part of the film relating events from Jackie's perspective, the sex act is implied at MM 85:00. The corresponding event from Hilary's point of view occurs at MM 55:20; however, Jackie's initial request to sleep with Kiffer occurs earlier, at MM 47:00.) This event from Jackie's point of view is barely recognizable as the same as what we had seen from Hilary's point of view. Hilary viewed the act as the effect of Jackie's uncaring manipulations—her desire to get what she (Jackie) wanted, irrespective of cost to those around her. From Jackie's perspective, there is no trace of the manipulations that loom so large from Hilary's point of view. Rather, the sequence of events leading up to sex is: Kiffer comes into Jackie's room, notices that she is very upset, and comforts her. Sex between the two of them isn't shown, but we can easily imagine it as the continuation of this scene. There is no hint that it is anything other than a spontaneous act on both their parts.

The second event that differs sharply in interpretation is the nighttime conversation between the two sisters, as Hilary wakes Jackie up to announce her engagement to Kiffer. (This begins at MM 35:20 from Hilary's point of view and MM 73:00 from Jackie's point of view.) From Hilary's point of view, Jackie is very cruel. When asked why she is marrying Kiffer, Hilary responds, "Because he makes me feel special." Jackie replies, "[T]he truth is, you're not special." Compare this with the conversation as related from Jackie's point of view. That same line ("the truth is, you're not special") is still there, but its meaning has changed significantly. Here it is Hilary who is the cruel one.

The final event I would like to consider occurs shortly after Kiffer barges into the du Pre home. (Hilary's take on this begins at MM 30:55, Jackie's at MM 72:50.) Even at this early juncture (not very much fictional time has elapsed since the wedding in Italy when the two perspectives started to diverge), clear differences are noticeable. Missing from Hilary's version of events is any sense that Jackie is disappointed by Hilary's choice to spend time with Kiffer, even though Jackie has come back home to see her.

If you are like me, your initial reaction is to try to reconcile the diverging stories, discovering the hidden truth that both versions of events were based upon. This reaction discloses an objectivist leaning: one assumes there are facts about what happened and one tries to use the conflicting stories as clues to discovering the facts. However, it is not at all obvious what this "hidden truth" would be.

In general, there are four alternatives we can take in order to reconcile the differences:

1. We can reject one of the interpretations as untrue and based on misinformation.
2. We can reject one of the interpretations as untrue and the result of lying.
3. We can reject one of the interpretations as untrue and the result of self-deception.
4. We can accept both of the conflicting interpretations as true by adopting a relativistic stance.

The first three options explain the differences as the result of error of some sort or other: one (or both) of the characters simply failed to represent the mind-independent world accurately. *Hilary and Jackie* does not *force* us to adopt the fourth, relativistic option, but the multiple-perspective structure of the film holds relativism out as an avenue that deserves exploring. So, here we go.

One advantage of discussing cognitive relativism in the context of a concrete example is that it clothes the various arguments for and against cognitive relativism in a form that is more accessible. Too often, relativism is discussed at a very high level of abstraction, and one is not sure *what* the various participants in the discussion have in mind when they speak of "differing perspectives."

The best way to get a foothold on this topic is by examining the main empirical argument for cognitive relativism. This argument begins with the pervasive differences of opinion one observes among people, coupled with the claim that there is no objective standard to use in adjudicating between the differing views—no objective standard to use in deciding which view is true and which view is false. Clearly, different opinions are offered by Hilary and Jackie. Does a difference of opinion by itself constitute evidence in favor of cognitive relativism? I think not. This can be seen by considering a related argument, one that shows the structural unsoundness of inferring cognitive relativism based solely on a difference of opinion.

This related argument runs as follows:[12] Different individuals have different views on whether the earth is flat or not. In general, there is a high degree of intracultural agreement on this question. Thus, among adults within a given culture, the probability that an individual holds the flat-earth hypothesis is closely correlated with whether her cultural peers hold this hypothesis. (Since conceptual schemes play a large role in cognitive relativism, and since conceptual schemes are largely culture-specific, this intracultural agreement is potentially relevant to the argument—it strengthens the relativist's case.) However, intercultural diversity and intracultural uniformity on the question of the earth's shape do not entail that there is no objective fact of the matter about whether the earth is flat or not. A consistent cognitive objectivist can say that some cultures (namely, those cultures in which the flat earth hypothesis is widespread) are just mistaken on this point. The burden of proof is on the relativist to show how difference of opinion implies relativism; so, the objectivist's response is not begging the question. In general, mere difference of opinion does not constitute evidence in favor of relativism. In order to argue for cognitive relativism, we must be offered more; we must be offered reasons to believe that there is no way of adjudicating between the differing views.

Hilary and Jackie does just that. As viewers, we are offered not just difference of opinion but also enough of Hilary's and Jackie's history to understand how and why their later conceptual schemes diverged. Consequently, the film does offer us reasons to believe that *both* sisters' account of events are true.

So far, all I have done is catalog a list of differences between Hilary's and Jackie's takes on events. As stated above, this sort of difference does not, in itself, argue for cognitive relativism. For that, we must be presented not only with a difference of opinion but also with some reason to think the difference is the result of incompatible but equally valid conceptual schemes. Otherwise, the cognitive objectivist can dismiss the differences as being the result of misinformation or deception of some sort. *Hilary and Jackie* provides us with evidence of differing conceptual schemes. We see that differences in interpretation of later events can be traced back to differing experiences during the time period when the two sisters are separated. Given these previous experiences, Hilary's take "makes sense," as does Jackie's, even though the two are at odds with one another.

There are three events that provide us as viewers with information about how and why the two sisters' interpretations of later events diverge. In each case, one of the sisters lacks relevant information about what is happening with the other. The three events all occur fairly early in fictional time after the Italian wedding. Indeed, the first event to be discussed happens that very next morning after the wedding, as first Jackie wakes up, then Hilary. In some ways, Hilary's take on these events stretches credulity, but I will disregard that as within the bounds of artistic license. (For this event from Hilary's perspective, see MM 23:40, for Jackie's, see MM 64:10.) Hilary wakes to find Jackie already gone. Hilary's reaction shows that this was not something she had expected. (This is the aspect that, I believe, stretches believability—that Hilary would not have been informed of Jackie's upcoming concert in Berlin and the need for an early departure.) From Hilary's perspective, Jackie had abandoned her there, without bothering to wake her or even write a "goodbye" note. When we finally get around to seeing Jackie's take on things, we start with exactly this event. Jackie is awakened by a man telling her she is running very late. She wants to wake Hilary and say good-bye but is told that there is no time for that. She receives assurance that Hilary's transportation back to England has already been taken care of.

The second event that helps us understand why the two sisters' conceptual schemes diverged involves the package of laundry. (See MM 27:00 and 71:00 for Hilary's and Jackie's takes, respectively.) In some ways, this event is emblematic of the whole film. Jackie, desperately homesick, is overjoyed to receive a reminder of home in the form of the familiar smell of her cleaned clothes. For her, the washed laundry has much more import than merely having clean clothes to wear again. Hilary, unaware of Jackie's current mental state, interprets the dirty laundry as evidence that Jackie doesn't care about the family she has left behind. To the extent Jackie thinks about them at all, it is as someone to do her laundry. I say this is emblematic of the whole film because it shows not only how different prior experiences can lead to different interpretations of shared events, but also how those differences in interpretations tend to reinforce the differences.

The final event that helps to explain how the two sisters' conceptual schemes diverged is Jackie's first noticing that something is wrong with her. Recall the chronology leading up to Jackie's unannounced arrival at Hilary and Kiffer's country home. Jackie has altered perception (MM 81:50). Jackie breaks the glass backstage and notices that her hand is shaking badly (MM 82:40). Jackie appears to know that something is seriously wrong with her—something that may make it impossible for her to continue playing the cello. She tries to talk about it with Danny, asking him how he would react if she were to give up the life of a concert cellist and become an "ordinary" person. Danny's response is very discouraging (MM 83:20). Hilary is not aware of any of this.

Do these differences in take amount to a difference in conceptual scheme? When I introduced the notion of a conceptual scheme in section 2.1, I used somewhat simplistic examples as illustration. The way I described it there, two people have differing conceptual schemes if they segment their respective perceptual streams differently. For example, I interpret a set of beige and black color patches as a telephone (a distinct object). Someone else (someone who lacks the concept of a telephone) interprets a similar set of beige and black color patches as a part of the desk. The example involving the devil is slightly more nuanced. I do not interpret events as the work of the devil; the concept of the devil plays no role in constructing a coherent world out of my perceptual stream. Someone else *does* use the concept of the devil in constructing a coherent world out of his perceptions. In that world, the devil is an active (if unseen) agent, causing various events to occur, and, perhaps, preventing the occurrence of others. The examples of differing interpretations I have drawn from *Hilary and Jackie* are not so straightforward as the examples I used in introducing what it means for two people to have different conceptual schemes. The most important respect in which the two sisters' interpretations differ regards the motives each imputes to the other sister in making sense of that sister's behavior. There seems also to be differences in what each sister pays attention to. Thus, in certain shared scenes (for example, the nighttime conversation in which Hilary announces her engagement), elements from one version of events are missing in the other and vice versa. These differences *do* amount to a difference in conceptual schemes, because the mutually incompatible world that each sister constructs is internally coherent and differs from the world constructed by the other sister in predictable ways. In Hilary's world, some of the bad things that befall her are the direct result of the actions of her self-absorbed sister. In Jackie's world, the loneliness and fear she feels are not assuaged when she seeks comfort from Hilary. If anything, Hilary's rejection of her only heightens those feelings.

2.4 Comparing Conceptual Schemes

Whose take on events was superior: Hilary's or Jackie's? Does this question even make sense? Whenever I discuss *Hilary and Jackie* with others, I find most people in agreement with Hilary's way of interpreting events. Hilary is the "good guy," the long-suffering victim, and Jackie is the "bad guy," the one who manipulates and uses others to get her way. While the typical viewer reports that her picture of Jackie softened somewhat after seeing things from Jackie's point of view, the bias in favor of Hilary and her perspective remains. (It would be interesting to see whether reversing the order of presentation of perspectives had any effect on this trend.) When asked *why* they voted in favor of Hilary's perspective as most accurate and/or trustworthy, the answer varies. Most people say something like, "Hilary's interpretation of events strikes me as most plausible." However, when asked to elaborate, or to cite a particular event and explain why Hilary's interpretation is more plausible than Jackie's, no answer is forthcoming.

How have philosophers approached this question? Is it possible to adjudicate between differing conceptual schemes? All cognitive relativists would say that, since no conceptual scheme is the objectively correct one, it is not possible to adjudicate based on dismissing all conceptual schemes but one as objectively mistaken. Cognitive relativists sometimes refer to a series of famous drawings as a means of illustration. Consider figure 2.1. What is it a drawing of?

Figure 2.1   *Figure 2.2*

Is it a duck looking up and to the right or a rabbit in profile looking to the left? What about figure 2.2? Is it an old woman looking to the left and slightly forward, or a young woman looking to the back and slightly left? If you are like most people, you are able to see figure 2.1 as either a duck or a rabbit, but not both simultaneously. Rather, your interpretation of the drawing shifts back and forth. At first, this shifting back and forth is beyond your conscious control. If you try, though, you should be able to "will" yourself to see it either one way or the other, depending on which features of the drawing you attend to; the same goes for figure 2.2.

The point that cognitive relativists make in putting these drawings forward as examples is that there is no objective fact about whether figure 2.1 is a duck or a rabbit. So, one cannot simply dismiss either of the two interpretations as being mistaken. One way in which the duck/rabbit drawing is unlike the difference between conceptual schemes is that, usually, you cannot will yourself to switch from one way of interpreting the world to another. In this respect, a second pair of drawings gets closer to what the cognitive relativist has in mind. Consider figures 2.3 and 2.4.

What is figure 2.3 a drawing of, a bird or an antelope? Now consider the same line drawing as in Figure 2.3, this time in the context of a flock of birds. If you are like me, you can discern the surrounding context "pulling" your mind toward the bird interpretation of the drawing. You can no longer flip at will between viewing the drawing as an antelope or as a bird. This is much closer to the role that an individual's conceptual scheme plays in determining how that individual views the world, according to the cognitive relativist. Raw sense data are ambiguous—they can be coherently interpreted in many different ways. Just so, figure 2.3 is ambiguous. The particular way an individual interprets the world depends on all sorts of other variables, including the individual's past experiences, what the individual is currently paying attention to, and other things going on within the individual's perceptual stream.

Figure 2.3   *Figure 2.4*

2.5 Truth Relativism

Cognitive relativism is not one single theory; rather, it is a family of theories. In this section, I focus on the least radical of these: truth relativism; section 2.6 will take up the more radical forms of cognitive relativism.

The first two forms of relativism I want to consider are not actually forms of *cognitive* relativism at all. **Physical-perspective relativism** is the view that whatever someone perceives must be perceived from a particular physical vantage point: there is no such thing as "a view from nowhere." Since physical perspective relativism does not question the existence of objective truth, it is not a form of cognitive relativism. **Weak conceptual relativism**, the view that perception must occur within the framework of some conceptual scheme or other, is also not a version of cognitive relativism, for it leaves open the possibility that some conceptual schemes are objectively incorrect.

Truth relativism denies the second objectivist thesis, the correspondence theory of truth, which claims that the truth of a statement is determined by whether or not that statement corresponds to one of the facts true of the mind-independent world. Rather, according to truth relativism, the truth or falsity of a statement must be judged relative to a particular conceptual scheme. Truth relativism differs from more radical forms of cognitive relativism in holding that rationality is universal and can be used in judging the adequacy (but not the objective truth) of competing conceptual schemes. Note that truth relativism does not deny the existence of a mind-independent world. That is, it does not deny the first of the two objectivist theses. Yet, if the truth relativist believes in the existence of a mind-independent world, how can he then justify *not* using that mind-independent world as the standard against which to judge the truth or falsity of judgments? Some truth relativists would answer this question by arguing that the concepts we use in segmenting sensory data and in forming judgments are *qualitatively* different from the way the mind-independent world really is. The mismatch between our concepts and the nature of the mind-independent world is so great that the correspondence theory of truth is not an option.

Other truth relativists reject the correspondence theory of truth because they say a criterion of truth must be applicable in practice, and skeptical arguments have shown that we could not possibly *apply* the correspondence theory of truth, for we can never know what this mind-independent world is really like. Since knowledge of objective truth is beyond our grasp, we should make do with the relativistic notion of truth that truth relativism offers.

2.6 Nietzschean Perspectivism and Postmodernism

Truth relativism is not the most radical form of relativism, however, for it holds out the possibility that different conceptual schemes can be ranked based on their overall rationality. Indeed, truth relativism holds out the possibility that some conceptual schemes can be rejected outright as irrational. To get to these most radical forms of relativism, we must combine truth relativism (relativism concerning how the truth value of individual statements is determined) with relativism of rationality (relativism concerning what makes a conceptual scheme well justified).

In looking at the family of theories that make up cognitive relativism, the next level up in terms of radicalness is **relativism of rationality**. What counts as a good reason for adopting a particular conceptual scheme? According to this form of relativism, there is no straightforward answer to this question, either because the notion of rationality is itself relative to a conceptual scheme, or because rationality as that notion is understood within the Anglo-American tradition is not a universal standard—many conceptual schemes lack anything roughly approximating our notion of rationality. According to the relativity of rationality, "what warrants belief depends on canons of reasoning . . . that should properly be seen as social norms, relative to culture and period."[13]

In its most extreme form, relativism of rationality even questions whether the laws of logic have any sort of objective status. According to **relativism of logic**, laws of logic (for example, the law of noncontradiction—that it is not possible for a statement to be simultaneously true and false) are merely social norms; they do not reflect laws governing the mind-independent world. The most radical relativists do not even require that I be minimally consistent in my beliefs, assuming my conceptual scheme does not recognize the law of noncontradiction. In the words of Walt Whitman, "Do I contradict myself? / very well then I contradict myself, / (I am large, I contain multitudes.)"[14] In the rest of this section, I look at the two most radical members of the cognitive relativism family: Nietzschean perspectivism and postmodernist relativism.

While few nonphilosophers are familiar with Immanuel Kant, **Friedrich Nietzsche** (1844–1900) is almost a household name. (I'm less confident that his views are as well-known as his name.) Nietzsche lived in the nineteenth century; thus, he predates the birth of postmodernism. However, he is the first major philosopher to espouse relativism of rationality, the point of departure for postmodernism. Indeed, he was also prescient of postmodernism in emphasizing the role language plays both in fixing our conceptual schemes and in creating the very idea of objective truth.

Nietzsche had a rather strange writing style, preferring to express his ideas with highly elliptical prose and copious self-contradictions. Some have argued that this writing style was exactly what was called for, given the message: Nietzsche wanted to jar his readers into seeing that many of the things they currently believed were not objectively true, without thereby putting something equally untrue in their place.[15] The use of multiple perspectives, in both film and literature, serves a similar purpose. We, as viewers, are shown several incompatible descriptions of the world and asked not to pick which one is the objectively correct one (or even which is closest to objective truth) but to conclude that they are all true relative to the perspective of their respective narrators. As Nietzsche tells us,

There are no facts, only interpretations.

As though there would be a world left over once we subtracted the perspectival![16]

Contrary to the implication of the second quotation above, he was no idealist: there *was* a world left over after the subtraction of the perspectival. As Arthur Danto notes in writing about Nietzsche, "[T]here was a world which remained over, tossing blackly like the sea, chaotic relative to our distinctions and perhaps to all distinctions, but there nevertheless. . . . A blind, empty, structureless thereness."[17] So, Nietzsche's conceptual relativism was the result of what he saw as a qualitative mismatch between our distinctions (that is, the concepts we use in structuring the world of experience) and the mind-independent world.

Because of his repeated emphasis on the ineluctably perspectival nature of all observation and knowledge, Nietzsche's version of cognitive relativism has come to be called "perspectivism." But Nietzsche didn't stop there, with merely a *negative* description of what the world *wasn't*. His perspectivism had a positive aspect as well. To the extent that you can say what it *is*, the world is "made up of points of origin for perspectives, . . . occupied by active powers, wills, each seeking to organize the world from its perspective, each locked in combat with the rest."[18]

Does this mean that every conceptual scheme is as good as every other one? Nietzsche would answer: no. The wills are in combat. The victor shall be the will whose perspective incorporates the conceptual scheme that most facilitates life. For Nietzsche, "Truth is that sort of error without which a particular class of living creatures could not live."[19] So, Nietzsche does not use some objective standard of rationality in judging the adequacy of a conceptual scheme, but rather a pragmatic standard: a conceptual scheme is adequate if it allows me to thrive.

While postmodernism's intellectual roots can be traced back to Immanuel Kant, its history as a distinct school of thought begins in the mid-twentieth century within philosophy and literary criticism in France and Germany, as a reaction to the devastation of the Second World War. For the postmodernists, Hiroshima and the Holocaust showed without a doubt that humanity is not progressing toward some objective goal, as the modernists' inherent faith in the universality of rationality had led many to believe.

Postmodernism's starting point is the claim that there are no objective standards either for determining the truth or falsity of individual judgments or for judging the adequacy of conceptual schemes. Members of the mainstream Western tradition mistakenly believe in objective standards because our language has created the myth of a mind-independent world against which judgments can be compared. According to

Gene Blocker, one of the goals of postmodernism is to expose this myth of the mind-independent world *as a myth*

> by "deconstructing" language, that is, by showing first the gap between word and object, language and reality, and then by showing that the so-called reality is simply created by the language itself. Deconstruction shows how language has constructed what we call "reality"; it then deconstructs these linguistic constructions. What this basically accomplishes, where successful, is to expose as myths linguistic descriptions which masquerade as reality—the myth of [the correspondence theory of truth], the myth of universal cross-cultural objectivity and rationality, the myth of neutral, value-free scientific investigation, and so on. . . . The things we refer to are not real, objective parts of reality; they are just ways of speaking which have caught on, become popular and then "internalized" so that we wrongly assume they accurately describe and reveal an independent reality.[20]

Even the distinction between what is or is not a value judgment is overthrown. According to postmodernism, all judgments are colored by human values and emotions. Even if the notion of a "disinterested observer" made sense, there is no neutral, value-free vocabulary in which to express judgments. As noted in the quote above, even science, presumed by many to be the epitome of rationality and the search for objective truth, is value-laden. As such, Alison Jaggar notes, "the conclusions of western science thus are presumed . . . [to be] uncontaminated by the supposedly 'subjective' values and emotions that might bias individual investigators. . . . [However,] it has been argued that it does not, indeed cannot, eliminate generally accepted social values."[21]

The upshot of **postmodernist relativism** is the legitimization of *all* points of view. There is no such thing as objective truth. There is no such thing as universal rationality. The canons of logic are merely one set of social norms among others with no special claim to universal acceptance. Many postmodernists even reject the possibility of employing pragmatic criteria for adjudicating between conceptual schemes.[22] Taken to its extreme in postmodernism "[t]here are no external standards nor even internal standards of personal or cultural consistency and coherence to restrict us. We are therefore free to go with what seems at the moment compelling to us and we are guided in our articulations only by the desire to persuade, to gain a receptive following."[23]

To many objectivists, and even modernist (truth) relativists, this sounds like intellectual anarchy. It should therefore come as no surprise that the postmodernist challenge to modernism's assumption of the universality of reason has been greeted with great apprehension within mainstream Anglo-American philosophy.

Is *Hilary and Jackie* a film that can be used to support the postmodernist cause? Yes and no. On the affirmative side, it presents not one complete and consistent picture of the world but a pair of perspectives; this much is in agreement with postmodernism. On the negative side, whether this was intentional or not, *Hilary and Jackie* seems to prefer one interpretation at the expense of the other—Hilary's perspective is judged as objectively better. (Although, I have also noted, however, that viewers were unable to explain what about the film led them to that conclusion.)

Just as postmodernist philosophers hold that there are no objective facts, postmodernists within literary and film criticism hold that there is no such thing as *the* meaning of a work of art (for example, a film). Thus, if some viewers interpret *Hilary and Jackie* as a postmodernist film, then it is for them. "Meaning" arises only in the confluence of a work of art and a point of view.

2.7 Sources of Disparity in the Narrative

Even if one rejects one (or both) of the perspectives offered by Hilary and Jackie as untrue, the question still remains: Why do the perspectives disagree with one another? Philosophers, psychologists, and, more recently, neuroscientists have theorized about how raw sense data is worked up to generate the world of experience. Each of these disciplines has something to contribute to a discussion of the question.

Psychological experiments have shown that research subjects' visual experiences are informed by expectations arising from the concepts a subject uses to categorize visual data. These expectations play a role in determining what the subject reports having seen. The classic example of this is the card-viewing experiment conducted by Jerome Bruner and Leo Postman.[24] Interspersed among normal playing cards were several "anomalous" cards—for example, a black four of hearts. After seeing each card for a brief period of time, the subject was asked to identify the card just seen. As Thomas Kuhn notes about the experiment, "For the normal cards these identifications were usually correct, but the anomalous cards were almost always identified, without apparent hesitation or puzzlement, as normal. The black four of hearts might, for example, be identified as the four of either spades or hearts. Without any awareness of trouble, it was immediately fitted to one of the conceptual categories prepared by prior experience. One would not even like to say that the subjects had seen something different from what they identified."[25]

Assuming this result can be generalized to more natural viewing contexts, the upshot is clear: expectation effects play a major role in the processing of sensory data. What I see is determined in some measure by what I expect to see.

A second, more familiar, source of differing perceptual experiences relates to the level of expertise of the perceiver. For example, someone knowledgeable about music can identify patterns that go unnoticed by less learned observers. Those with prior musical training hear major chords *as* major chords and can identify within the chord the individual notes that make it up. To me, a musical novice, a major chord is not heard as a major chord but as an unstructured, generally "harmonious" sound. In some sense, the person knowledgeable about music "hears" something different from what I hear, even though we are receiving identical raw sound data.

The third example of differing perceptual experiences involves the interpretation of ambiguous raw sense data. We have already discussed, in section 2.4, how our minds can interpret a single drawing in two different ways—one moment the drawing is a duck, the next, a rabbit. With a little practice, an observer can even will herself to see it one way or the other.

What all three of these examples give evidence for is the thoroughly integral role that concepts play in our observations. In the case of the ambiguous duck/rabbit drawing, it is not that we first see the drawing, then apply the concept *rabbit* to it. Rather, the seeing of the drawing is the very same event as the applying of the concept *rabbit*. This result appears to hold in all instances of observation. The musically learned do not hear sounds and then apply the concept *major chord*. Rather, the sound is heard as a major chord (the hearing is part and parcel of the application of the concept). Similarly, when research subjects identify a black four of hearts as a four of spades, it is because they are (mistakenly, it turns out) seeing the card as a four of spades.

What accounts for our ability to tune our powers of observation in this way? Recent results in the neurosciences may shed some light on this question. The human brain is an incredibly complex organ. It is also an incredibly plastic organ, capable of massive self-tweaking as the individual learns. The totality of differences in the cognitive abilities of a young child on the one hand and an adult on the other is accounted for by this tweaking over a long period of time. The sensory pathways in the nervous system (those parts of the brain and peripheral nervous system given over to the processing of sensory information) are especially plastic. Consider the visual pathway as a case in point. Light enters the eyes and is projected onto the surface of the back of the eye—the retina. The retina contains within it cells that are sensitive to how much and what color light is present in their immediate vicinity on the retina. The optic nerve communicates this information to the brain. There are several levels of processing of visual information in the brain. The details are not important. What *is* important is the fact that, all along the way, the individual cells that take in, transport, and process the visual information are capable of adapting over time. At least some of this adaptation, this cellular-level learning, is driven by things that are going on in other parts of the brain. It appears as though this plasticity reaches even to the light-sensitive cells on the retinal surface itself. If this is correct, it goes part of the way to explaining why the application of concepts to visual data is so "natural," and so hard to circumvent—the result of past experience changes even our eyes! Admittedly, it is very unlikely that retinal cell adaptation is driven by such high-level mental processes as concept formation and learning, but the possibility that conceptual schemes are at least in part realized in the brain by changes in the sensory pathways is tantalizing.

What accounts for the differences in perspectives in *Hilary and Jackie*? Gleaning intentions from observable behavior is a tricky business. This is especially so when past experience leads one of the observers to adopt some assumptions about the other person's motivations. It seems to me that the most likely explanation for the differences we see when comparing Hilary's and Jackie's interpretation of events is due to a combination of factors. Several pivotal events (for example, the episode involving the package of dirty laundry) lead Hilary to adopt certain not-very-flattering assumptions about Jackie's motivations. These assumptions later play out in what Hilary pays attention to and how Hilary interprets ambiguous data. The nighttime conversation between the two sisters in which Hilary announces her engagement to Kiffer is useful to consider as an example. Jackie's remark—"the truth is, you're not special"—is ambiguous. According to Hilary, it meant, roughly, "you are a boring, ordinary person." According to Jackie, it meant "you can't understand how difficult my life is." In context, both interpretations make sense. They are both consistent with the surrounding conversation, as each attended to and remembered it. This surrounding context is like the background in the ambiguous bird/antelope picture—it draws the mind of the two characters into interpreting the ambiguous sentence in different ways. It is as if Hilary is interpreting the drawing of the bird/antelope with other birds in the background, whereas Jackie is interpreting it with antelope in the background.

The scene in which Jackie and Kiffer have sex shows a similar structure. For Hilary, this action is the culmination of Jackie's repeated manipulations, beginning with the conversation among Hilary, Jackie, and Kiffer on the evening of Jackie's arrival at their country home. This evening conversation is missing from Jackie's story, presumably because for her it was an unimportant event. Jackie was obviously quite drunk at the time (even Hilary's take on things admitted that), and she blurted out something on the spur of the moment, did not act on it, and quickly forgot about it. For Jackie, the evening conversation was unrelated to her later having sex with Kiffer. For Hilary, previous events caused her to infer the linkage between the conversation and sex. Is there an objective fact of the matter here? It is hard to say. Both Hilary's and Jackie's perspectives are internally consistent, and they both fit the data.

With *Hilary and Jackie* we get something approximating an argument for truth relativism. Even if there is such as thing as "objective truth," it is beyond our grasp. The criterion for truth should therefore be not this unknowable "correspondence with the mind-independent world" but consistency with the observed world, relative to a particular conceptual scheme. It is unclear whether *Hilary and Jackie* also means to argue for relativism of rationality, according to which there are no universal criteria for deciding which of several competing conceptual schemes is better.

2.8 Is Relativism Correct?

So far we have been trying to understand what cognitive relativism is without worrying much about whether it is correct. In this closing section, I turn to this issue. Is

cognitive relativism correct? What arguments can be given in its favor? What arguments can be given against? Which side makes the best case?

The two main arguments standardly given for cognitive relativism have already been
discussed in some detail; I shall merely summarize them here. The main *empirical* argument for cognitive relativism is that different (groups of) people have different views—
on what sorts of things exist, on how certain things are expected to behave, and so on.
A multiple-perspective film attempts to demonstrate this difference by giving us (the
film's viewers) access to the world of experience of various characters so that we can
see for ourselves how they view the world differently. The main *theoretical* argument
for cognitive relativism starts from the premise that all observation is theory laden. We
cannot view the world except through the lens of a conceptual scheme. ("Percepts
without concepts are blind.")

The objectivist can respond to these two arguments by granting some of the cognitive relativist's claims, while denying others. For example, the objectivist can grant
that different people have different views, while denying that these differing views are
inconsistent with either of the objectivist theses. Similarly, the objectivist can grant
that all observation is theory laden, without following the cognitive relativist on to the
assumption that *subjective* truth (that is, truth relative to the world of experience created via a network of concepts) is all there is to truth. Maybe this "meeting the relativist halfway" is what MacIntyre had in mind when he suggested that relativism
"embodies some not-to-be-neglected truth."

There are other arguments that have been put forward in support of cognitive relativism. One of these, discussed below, has been effective at making the view popular
among nonphilosophers. Cognitive relativism has achieved a moderate level of acceptance among Anglo-American intellectuals in recent years. It is common nowadays to
hear the term *paradigm shift*,[26] or to describe individuals as "living in different worlds."[27]
I believe there are several factors responsible for relativism's increasing popularity.
One of these is relativism's perceived connection to tolerance and liberalism. Increasing contact with far-flung societies and with American subcultures has shown that the
mainstream Anglo-American way is not the only way. Cognitive relativism allows us
to avoid discord: it allows us to say "everybody is correct." I find this line of argument
questionable on several accounts. First, trying to justify a substantive philosophical
theory by pointing out the perceived social benefits that would accrue if the theory
gained widespread acceptance is not a legitimate method of argument. Second, it is
not clear that relativism has the nice liberal implications its adherents assume.

In a pluralistic country like the United States, tolerance is an absolute necessity.
Some argue that one way to foster tolerance is to convince everyone that cognitive
relativism is correct. If there is no such thing as absolute truth, but only truth relative
to a conceptual scheme, then two individuals can both be right on some issue, even if
those two individuals disagree with one another. I am less likely to act intolerantly

toward someone with whom I disagree if I think that that person's views may be true (relative to their own conceptual scheme, of course). While the above line of reasoning looks good on the surface, I believe it has one serious flaw—that is the form of tolerance that emerges from relativism is not very attractive. It should not be confused with the form of tolerance that emerges from traditional liberalism.

Let's take a closer look at tolerance à la relativism. Suppose that I am someone who categorizes members of certain races as fully rational and members of other races as less than fully rational. Suppose further that I am someone who holds that I have serious moral obligations only to creatures that are fully rational. Thus, I believe that I don't have serious moral obligations to members of some racial groups. As a result, when I make decisions, I may not take their well-being into account to the extent I take into account the well-being of those I judge to be fully rational humans. A consistent cognitive relativist would have to admit that a racist conceptual scheme is not *objectively* better or worse than any other. Thus, a consistent cognitive relativist cannot reject my conceptual scheme on the grounds that it is mistaken. Similarly, a consistent cognitive relativist cannot object that those actions of mine based on my racist categorization of humans are done in error, so long as my actions are consistent with my racist conceptual scheme. Even more importantly, *moral* condemnation of my racist actions is beyond the reach of the cognitive relativist.

This is the version of tolerance that arises out of cognitive relativism: so long as someone is acting in a way that "makes sense" given her (or her culture's) conceptual scheme, that person is not acting in an incorrect or immoral manner. But this is not a version of tolerance that is very appealing, for it requires that I tolerate individuals and societies, no matter what they do. Genocide, human slavery, the subjection of women—all of these things have been practiced by some societies. (Alas, some societies continue to practice them even now.) The consistent cognitive relativist must tolerate these sorts of practices, along with the less objectionable ones. Contrast the version of tolerance emerging out of relativism with that emerging out of traditional liberalism, according to which individuals may act as they like as long as they do not infringe on the rights of others. It is this latter version of tolerance that is required to prevent a society from succumbing to either tyranny by the dominant group or Balkanization as the society rips apart into its separate subcultures. If a stable pluralism is a benefit for a society (as I believe it is), then it is not relativism but objectivism that is most likely to achieve it.

So, the argument for cognitive relativism based on its relationship with tolerance is actually an argument *against* cognitive relativism. Are there other such arguments? One problem the cognitive relativist faces is explaining just what intellectual investigation (within both the sciences and the humanities) is striving for, if not knowledge of the objective truth. It seems as though we already have knowledge in the relativist sense, so what's the point of continuing the search?

A second difficulty for cognitive relativism is explaining why science and technology have been so successful. This difficulty is especially acute for postmodernism, which classifies science as "just one among many equally good approaches to improving our understanding of the world." The postmodernist responds by noting that science and technology are successful relative to their own criterion for success (namely, controlling the environment); but not necessarily successful relative to some other criterion (for example, living in harmony with the environment). One person's idea of success is another person's idea of failure. I will leave it for you, the reader, to decide whether this response is adequate.

By far the most oft-cited criticism of cognitive relativism is that it is self-refuting.[28] If the truth of all judgments is relative, then the truth of the judgment "cognitive relativism is correct" is itself relative: it is true according to some conceptual schemes and false according to others. If one goes the extra step to relativism of rationality, those conceptual schemes in which conceptual relativism is true have no better claim to our allegiance than those conceptual schemes in which it is false. Thus, for the relativist about rationality, I (a person with a conceptual scheme that makes cognitive relativism false) can truly say that cognitive relativism is false.

Discussion Questions

1. Are value judgments really qualitatively different from nonvalue judgments?
2. What are the similarities between Berkelian idealism (discussed in section 1.6) and cognitive relativism? What are the differences?
3. What is the relationship between skepticism and relativism? Does cognitive objectivism manage to avoid both?
4. Does the individual who understands his experience as involving the work of the devil "live in a different world" from the individual who does not? Are they members of different cultures? What *is* a culture, anyway?
5. Did you start out the chapter as a cognitive relativist? Or now, after having finished the chapter, are you a cognitive relativist? If your view changed, why did it change? Does relativism embody some "not-to-be-neglected truth," as MacIntyre suggests?
6. As you were watching *Hilary and Jackie* did you find yourself assuming that Hilary's account of events was the most trustworthy of the two? If so, can you isolate what led you to this conclusion?

Annotated List of Film Titles Relevant to Relativism

Rashomon (1950). Directed by Akira Kurosawa. Starring Toshiro Mifune, Masayuki Mori, Machiko Kyo, Takashi Shimura, Minoru Chiaki.

Rashomon, like *Hilary and Jackie*, is a multiple-perspective film: it tells the same story several times over from the point of view of different characters.

Citizen Kane (1941). Directed by Orson Welles. Starring Orson Welles, Joseph Cotten, Ray Collins, Dorothy Comingore.

Citizen Kane is the reconstruction of one man's life, as told from the points of view of several people who knew him. Rosebud, the enigmatic dying last word of the title character, sets a newspaper reporter off on a quest to understand what the word signifies by interviewing several of Kane's associates. In the process, he discovers that each interview subject presents a very different version of the man. Whose portrayal is most accurate? Does that question even make sense?

Go (1999). Directed by Doug Liman. Starring Sarah Polley, Desmond Askew, Katie Holmes.

Drug deals, sex, violence, pyramid schemes, a road trip to Las Vegas, supermarket check-out cashiers: these elements are thrown in the hopper, shaken, and strewn out to form the backbone of a multiple-perspective film. *Go* has the fast-paced, almost frenetic feel typical of young directors weaned on music videos. It's a fun, darkly comic ride.

Courage Under Fire (1996). Directed by Edward Zwick. Starring Denzel Washington, Meg Ryan, Matt Damon.

A classic example of the multiple-perspective film.

He Said. She Said (1991). Directed by Ken Kwapis, Marisa Silver. Starring Kevin Bacon, Elizabeth Perkins, Sharon Stone.

This lightweight comedy attempts to answer the question, Do men and women live in different worlds? It offers the male and the female perspective on a love affair that develops between two polar-opposite newspaper editorial writers.

Annotated List of Book Titles Relevant to Relativism

MODERN "CLASSICS" IN THE HISTORY OF COGNITIVE RELATIVISM

Immanuel Kant

Critique of Pure Reason, first published in German; 1st edition 1781, 2nd edition 1787. This is where cognitive relativism in the modern era comes from (even though Kant would deny it). The standard scholarly version of the *Critique*, translated by Norman Kemp Smith, is available in its entirety online at <http://www.hkbu.edu.hk/~ppp/cpr/toc.html> and <http://www.arts.cuhk.edu.hk/Philosophy/Kant/cpr>.

Prolegomena to Any Future Metaphysics, first published in German, 1783. Kant attempts to boil down the theory laid out in his *Critique of Pure Reason* in a form that will be more accessible than the larger work. The *Prolegomena* is also available in its entirety online at <http://www.utm.edu/research/iep/text/kant/prolegom/ prolegom.htm>.

Friedrich Nietzsche

Unpublished Notes, published posthumously in the German multivolume collection *The Works of Nietzsche* 1958. Citations of the *Unpublished Notes* here are from the third volume, as translated by Arthur Danto. Nietzsche is one of the most widely read (and widely misunderstood) Western philosophers. To precipitate out the philosophical substance from the surrounding literary fireworks, Danto's *Nietzsche as Philosopher* (New York: Columbia University Press, 1965) is an excellent source. The reader doesn't miss the flavor of Nietzsche's writings, while making Nietzsche's philosophy as clear as possible. For a full-service academically oriented Nietzsche site online that includes a biography and the complete collected works, see <http://turn.to/nietzsche>.

Thomas Kuhn

The Structure of Scientific Revolutions, (Chicago, University of Chicago Press, 1996; first published in 1962). While Thomas Kuhn's seminal work is generally considered as a work in the philosophy of science, it has been widely influential throughout philosophy. It is moderately easy reading; hence, it is accessible to the determined lay reader. In the book, Kuhn explores the relationship between conceptual schemes, theories, and observation and the nature of theory choice.

Collections of Essays and Single-Author Books on Relativism

Jack Meiland and Michael Krausz, eds., *Relativism: Cognitive and Moral* (Notre Dame, IN: Notre Dame University Press, 1982). An excellent collection of essays by the most important philosophers writing in the area of relativism.

Martin Hollis and Steven Lukes, eds., *Rationality and Relativism* (Cambridge, MA: MIT Press, 1982). Another very good collection of essays, with several contributions focusing on relativism within sociology and cultural anthropology.

Nelson Goodman, *Ways of Worldmaking* (Indianapolis: Hackett, 1978). Goodman argues that it is possible that several irreconcilable versions of the world can be right, and considers how taking relativism seriously would alter our standard understanding of "truth."

Paul Feyerabend, *Against Method* (New York: Routledge, 1988). Feyerabend starts with Thomas Kuhn and goes one better. In this work, Feyerabend argues that Western science is not a homogeneous set of methods; there is no universally applicable set of standards that can be used to adjudicate between conflicting theories (as Kuhn has argued).

Related Works

Hilary and Piers du Pre, *Hilary and Jackie* (originally entitled *A Genius in the Family*) (New York: Ballantine, 1997). This is the book on which the film is based.

Plato, *Theaetetus* and *Protagoras* originally published in Greek. These two dialogues by Plato (427–347 B.C.E.) discuss the ramifications of Protagoras's famous one-liner "Man is the measure of all things." Both are available in their entirety online at <http://classics.mit.edu/Plato/theatu.html> and <http:// classics.mit.edu/Plato/protagoras.html>, respectively.

Alburey Castell, Donald Borchert, and Arthur Zucker, eds., *Introduction to Modern Philosophy* (Upper Saddle River, NJ: Prentice Hall, 2001). A collection of essay-length works in modern philosophy, arranged by topic; chapter 9 is particularly useful.

PART II

Minds, Bodies, and Persons

3

Personal Identity

Being John Malkovich (1999) and *Memento* (2000)

Craig: It raises all sorts of philosophical-type questions, you know, about the nature of the self, about the existence of a soul. Am I me? Is Malkovich Malkovich? . . . Do you see what a metaphysical can of worms this portal is?

—from *Being John Malkovich*

Teddy: You do not know who you are.
Leonard: I'm Leonard Shelby. I'm from San Francisco.
Teddy: That's who you *were*.

—from *Memento*

Are you the same person now as you were on the day you were born? I've yet to meet a person who answered this question in the negative. However, explaining how this identity over time is possible is a rather tricky issue. After all, the *physical* changes your body has undergone between your birth and the present are striking: it is possible there is not a single atom that your current body shares in common with your infant body. Perhaps (at least, for humans) identity over time is not tied to your physical sameness but to your mental sameness. However, even if we focus on your *mental* properties, explaining how you have remained the same person from your birth until now is difficult. Can you (now) remember being an infant? Do you (now) share any specific beliefs or desires with your self as an infant? It seems that explaining this identity over time with reference to sameness of mental properties won't work either. What other options are available? Maybe you possess an immaterial soul that persists through your life unchanged, and it is by virtue of this that you are the same person as you were at birth? Will this explanation work without introducing even more problems? These are the sorts of questions that fall under the topic "personal identity." Their answers have ramifications for our basic self-understanding, for they imply who and what we are as individuals.

3.1   The Conceivability of an Afterlife

What does it mean to say "You will survive the death of your body"? As a first approximation, "You will continue to exist, even after your body dies" is pretty good. A better approximation, one that fits in with the way personal identity will be discussed in
the rest of this chapter, is "There will be someone who exists after your body dies, and
that person will be *identical to you*."[1]

The word *identical* in English is ambiguous. In some contexts, to say two things are
identical is to say they are very similar; this is the sense used in the context of *identical*
twins. The second sense of *identical* means "one and the same"; this is the sense meant
in describing Clark Kent as *identical* to Superman. It is this second sense that will concern us in this chapter. What does it mean for person A to be identical to (that is, one
and the same person as) person B? Or, as in the case above, what does it mean to say
that some person who exists after the death of your body is identical to you?

Many religious traditions include a belief in an afterlife. I am not interested here in
discussing whether or not belief in an afterlife is true, or even whether it is well-
founded. Rather, I want to discuss whether this belief is *possibly* true. To see what I'm
getting at, consider the sentence "Green ideas sleep furiously." Even though the individual words that constitute this sentence are familiar and the sentence as a whole is
grammatical, still, the sentence doesn't make any sense. I cannot conceive of what a
world would be like in which this sentence was true. Ideas just aren't the sort of things
that can sleep, much less sleep furiously. Nor are ideas the sort of things that can be a
color, green or otherwise. There seems to be some sort of category mistake going on
in the sentence. One way to describe this mistake is to say that the sentence is not only
false, it is conceptually impossible. Another way to describe the mistake is to say that
the sentence expresses something that is inconceivable.

On first glance, the sentence "You will survive the death of your body" isn't like the
sentence "Green ideas sleep furiously" at all. For one thing, many people assent to the
former sentence, whereas no one would assent to the latter. More importantly for our
purposes here, I can conceive of what a world would be like in which the former sentence is true. (Or, at least, I think I can.) If this claim about the conceivability of the
sentence "You will survive the death of your body" remains unchallenged, that would
say a lot about what makes you *you*.

Under everyday circumstances, how do you identify a person from one time to
another? Let's suppose you have a friend named Trina whom you haven't seen in several years. What sort of evidence would lead you to believe that someone you see
from across the room at a party is your friend Trina? The most important attribute we
use in identifying someone is physical appearance. So, in the example from above, you
would remember what Trina looked like and ask yourself what (dis)similarities you
see in Trina's appearance and the appearance of the person across the room. You may

even walk closer to get a better look. Obviously, we don't require exact similarity in appearance; otherwise, we couldn't recognize someone after that person got a haircut. But there are parameters about how much someone can change in their appearance and still be readily recognized as the same person.

What does this example tell us about our everyday understanding of personal identity? First and foremost, it tells us that someone's observable physical attributes—primarily, what she looks like or what her voice sounds like—matter a great deal in our judgments about personal identity. But physical similarity is not the property that *determines* personal identity. If I find out that the person I see from across the room is not Trina, but her identical twin sister Greta, I would immediately cease believing she was Trina, despite the physical resemblance. (If physical resemblance were all there was to personal identity, we would judge identical twins as being one and the same person.) It seems as though physical resemblance is a stand-in for the property that *truly* determines identity. This underlying property is *physical continuity*, and according to the **physical continuity theory** of personal identity, you are the same person you were at birth if your body has existed continuously from then until now. We use similarity of physical appearance as a stand-in for physical continuity because physical appearance is all we have available to us. I rarely see someone continuously for more than a few hours, yet I can easily note similarities in physical appearance, even when it has been years since I have seen someone. Experience has taught me that, for non-mass-produced objects (humans, for example), when I see an object at time t_1 and an object at time t_2 and notice that the two objects look *very* similar, they are usually one and the same thing.[2]

But if physical continuity is what is required for personal identity, then the sentence "You will survive the death of your body" is inconceivable. After death, your body will cease to exist as a body. Admittedly, the atoms that constitute your body will continue on, but they will not form a body. A physical transformation will occur that prevents continuity. Just so, if I take a pencil and grind it up into a fine dust, the pile of dust that results is not the pencil. The original pencil has ceased to exist. Perhaps the pencil could have survived less drastic changes—having a notch made in it or having the end cut off. It would still be the same pencil. But grinding it into a pile of dust is too radical a change for the resulting matter to be identical to the original pencil.

The decomposition (or incineration) of a human body is as radical a change as the grinding up of a pencil. So, if a human body dies at time t, the person whose body that is ceases to exist at. t (or shortly thereafter). In other words, if we assume the physical continuity theory for person identity, continuing to exist after the death and disintegration of one's body is a conceptual impossibility.

But, the notion of an afterlife seems possible to most people, even to those who reject it as implausible or unlikely. That tells us that most people do not tie personal identity to physical continuity, but to something else—something that could persist through the physical transformation that occurs at death.

Some philosophers have argued for the **psychological continuity theory** of personal identity. According to this theory, what makes me *me* are my psychological characteristics. I am the same person I was last year because there is a cluster of psychological properties that exists continuously from then until now. Different philosophers disagree over what this cluster consists of. Some say it is a stream of consciousness; however, this interpretation of the psychological continuity theory has problems dealing with discontinuities in the stream of consciousness that occur during sleep. Others say it is high-level psychological properties such as my personality, disposition, value system, long-term desires, and so on—the sorts of attributes that generally change very slowly over time. Yet others say psychological continuity is achieved by memory. I am the person I was last year because I can remember having some of the perceptions and thoughts that that person had. I am the person I was two years ago because the person I was last year can remember having some of the perceptions and thoughts that that person from two years ago had. Memory is used as the transitive link that ultimately identifies me as identical to that person who was born many years ago. These three versions of the psychological continuity theory need not be taken in isolation: it is possible to construct a hybrid version of the theory that uses two or three of these clusters. So, for example, if continuity of memory fails (as we shall see in the case of Leonard Shelby, the protagonist in *Memento*), continuity of stream of consciousness could be used to link together a memory-fragmented mental life.

The psychological continuity theory fares somewhat better than the physical continuity theory in allowing for the possibility of an afterlife. It is not clear how the psychological clusters mentioned above could persist after my death; however, it is at least not impossible that they continue after the body has ceased to exist. (Remember, all we are looking for in this section is a theory of personal identity that allows the sentence "You will survive the death of your body" to be possibly true.)

Within many religious traditions, the thing that continues to exist after death is assumed to be the individual's immaterial soul. Being immaterial, it is not affected by the decomposition of the body after death. According to the **same-soul theory** of personal identity, what makes me *me* is my soul. It is somehow or other attached to my body during my lifetime, then becomes disattached at death, continuing to exist either in disembodied form or by reattaching to another body.

The problem with both the psychological continuity and the same-soul theories of personal identity is explaining why, in everyday circumstances, we place so much emphasis on physical attributes in determining identity. While immaterial souls could survive transformations of their host bodies, they (being immaterial) cannot be seen, heard, or sensed in any way. If we consistently applied the same-soul theory, someone's physical appearance should be irrelevant in deciding who that person is. Similarly, psychological attributes cannot be seen directly; they must be inferred by looking at someone's behavior. Yet, even when people are not behaving at all because they are sleeping, we do not infer that they have ceased to be who they are. Admittedly, in cases when someone's behavior deviates significantly from how that individual usually behaves, we describe him as "not being himself." However, this usage is metaphorical, of course. "Tom isn't himself today" does not mean that this person in front of me (that is, Tom) isn't really Tom after all.

We shall return to these and related points in later sections. For now, though, it is sufficient to note that, of the three theories of personal identity discussed so far, the physical continuity theory comports best with our everyday usage; however, it runs afoul of the widespread belief in the conceptual possibility of an afterlife.

3.2 The General Problem of Identity over Time

Establishing criteria for personal identity (that is, what it means for person A to be identical to person B) is just a special case of a more general topic. By virtue of what is object A identical to object B? On first glance, identity for inanimate objects seems straightforward. For one thing, we needn't worry about squaring our theory with issues involving an afterlife. (It was the need to make space for the conceptual possibility of an afterlife that was the major problem for the physical continuity theory of personal identity.) Thus, why not just say, for object A and object B, they are identical if object A is physically continuous over time with object B? (For example, the phone that was on my desk yesterday is identical to the phone that is on my desk today if they form a physically continuous object.) Unfortunately, even for inanimate objects, the story isn't quite this simple. Consider the following examples.[3]

You are taking a course in car maintenance from a teacher with a rather unorthodox teaching style. In this course, you are to take a car apart piece by piece, carefully labeling each piece; then, once the car is thoroughly disassembled, you are to put it back together. Let's suppose you manage to do this—that is, you manage to put together the parts in just the same way they were originally put together. Is the car after this exercise *identical* to the car before? If you are like me, you will answer, "Yes, they are one and the same car."

After learning so much about car maintenance, you decide to service your car yourself. Your radiator starts to get a little rusty, so you buy a new radiator and install it. (It doesn't really matter in this case, but, suppose you throw the original radiator out on the junk heap in your backyard.) The car with the replaced radiator is still the same car: changing this part hasn't changed its identity. The next item on your car to need replacement is the right front tire, which you replace. Again, changing this tire does not affect the car's identity. Then the clutch gets a little sloppy, so you decide to replace it before it breaks and leaves you stranded. Yet again, it's still the *same* car after the replacement as before. The process of gradual replacement lasts over several years, and, after each replacement, it's still the same car as before. By the end of the process, *every single one of the car's original parts has been replaced.* Even the frame and the body have been replaced. Now, compare the car before you started working on it to the car after the last original part is replaced. Are they the same car? Again, if you are like me, you will answer, "Yes, they are one and the same car."

If you disagree with me on this (that is, if you think the car resulting from the gradual replacement of all of its parts is not identical to the original car), when during the gradual replacement process did the car stop being identical to the original car? Remember, at each stage, we are only replacing one part. To justify your view, there has to be *some part* whose replacement was crucial in changing the car's identity. What part would that be? More importantly, what is so special about that part that makes its replacement alter the identity of the car? Maybe you think a car's body is so crucial to the identity of a car that a car could not survive having its body replaced, in the same way as a pencil could not survive being ground into dust. Suppose I say we replace the body gradually. First we replace the driver's side door. Then, several months later, we replace the right front fender, then six months later we replace the rear bumper, and so on. (If you think it is not the car body, but some other part that is crucial to a car's identity, I could run the super gradual replacement argument on that part, too. It might require me to retell the story such that major cutting and welding was required, but it doesn't change things substantially.) When during this process does the car lose its original identity? Again, the burden is on you to point to either some special part or special *threshold* percentage of replacement that changes the car's identity.

I shall assume that everyone is in agreement in the gradual replacement case: the postreplacement car is identical to the original car. Now comes the twist. I mentioned above in the gradual replacement case that, as you replaced parts, you threw the original ones out onto the junk heap in your backyard. So, at the end of the gradual replacement process, you have all the original parts in a heap. Now, with all this car repair knowledge, you decide to take on the ultimate challenge: to see if you can put all the original parts back together. You manage to do just that. Now you have two cars. Which car is *identical* to the original car—the one with the replaced parts or the rebuilt one with the original parts? After all, they can't both be identical to the original car.

If you think it is possible that they are both identical to the original car, think some more about what *identical* means in this context. (Remember, the sense of *identical* we are working with is the sense in which Clark Kent is *identical* to Superman.) Let's call the original car (before you started working on it) car A, the car that resulted from gradual replacement of parts is car B, and the car that resulted from reassembling the original parts is car C. Clearly, car B is not identical to car C. (Remember, *identical* here means one and the same as). So, it cannot be the case that car A = car B and car A = car C, since car B ≠ car C. Either car B is not the continuation of car A, or car C is not the continuation of car A, or neither of them are.

This example shows that, even for inanimate objects, finding a theory for object identity over time is a rather tricky matter. In the case of humans, it is so much the trickier, since we humans have not just a physical nature but also a psychological nature. The possibilities for finding counterexamples to a theory of personal identity are that much greater. In some ways, the two focus movies for this chapter do just that: they present some atypical situations involving humans and ask us as viewers to decide what we make of them. Are the identities of the protagonists affected by the things that happen in the movies?

3.3 An Overview of the Movies

BEING JOHN MALKOVICH (1999). DIRECTED BY SPIKE JONZE.
STARRING JOHN MALKOVICH, JOHN CUSACK, CATHERINE KEENER,
CAMERON DIAZ.

Being John Malkovich offers a fun romp through the topic of personal identity. In the movie, Craig Schwartz, an accomplished puppeteer, discovers a secret passageway that leads to the sensory stream of another human—the actor, John Malkovich. Whoever enters this passageway experiences everything John Malkovich experiences for the space of fifteen minutes. After this fifteen minutes, the individual is spit out alongside the New Jersey Turnpike. At first, Craig sees this primarily as a great opportunity for making money. Everyone is curious about what it would be like to see the world through someone else's eyes; many would be willing to pay for the chance, even if it only lasts a short time.

A bizarre love triangle that erupts along the way leads Craig to want exclusive possession of the passageway. He not only manages to gain exclusive use, but his knowledge of puppeteering allows him to control John Malkovich's body in addition to experiencing John Malkovich's sensory stream. The title of the film hints that one way of interpreting what is going on is that Craig succeeds in *being* John Malkovich. That is, Craig becomes identical to him.

Being John Malkovich is a lighthearted comedy that never takes itself too seriously. The plot's twists and turns are self-consciously silly. Nevertheless, the movie is useful for asking whether, under these circumstances, we would assent to the claim that Craig becomes John Malkovich. And if so, what does that answer tell us about the concept of personal identity?

MEMENTO (2000). DIRECTED BY CHRISTOPHER NOLAN.
STARRING GUY PEARCE, CARRIE-ANNE MOSS, JOE PANTOLIANO.

For those who hold some version of the psychological continuity theory of personal identity, *Memento* raises some very interesting questions. The film focuses on two days in the life of Leonard Shelby, a man who has a form of amnesia that prevents him from remembering anything for more than a few minutes. He has normal memory of events that took place before the incident that put him in this condition, but not events that happened recently. As he describes his own subjective state of mind, he can no longer "feel" the passage of time; he has the present and the remote past, and that is all.

Memento is structured to try to give us, the viewers of the movie, the same subjective feeling of fragmentation of self as Leonard experiences. To do this, the film moves backward through fictional time: the first scene we see is the last thing that happens; the next scene we see is the thing that happened second to last, and so on. Interspersed among the scenes that are progressing backward in chronological order are about a dozen scenes shot in black and white that are flowing forward in chronological order. The result for the viewer is extreme disorientation. While we know what happens later to Leonard (because we've already seen it), we don't know what has happened in the past that led to the current scene — much as Leonard himself "knows" what is happening in the present but has no clue about how he got there. (I put the word "know" in quotes because, as *Memento* argues, it is unclear whether Leonard's experience of the present, lacking as it does all relevant historical context, really constitutes knowledge.)

Leonard tries to cope with his condition, tries to supply himself with historical context, by leaving himself mementos — all sorts of mementos: little notes to himself written on pieces of paper, and pictures of his acquaintances to tell himself what names go with what faces, who to trust and who not to trust. For really important long-term mementos, he uses tattoos — all over his body. While incomplete, these mementos from his fragmented past allow him to set short-term goals and decide what to do next. The overarching long-term goal implicit in his tattoos drives the movie's plot.

Who is Leonard Shelby? Did he (the person) survive the incident, or did he disappear with his ability to form new memories? One option *Memento* raises is that the original Leonard doesn't exist anymore. His body is occupied by a series of persons who only last a few minutes each — the maximum span of time that he can remember something. The little notes and pictures he leaves for himself in the future, even the "notes" he leaves on his body in the form of tattoos, are not the right sort of link required for personal identity.

As mentioned above, *Memento* is (intentionally) a very confusing movie. It is possible for the viewer to piece together events in the correct chronological order if you treat the movie as a sort of puzzle. While it is tempting to do this, don't spend too much energy trying, because that's not the point. Once you have the general idea, let yourself become confused along with Leonard. Save puzzle solving for subsequent viewings.

3.4 *Does Craig Succeed in* Being John Malkovich? *Does Leonard Succeed in* Being Anybody?

Both *Being John Malkovich* and *Memento* offer fertile ground for becoming clearer on how our everyday concept of personal identity would be extended to cover atypical cases. Which extensions we are willing to allow may tell us something about the concept that is relevant in more usual circumstances. Also, the insight that the movies give us into the protagonists' view "from the inside" will prove useful in sections 3.5 and 3.6, where we shall piece together the arguments implicit in both films.

While the situation described in *Being John Malkovich* is pure make-believe, Leonard's condition in *Memento* (anterograde amnesia or short-term memory loss) is a rare but well-documented disorder. For our purposes, though, both cases will be treated as hypothetical.[4] Assume that someone like Leonard exists. What would you say about him? What does he say about himself? Is he the same person from one hour to the next? Philosophers often rely on thought experiments of this sort—that is, hypothetical examples that test the extension of a concept. So, here we go.

As the second quote that opens this chapter illustrates ("I'm Leonard Shelby. I'm from San Francisco"), Leonard claims to be the same person as he was before the incident.[5] From the inside, it feels to him as though he is identical to that man who had a wife and worked as an insurance claims investigator. But what is this "feeling of identity"? Recall David Hume's remarks on this topic, discussed in section 1.5. Hume notes, "[W]hen I enter most intimately into what I call *myself*, I always stumble on some particular perception or other, . . . [however], I never can catch *myself* at any time without a perception, and never can observe any thing but the perception. . . . The mind is a kind of theatre, where several perceptions successively make their appearance; pass, re-pass, glide away, and mingle in an infinite variety of postures and situations. There is properly no *simplicity* in it at one time, nor *identity* . . . whatever natural propension we may have to imagine that simplicity and identity. The comparison of the theatre must not mislead us. They are the successive perceptions only, that constitute the mind."[6]

According to Hume, the self is not something we can perceive directly, either by looking very closely at our perceptions or by introspecting. What, then, is generating this "feeling of identity" that we all (Leonard included) experience? The most likely source is memory. We can remember things that happened to us in the past, just as Leonard can remember having a wife. In our case (that is, for people with normal memory), this version of the psychological continuity theory can be run without difficulty. But for Leonard, a serious problem arises. Let's grant Leonard that, at the point in time when he tells Teddy "I'm Leonard Shelby. I'm from San Francisco" he is really identical to the preincident Leonard Shelby. The next day, Leonard has no memory of this conversation with Teddy. (Since he slept during the night, neither the transitivity of identity across memory links nor the continuity of stream of consciousness options will work to link Leonard who talked with Teddy and Leonard who brushed his teeth that next morning.) If Leonard were asked that next day, he would still insist he was identical to the preincident Leonard Shelby, the insurance claims investigator. But, this can't be true according to the psychological continuity theory of personal identity, for now there are *two* Leonards who aren't identical to one another. Each day in Leonard's postincident life has no memory links to any of the preceding days in Leonard's post-incident life. According to the memory version of the psychological continuity theory, I don't need a *direct* memory link to myself as an infant in order to be identical to that infant, but my infant self does need to be accessible via a series of memory links. In Leonard's case, these intermediate memory links from one day to the previous one are missing. Admittedly, Leonard does have remote links to his preincident life, but the memory version of the psychological continuity theory requires more than that—it requires that one can link up with each time slice of one's previous self via memory. *That* is what fails when comparing the Leonard who talked with Teddy and the Leonard who brushed his teeth that next morning. This is the same general problem of identity over time isolated in the examples about the car discussed in section 3.2—two distinct things cannot be identical to one and the same thing: both cars (the one resulting from the gradual replacement of parts, the other from rebuilding the original parts) cannot be identical to the original car.

One might describe the case of Leonard differently, since the postincident portions of the two Leonards (that is, the Leonard who talked with Teddy and the Leonard who brushed his teeth that next morning) do not overlap in time. Still, the impossibility of two distinct things being identical to the same thing blocks this way out. To see why, let's go back to the car case. You gradually replace all of the original parts on your car, being careful both to replace them before they become nonfunctional and to save the old parts. Now, your car has none of the original parts. You start to reassemble the (old) parts that have been sitting on your backyard junk heap, when you think, "I can't reassemble the old parts while the new-parts version of the car still exists; otherwise, I won't be able to decide which car is identical to the original car." So, to avoid problems, you melt the new-parts car down to molten metal and rubber. (Cars cannot survive this kind of physical transformation, just as pencils cannot survive being ground into piles of dust.) Only then do you reassemble the old parts. Have your actions kept the problem of identity from arising? No, because even though the new-parts car has ceased to exist when the reassembled car emerges, the two *distinct* cars are vying for identity with the original car. (Clearly, the car that gets melted down is not identical to the car that gets reassembled; so the fact that one of the contenders for identity has been destroyed is irrelevant.) Just so with Leonard. One person can only be identical to himself, not to many distinct others. Another way of putting it is that Leonard's memory lapses produce too many distinct contenders for being the postincident continuation of the preincident Leonard.[7]

Maybe, though, this problem with identity over time exemplified in the case of the two cars is just a philosopher's puzzle. Is there anything else about Leonard's condition that could raise difficulties in assenting to his claim that he is identical to Leonard the insurance claims investigator? There are two additional problems here.

First, because Leonard lacks so much historical context, it could be argued that he doesn't even have a meaningful present. Leonard must look at the various mementos he has left for himself to understand what he is doing. One sees in both the example involving the chase scene with Dodd (at minute mark 49:40)[8] and his waiting in ambush for Dodd in the bathroom with the "weapon" (MM 46:00) just how isolated the present as he experiences it is. Normally, people don't need to look at their bodies to know who they are. I don't need to look down at my body or to look at myself in the mirror to know that I am me. Strangely, in one sense, Leonard does. His body, and especially his tattoos, provide a critical link between his current self and his past.

Furthermore, Leonard shows by his own actions that even he doesn't believe that his future self is the same person as his present self. One sees this most clearly in his setting the Leonard of the future up to kill Teddy. Given the mementos from the past that help him to understand his present, Leonard is making a perfectly logical inference when he writes HE'S THE ONE KILL HIM on the back of Teddy's picture. However, once one knows the origin of some of those mementos (in particular, the source of the license plate number of his target's car), the illusion that the mementos are simple reminders to serve as a crutch for his faulty memory is broken. When Leonard writes down Teddy's license plate number, he knows his future selves are totally isolated from his current self. It is as if he is leaving messages not for himself but for some future person, much as one might send a message to members of some future generation in a time capsule. Even though he (Leonard in the present) is *able* to kill Teddy (after all, he has a gun), he is *unwilling* to kill him, so he sets someone else up to do it (namely, the Leonard of the future).

The preceding analysis points in the direction that Teddy was correct: the original Leonard ceased to exist during the incident. What is now "occupying" Leonard's body is a freakish succession of persons who are isolated from the original Leonard and from one another. Recall Teddy's last words before Leonard shoots him: "Let's go down here; then you'll really know who you really are." (Recall that what was "down there" was Jimmy's strangulated, naked body.)

There are important parallels between Teddy's way of viewing Leonard and Sammy Jankis's wife's way of viewing Sammy. In the black and white flashback to the scene in which Sammy's wife comes to visit Leonard in his office, the wife asks Leonard his personal opinion of Sammy's case. If she could get some assurance that the *old* Sammy is gone, she could move on and try to love this *new* Sammy. Here, it seems to me that she is not speaking metaphorically: she thinks it possible that the new "occupant" of her husband's body is not her husband but someone else—someone new.

Now, contrast Leonard's feeling like he's Leonard Shelby before the incident with how Craig responds to being inside the Malkovich portal. Recall that during his first visit to the portal, he lacked control over John Malkovich portal—all the passageway provided at that point was fifteen minutes worth of passive access to Malkovich's perceptual stream. Craig was clearly aware of the distinction between himself and Malkovich. Even after Craig learned how to control Malkovich's body, he described the sensation as "wearing a really expensive suit." Craig recognized the body he was occupying as something foreign, something distinct from himself. After several months at the helm, Craig still recognized himself as being distinct from Malkovich. This is shown in his reaction to the phone call from Dr. Lester, threatening him that if he (that is, Craig) doesn't leave at once Maxine will be killed. Craig does *not* respond with "What on earth do you mean 'I had better leave John Malkovich's body, or else'?—I *am* John Malkovich!" What is Craig missing "from the inside" that explains his denial of identity to Malkovich? Memory. At the point in time when Dr. Lester calls, Craig's memories could be broken into two isolated sets: (1) memories had over the past several months as John Malkovich, and (2) all memories of events before that as Craig. There are no memory links between Craig in the portal and John Malkovich before Craig entered the portal. This is quite different from Leonard's case. Leonard in the present lacks memories of being Leonard yesterday; however, he has many memories of being Leonard before the incident. That is why he so naturally asserts that he is Leonard Shelby from San Francisco (even though we, from the outside, find difficulty with this claim).

This discussion lends additional credence to the importance of memory in establishing personal identity, both from the inside (identifying who you, yourself, are) and from the outside (identifying who other people are, at least in atypical cases). If one assumes that the physical continuity theory of personal identity is correct, one cannot make sense of Craig's continuing to exist while in the portal. According to this theory, Craig ceased to exist when he entered the portal, because his body ceased to exist. Similarly, the physical continuity theory implies that the postincident Leonard is unambiguously identical to the preincident Leonard.

3.5 Three Theories of Personal Identity

In section 3.1 I introduced the three main theories for personal identity put forward by philosophers: the same-soul theory, the psychological identity theory, and the physical continuity theory. In this section, we will look at these theories in more detail, using the two focus movies as points of reference.

According to the physical continuity theory of personal identity, person A is identical to person B if person A's body is physically continuous with person B's. But what does this mean? Does it mean that any difference between person A and person B implies they are not identical? This is much too strong, for then my merest movement would cause me to cease existing. Are there any physical attributes that persons have that remain unchanged over long periods of time? The only plausible candidate here is DNA. I now have the same DNA as I had at birth. I will continue to have this DNA until my death. Maybe we should link personal identity to DNA. This has a couple of problems. For one, DNA is a recent discovery, whereas the concept of personal identity predates it by many millenia. More importantly, though, this construal of the physical continuity theory would make sets of identical twins and clones into nondistinct persons. Even if I look very much like my identical twin sister, we are nevertheless distinct persons.

But, if DNA won't work to ground personal identity, what next? Maybe we shouldn't be looking for a property or properties that remain unchanged over the life of an individual. Maybe we would be better off trying to specify the extent to which someone can change and still be the same person. The standard interpretation of the physical continuity theory does just that—to say that A and B are physically continuous is to say that, over time, A "traces [a] physically continuous spatio-temporal path" to B or vice versa (depending on whether A preceded B in time or not).[9]

This theory doesn't mesh very well with the viewer's natural reaction to either film. According to it, the Leonard who talked with Teddy is identical to the Leonard who brushed his teeth that next morning, who is identical to Leonard before the incident. Likewise, anyone who enters the portal in *Being John Malkovich* ceases to exist. There is no way within the confines of this version of the physical continuity theory to make sense of personhood apart from a physical body: no distinct body, no person. Recall the way the portal in *Being John Malkovich* worked—the bodies of those who enter it disappear, only to reappear along the New Jersey Turnpike some time later. A consistent follower of the physical continuity theory would have to say that those individuals spit out along the New Jersey Turnpike are brand new people. In particular, they were not identical to anyone who entered the passageway. Why? Because they are not physically continuous with them. What happened to Craig? He disappeared suddenly. Eight months later, someone who looked very much like him came into existence; but, because this later individual was not spatiotemporally continuous with the earlier one, they were not one and the same person. What happened to John Malkovich? He acted funny for eight months.

The same-soul theory is the second of the three theories of personal identity to consider. In section 3.1 I noted that this is the theory of personal identity that fits in most easily with the widespread belief in the possibility of an afterlife. It is based on a view of what the world is like that is called **Cartesian dualism.**[10] According to this view, two distinct types of "stuff" exist. One of these—matter—is the type of stuff that makes up physical objects. My desk is made of matter; my body is made of matter. The second type of stuff is immaterial—it is just as real as matter, even though it is immaterial. My soul is an example of this type of stuff. According to Cartesian dualism, matter and soul are totally independent in existence. There can be soulless matter (for example, my desk) and disembodied souls (for example, my soul after the death of my body). What is essential about me is not my body or any other characteristic of my physical being, but my soul. Within this view, it is conceptually possible that I existed before my body was conceived, just as it is conceptually possible that I will continue to exist after my body disintegrates. It is unclear how to apply the same-soul theory to *Being John Malkovich* and *Memento*, because souls are, by their very nature, not the sorts of things one can perceive. Think about how a consistent same-soul theorist would answer the question, Which soul was occupying John Malkovich's body—Malkovich's, or Craig's, or both? Similarly, in Leonard's case, Did Leonard's original soul cease to exist after the incident, only to be replaced by a new one—or even a succession of new ones? Because souls are not perceivable, there can be no reason for arguing one way or the other based on what we see in the movies. Souls are very enigmatic beasts. How can I be confident in assuming that you are the same person you were yesterday or two seconds ago? Bodies are observable (both one's own and those of others). Even memory is observable in the first person. (While you cannot perceive my memories, I can.) But I cannot perceive my own soul, much less yours.

That leaves us with the psychological continuity theory of personal identity. This theory comes in several different versions. According to one version, long-standing psychological characteristics (personality, dispositions, worldview, etc.) are what identify individuals over time. This version meshes well with *Being John Malkovich*—Craig continues to exist, even after he enters the passageway. He does, though, swap bodies along the way. The original Malkovich ceases to exist (or, at a minimum, is suppressed) once Craig gets control over the body. However, this version of the psychological continuity theory as applied to *Memento* is more equivocal. There's no reason to believe that Leonard before the incident was anything other than a bland and law-abiding citizen. Afterward, he became a killer. Was this metamorphosis the result of a change in personality, or was it that his circumstances changed radically and his old personality merely adapted? It is unclear. We aren't told enough about the preincident Leonard to answer this question. Even the extent to which his dispositions and long-term desires change is unclear. Certainly, after the accident, he gains the desire to avenge his wife's death. But, there is some evidence that he must "rediscover" this desire over and over again. He can't remember the significance of the name John G. for more than a few minutes. There is even evidence that he must "rediscover" the existence of his tattoos every few minutes. One scene in particular points very strongly in this direction. It occurs in the rest room of the diner in which he has just talked with Natalie (MM

22:00). While washing his hands, he sees a tattoo that reads REMEMBER SAMMY JANKIS and tries to wash it off. He is surprised when it doesn't. Likewise, on a couple of occasions, he stares in the mirror at the tattoos on his upper body as though he is seeing them for the first time. Is he also acquiring the desire for vengeance implicit in the tattoos as though for the first time? If so, then it is not at all clear what this version of the psychological continuity theory implies in Leonard's case.

What about other versions of the psychological continuity theory? According to the second version, it is a continuous stream of consciousness that is the backbone of personal identity. Presumably, thoughts last some finite amount of time. Perceptions likewise linger—not long, but they do not come and go instantaneously. The stream-of-consciousness version of this theory ties personal identity to the overlapping thoughts and perceptions that come and go through consciousness. The following diagram is useful for explaining how this is supposed to work.

In figure 3.1, A represents your sensing the smell of the dinner that is in front of you; B represents your intending to write "garlic" on your grocery list; C represents your thinking about what's on TV tonight, and so forth. The average person's mind is a very busy place, with many overlapping thoughts and sensations that come and go. No single thought lasts for very long, but the stream is continuous. According to some, the unity of this stream is what defines personhood. The analogy with a real stream is fitting. Particular molecules of water come and go, but the stream retains its identity despite the underlying flux.

The main problem with this version of the psychological continuity theory of personal identity is dealing with both typical and atypical breaks in the stream. When I fall asleep, the stream goes away (at least, while I'm not dreaming.) If I were ever to become comatose, the stream would go away. Who am I, then, when I wake up? If one ties identity solely to stream of consciousness, I am a new person.

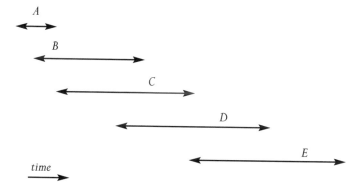

A

B

C

D

E

time

Figure 3.1

What about Leonard? As far as we can tell from the film, Leonard's stream of consciousness is normal. So, on this theory, so long as he doesn't lose consciousness, he remains the same person. As soon as he falls asleep, however, he ceases to exist. He is not identical to the person who wakes up later. For Craig, things are a little less straightforward. His stream of consciousness as he enters the Malkovich portal does not meld smoothly with John Malkovich's stream of consciousness just prior to that. Even though Craig begins having access to this different set of perceptions, there appears to be no overlap at all. If you use the name John Malkovich to designate the person associated with Malkovich's body before Craig enters the portal, then Craig never becomes John Malkovich.

Because of problems in dealing with breaks in continuity of the stream of consciousness, this version of the psychological continuity theory isn't very popular. Although, as we shall see, it can be used in tandem with the memory version of the theory with interesting results.

The standard interpretation of the psychological continuity theory uses memory as the ultimate determiner of identity. If person A can remember the thoughts and perceptions of person B, then person A is identical to person B. Memory according to this view can be applied transitively to establish identity; so, if I can remember the thoughts of person B (myself last year) and person B can remember the thoughts of person C (myself two years ago), then person A is identical to person C.

Craig remains Craig when he enters the portal, because he has memories of being Craig, not memories of being John Malkovich. The case from *Being John Malkovich* is straightforward.

Memento is a lot more interesting. Leonard after the incident can remember being Leonard before the incident. So, identity *seems* unproblematic. However, there are a couple of difficulties. One of these has already been discussed at length in the previous section. While Leonard after the incident is linked via memory with Leonard before the incident, he has no memory links with himself between the incident and the present. We could take advantage of the transitivity of identity through memory to some extent; Leonard in the present can remember the thoughts and perceptions of Leonard three minutes ago, who can remember the thoughts and perceptions of Leonard six minutes ago (even though Leonard in the present cannot), who can remember Leonard nine minutes ago, and so on. This is the way the memory version of the psychological continuity theory is supposed to work. However, in Leonard's case, we can't do this going back every three minutes to continuously link up Leonard in the present with Leonard prior to the accident because there are unbridgeable gaps between now and then. When he wakes up, he can remember nothing that has happened since the incident. He can't even remember what happened three minutes ago in order to start the linking up.

Some philosophers have tried a hybrid approach to psychological continuity. Either memory or continuation of a stream of consciousness can be used to establish identity.

But that won't help here either, for every day of his postincident life, Leonard's mind is a memory and stream of consciousness cul-de-sac. The British philosopher Derek Parfit has described a related case.

> *The Sleeping Pill.* Certain actual sleeping pills cause retrograde amnesia. It can be true that, if I take such a pill, I shall remain awake for an hour, but after my night's sleep I shall have no memories of the second half of this hour.
>
> I have in fact taken such pills, and found out what the results are like. Suppose that I took such a pill nearly an hour ago. The person who wakes up in my bed tomorrow will not be psychologically continuous with me as I am now. He will be psychologically continuous with me as I was half an hour ago. I am now on a *psychological branch-line*, which will end soon when I fall asleep. During this half-hour, I am psychologically continuous with myself in the past. But I am not now psychologically continuous with myself in the future. I shall never later remember what I do or think or feel during this half-hour. This means that, in some respects, my relation to myself tomorrow is like a relation to another person.
>
> Suppose, for instance, that I have been worrying about some practical question. I now see the solution. Since it is clear what I should do, I form a firm intention. In the rest of my life, it would be enough to form this intention. But, when I am on this psychological branch-line, this is not enough. I shall not later remember what I have now decided, and I shall not wake up with the intention that I have now formed. I must therefore communicate with myself tomorrow as if I was communicating with someone else. I must write myself a letter, describing my decision, and my new intention. I must then place this letter where I am bound to notice it tomorrow.
>
> I do not in fact have any memories of making such a decision, and writing such a letter. But I did once find such a letter underneath my razor.[11]

The case that Parfit describes (one-time retrograde amnesia) differs from Leonard's case in one important respect: there are not multiple, disconnected contenders for being identical to the individual before the onset of the amnesia. Even though Parfit cannot remember what he thought or did for that half hour before he fell asleep, that part of his mental life is linked by both memory and stream of consciousness with what immediately preceded it. In Leonard's case, each new day is not linked via stream of consciousness with anything, and only linked via memory to the remote past. In order for Parfit's case to be relevantly like Leonard's, he would need to take the anterograde amnesia–producing sleeping pill every few hours for the rest of his life. Despite these differences, Parfit's discussion provides a useful additional example of what is meant by "psychological continuity." Also, his mentioning of the notes to himself in the future should remind you of Leonard's way of coping with his disability.

3.6 *Evaluating the Theories*

Being John Malkovich argues for some version of the psychological continuity theory of personal identity. The film implies in several places that Craig continues to exist after entering the portal, but never succeeds in being John Malkovich. The best way to make sense of this is by noting the clear discontinuities in long-standing psychological characteristics, stream of consciousness and memory that separate the John Malkovich prior to Craig's entry from the John Malkovich after Craig's entry. If you apply any of the three versions of the psychological continuity theory here, the implication is non-identity (as the movie suggests). The main alternative, the physical continuity theory, implies that Craig ceases to exist when he enters the passageway, contrary to what the movie suggests.

Memento "opens up a can of worms" (to use Craig's colorful language in *Being John Malkovich*) for the memory-based version of the psychological continuity theory of personal identity. One topic related to this theory we've yet to broach is a secondary theme of *Memento*. Were Leonard's memories of his preincident self accurate? Several hints dropped along the way point toward a "no" answer, or, at least, raise the specter of doubt. Did Sammy Jankis really exist as Leonard seemed to remember him? How many attackers were there when his wife was killed? Was his wife really killed in that way? Maybe Leonard has, in constructing the story of Sammy Jankis, really told the story of his own wife's death.

The distinction between genuine and nongenuine memories was discussed in section 1.5 in the context of Hume's radical skepticism. In order to be genuine (1) a previous perception must have occurred; (2) that previous perception must be causally responsible for the current memory; and (3) the current memory must accurately represent the previous perception. Obviously, the psychological continuity theory of personal identity requires that, in order to serve as a link, a memory must be genuine—seeming to remember is not enough to identify the person seeming to remember as the earlier person whose thoughts and perceptions are being remembered. To see this, consider what the implications would be of allowing nongenuine memories in as an identity link. Some present-day person who seems to remember being Napoleon at the battle of Waterloo would *be* Napoleon. Any theory of personal identity that has this implication would be unacceptable. Leonard's confusion about what happened, even before the incident, casts doubt on the genuineness of much of what he claims to remember.

In many ways, though, we are not so unlike Leonard in this regard. How accurate is *your* memory? To what extent can your memory be swayed by suggestion? There is an immense literature within psychology on this topic.[12] Oddly, Leonard makes reference to this in his lunch conversation with Teddy (MM 23:00): "Memory's unreliable. . . . Memory's not perfect. It's not even that good. Ask the police. Eyewitness testimony is unreliable." But if memory in general is unreliable, and if (as Hume argues) there is no way in the present to check that any given memory is accurate, what does that say about the memory-based version of the psychological continuity theory of personal identity? One may be tempted to say that: even though I cannot know for sure whether a memory is genuine, presumably, there is a fact of the matter. If *I* was not really at the battle of Waterloo, then *I* am not Napoleon, even though I seem to remember being him. The problem with this is that it presupposes some route other than memory for establishing identity. What is at issue is my identity. By saying I was not *really* at Waterloo is begging the question.

Memento reinforces Hume's general skepticism about the unity of the self, even as viewed "from the inside"—we cannot see that unity itself; rather, we must infer it from memory. However, if this is to work, we must have some way of distinguishing between genuine and nongenuine memories. But we do not. Furthermore, because of the role that historical (remembered) context plays in giving meaning to the present, this skepticism about memory infects even the present. What I am doing right now depends on what intentions I formed in the past. The effect of Leonard's total lack of context provides the occasional comic relief in *Memento*, but it also points to a more general problem for making the psychological continuity theory of personal identity work, even for individuals with normal memory.

Discussion Questions

1. Do you believe in an afterlife? If so, by virtue of what will you be identical to your postdeath self?
2. Just after viewing *Being John Malkovich*, did you think that Craig succeeded in being John Malkovich? If so, what happened to the original John Malkovich?
3. Just after viewing *Memento*, did you think Leonard remained the same person throughout the movie?
4. What was your initial response to the examples involving the cars? Prior to hearing of the two-car case, did you agree that the reassembled car was identical to the original car? Was the new-parts car identical to the original car? What did your intuitions tell you in the two-car case (when both the new-parts and the reassembled car existed)?
5. While anterograde amnesia of the sort Leonard had is quite rare, some other brain abnormalities producing other forms of amnesia are quite common. One example is Alzheimer's disease. What attributes would a case of amnesia have to have to call into question someone's identity?
6. Given what you now know about personal identity, do you think it is possible for you to wake up tomorrow as somebody else?
7. Just for fun: can you reconstruct the actual sequence of events in *Memento*?

Annotated List of Film Titles Relevant to Personal Identity

Awakenings (1990). Directed by Penny Marshall. Starring Robin Williams, Robert De Niro.

Patients in a mental institution have been catatonic for years or even decades before being "brought back to life" by a new drug.

Regarding Henry (1991). Directed by Mike Nichols. Starring Harrison Ford, Annette Benning.

Henry suffers severe brain damage from a gunshot wound to the head. He cannot remember anything about his previous life.

Total Recall (1990). Directed by Paul Verhoeven. Starring Arnold Schwarzenegger, Rachel Ticotin, Sharon Stone.

While serving as one of the two focus films for chapter 1's discussion of skepticism, *Total Recall* also brings up issues within personal identity. Under that chapter's second interpretation, who is Quaid *really*? Under its third interpretation, what is the relationship between Quaid and his ego trip counterpart? How can Quaid distinguish between genuine and nongenuine memories?

Annotated List of Book Titles Relevant to Personal Identity

"CLASSICS" IN THE HISTORY OF PERSONAL IDENTITY

John Locke

Essay Concerning Human Understanding, first published in 1694. "Of Identity and Diversity" (chapter 27 of book II of this work) considers the three theories of personal identity discussed in this chapter and argues in favor of the memory version of the psychological continuity theory and against the same-soul and physical continuity theories of personal identity. The *Essay* is available in its entirety online at <http://www.ilt.columbia.edu/Projects/digitexts/locke/understanding/title.html> and <http://socserv2.mcmaster.ca/~econ/ugcm/3ll3/locke/Essay.htm>.

David Hume

A Treatise of Human Nature, 1740. Most of this book deals with skepticism; however, several sections (in particular, book 1, part 4, section vi) question the unity of the self. The scholarly standard for this work is the 2nd edition, put out by Oxford University Press in 1978. The *Treatise* is also available in its entirety online at <http://socserv2.socsci.mcmaster.ca/~econ/ugcm/3ll3/hume/treat.html>.

4

Artificial Intelligence

AI: Artificial Intelligence (2001)

Professor Hobby: I propose we build a robot who can love. . . . [A robot] with a mind. . . . [A robot] with an inner world—of metaphor, of intuition, of self-motivated reasoning, of dreams.

Assistant: If a robot could genuinely love a person, what responsibility does that person hold toward that [robot] in return? It's a moral question.

Gigolo Joe: They made us too smart, too quick, and too many. We are suffering for the mistakes that they made. Because, when the end comes, all that will be left is us. That's why they hate us.

—from *AI: Artificial Intelligence*

The recent development of advanced computers capable of performing some tasks at the same level as (or sometimes, even better than) their human makers has opened up a whole series of questions. Even before the advent of the computer age, filmmakers, and, before them, novelists, have seen fiction as a suitable means for exploring these questions. Thus, Mary Shelley's nineteenth-century novel *Frankenstein*, while it deals with an organic "monster" rather than one made of silicon chips and metal, shares much in common with later novels and movies about advanced robots and their relationship with their human makers. A recent contribution to this long line of fictional works, Steven Spielberg's film *AI* explores many of the questions at the intersection of philosophy and artificial intelligence. Could a highly advanced robot be a person (in the sense of having various moral rights, such as the right not to be harmed without just cause)? What does it mean to be a person, anyway? Is having a mind a prerequisite for personhood? Is it possible for something made of silicon, wire, and metal to have a mind?

Many futuristic science-fiction movies involving computers describe a world in which robots are in competition with the human species for dominance of the world. Is this a likely scenario? Can we reasonably expect this sort of situation to arise in the real world, given what we currently know about computers? If so, is it something we (as humans) should fear? Maybe, the transition from biological organisms to nonbiological organisms is just "evolution taking its course." Is there something we should be doing now to make sure that some future computer-caused catastrophe for the human species doesn't happen? What does "reasonable prudence" require of us today?

You can see the philosophical fertility of movies about highly developed computer robots. Several of these questions have been around since the days of Plato in ancient Greece. So, they are nothing new to philosophy; however, the development of computers over the past half century, coupled with science-fiction depictions of the future trajectory of computer research, has brought these questions into focus for many nonphilosophers. This chapter will examine how contemporary philosophers have answered these questions, using the film *AI* as a sounding board. As usual, the first several sections of this chapter are general and may be read prior to watching the movie. The material beginning with section 4.4 should only be read after watching *AI*.

4.1   What Is Artificial Intelligence?

For some, May 11, 1997, marks a significant date in the relationship between computers and humanity, for that was the day on which "[i]n brisk and brutal fashion, the IBM computer Deep Blue unseated humanity . . . as the finest chess playing entity on the planet. . . . Garry Kasparov, the world chess champion, resigned the sixth and final game. . . ."[1] Deep Blue's defeat of history's greatest chess player stunned the world. Was this threshold event a sign that computers had achieved a level of intelligence on a par with that of humans? Hardly. However, it did highlight just how far computers had come since their invention a mere fifty-five years earlier.[2]

At the beginning, computers were employed primarily to perform the sorts of massive calculations that humans found tedious and time-consuming. Computers made excellent number crunchers, capable of performing highly complex series of calculations in much less time than a human would require—and without error. Soon, though, researchers started seeing other applications for computers. Could other tasks (for example, playing games such as chess) be formalized in such a way that the computer's great calculating ability would be exploited within these domains as well? Thus, artificial intelligence (AI) was born not long after the general-purpose programmable computer was invented.

The term *artificial intelligence* was coined in the mid-1950s as the name of the research area (increasing a subarea within computer science) whose aim was to program computers so that they did things that, when done by humans, were thought to require intelligence. John McCarthy, the term's inventor, made a point of distinguishing between *artificial* intelligence and *fake* intelligence. For him, computers could display genuine (not fake) intelligence, even though that intelligence was the result of the activity of an artificial (that is, human-created) device.[3]

Game playing was seen early on as a suitable test bed for discovering whether computers could achieve humanlike levels of expertise in a quintessentially human activity. At least at first blush, game playing has many of the attributes one associates with intelligence: it requires a player to consider the consequences of acting one way versus another and to use that information to decide what to do. Doesn't a large portion of human decision making consist of exactly this sort of reasoning? If they could get computers to display this sort of reasoning, so argued the early AI researchers, that would be a major step toward achieving computer-based intelligence. Even though they were working on computers with miniscule computational power by today's standards, AI researchers met with some early successes. Checkers, while much less complex than chess, is still a challenging game for humans. It quickly succumbed to computerization. By the late 1950s, a computer could beat the world's best checkers player.

It may be useful at this point to peek inside a hypothetical game-playing program to see how these superhuman feats are accomplished. Most games (and virtually all board games such as backgammon, chess, and checkers) are defined by a start position, a set of rules that specify what counts as a legal move, and a goal state or states. So, in chess, the start position is the opening board position, the set of rules specify that there are two players who take turns moving the pieces around in certain ways (for example, the knight can move up two squares and over one, but it cannot move diagonally). The goal is to have your opponent in checkmate (a precise specification of "checkmate" would also need to be included in the rules). No surprises here. Let's consider a very simple chess-playing program. (I'll refer to it as Version 1.0.) One way to get a computer to "play" chess is to give the computer a way of representing the current board position and a way of randomly selecting one from among the legal moves that can be made, given that board position. Obviously, the level of play of such a program would be pathetic. A major step up (Version 2.0) in level of play could be achieved if we added a new capability to this chess program. Now, rather than randomly selecting a move from among the legal moves, the computer considers all the possible legal moves given the current position, then rates the moves in terms of how good they are. We'd need to add something to the program so that, for each of these legal moves, the computer had a way of calculating that move's "goodness." What sorts of attributes would we look for?[4] For help, we could ask master chess players for assistance. What do *they* look for in deciding whether a board position is to their own or their opponent's advantage? We would need to have them specify very precisely what they mean so that we could write our updated chess program to look for those attributes and rate each possible move accordingly. Version 2.0 of our chess program would still be easy to beat, even for not-very-good human chess players, but it could probably beat a novice.

What would really enhance our chess program is if we could give it the ability to take into account how its human opponent might react to one move versus another. It would be even better still if our program could take into account how the opponent might move and then what countermove the program would make. If nothing else, expanding the evaluation process into the future would uncover any checks or captures lurking just a move or two away. It is fairly easy to automate this process via iteration. Prior to actually picking a move, the program calculates all the possible legal moves it has to choose from. However, rather than applying the goodness rating now, as Version 2.0 did, the program holds off on that step. First, it calculates, for each legal move it might make, all the legal moves its opponent could make in reply. In theory, we could repeat this process as many times as we liked and only apply the goodness rating to each board position n moves into the future. (Let's call this fancy chess playing program Version 3.0.) Obviously, in applying the information we gain about the goodness of board positions several moves into the future, we'd have to write the program so that it assumed its opponent is trying to keep it from winning, but that part isn't hard. All of this sounds so straightforward that one wonders why it took computers so long to beat the world's best human chess player. We shall see shortly that there's more going on than meets the eye. But, for now, this simplified description gives you the flavor of how game-playing programs work.

There were many early successes in AI in domains other than game playing. Computer programs were developed that could solve logic problems, manipulate blocks in a virtual world based on simple instructions in English entered at the keyboard, achieve expert-level performance in domains like blood disease diagnosis and analysis of chemical structure, and solve equations in calculus that would leave the brightest MIT undergraduates scratching their heads. The claims of AI researchers that artificial intelligence was possible didn't sound so far-fetched after all.

Philosophers and psychologists saw in artificial intelligence a new way of thinking about the mind. If we really could make computers intelligent like us, what would that tell us about our own minds? Maybe we are really computers—not in the sense of being made of silicon chips and wire, but in the sense that our intelligence is realized in instructions that resemble those of a computer program.

While these early successes in AI were the impetus that started philosophers thinking about the mind in a new way, in the long run, they haven't resulted in the general, all-purpose intelligent computer that had been predicted. To see why, let's return to Version 3.0 of our hypothetical chess-playing program. I mentioned above that, *in theory*, the expansion of the set of future moves could continue indefinitely. There's a hitch, though. At the beginning of a chess game, there aren't very many legal moves. (On opening, each side has to choose from among exactly twenty legal moves.) Similarly, toward the end of a game, once most of the pieces have been captured and removed from the board, the number of legal moves is fairly small. In the middle of a typical game, there are many more legal moves available to each side. Admittedly, most of these moves are not good ones, but that's not the point. A bad but legal move is still a legal move, and what Version 3.0 of our chess program cares about is the set of legal moves. On average (taking into account the number of moves that are legal early on, in the middle, and late in the game), there are approximately thirty-five legal moves available to each player at any one time. If the chess program looks only at the current set of legal moves and applies the goodness rating to each of those moves, it only needs to consider (on average) thirty-five board positions (this was what Version 2.0 did). If it wants to look further in the future, the number of board position that must be evaluated quickly gets out of hand. For each move, the opponent can make (on average) thirty-five legal countermoves. That means that, if Version 3.0 of the chess program only considers one move/countermove pair, it will have to evaluate (on average) $35 \times 35 = 1,225$ board positions. If it looks one more move into the future before applying the goodness rating (move + countermove + counter-counter-move), it will have to consider $35 \times 35 \times 35 = 42,875$ board positions. In general, to look n moves into the future requires the program to evaluate 35^n positions. This number gets very big, very quickly as n increases. This "combinatorial explosion" explains why, even with current supercomputers, it is impossible to produce a really good chess program using this brute force method for determining which move to pick. Deep Blue, the chess program that beat Garry Kasparov in 1997, ran on a state-of-the-art computer built especially for the purpose and could evaluate 200,000,000 board positions per second (sixty billion in the three minutes that each player has to pick the next move). However, even at this speed, Deep Blue could only search around seven moves into the future if it used this brute force technique.[5] ($35^7 \approx$ 60 billion.) Checkers, a game with a much smaller number of legal moves per board position, is amenable to this approach, which is why it was so (relatively) easy to produce an expert-level checkers program, even with the computers of forty-five years ago.

What lessons has AI (and philosophy) learned from game-playing programs? One thing that is quite clear is that humans don't solve problems using the brute force search described above with Version 3.0 of our chess-playing program. Garry Kasparov, in deciding which move to pick, does a much more limited search. (At top speed, human grand masters can evaluate approximately three board positions per second.) Instead, he relies on "hunches" and "intuition"—the implicit knowledge gained from playing and studying the equivalent of tens of thousands of chess games during his life.

Some computer scientists and philosophers have argued that game playing is in reality a very poor test bed for AI, because the attributes of domains such as chess and checkers are so different from the sorts of tasks that take up the bulk of the average human's day. Game-playing programs have been a singular success precisely because of these attributes. The rules of a typical game are small in number and very clear-cut.

Even if you've never written a computer program in your life, you could probably specify the rules of checkers with enough precision that those rules could be easily written in computer-usable form. Furthermore, the goal states of games are (usually) very easy to specify with precision—hence, easy to encode in a computer program. Games are highly atypical human activities, because they neither require the integration of huge amounts of diverse knowledge nor suffer from the ambiguity one sees in other human activities such as language comprehension, vision, and planning. I warned above that one should not make too much of Deep Blue's victory over Kasparov—Deep Blue has not achieved a level of intelligence on par with that of a human. Kasparov can understand language (several languages, actually); he has normal vision; he can see and recognize things in his environment, name them, understand what they do or what they are for. He can manipulate them in various ways and use them to achieve goals, both short- and long-term. All Deep Blue can do is play a very good game of chess. It can do absolutely nothing else. It can't even "see" the chessboard or move the pieces—for that, it requires human assistance.

The current state of the art in AI in some of these more typical human domains is still quite modest and is likely to remain so for the foreseeable future. The average three-year-old child can out-perform the most advanced computer-controlled robots in navigation through cluttered environments and manipulation of objects. The average three-year-old is also better at picking out salient features of the environment based on visual information, recognizing objects from one point in time to another, learning by example, and language comprehension. Indeed, it seems fair to say that, for all "general-purpose" tasks, an average three-year-old can out-perform the most advanced AI system.

How long this human superiority will last is a subject of hot debate. The example from game playing shows us that raw computational power is not the decisive issue. Rather, the weakness of current AI systems lies in the software—in the program, not the computer on which the program is running. How long it will take AI to address these weaknesses is hard to judge, if, indeed, they can be addressed at all. In the meantime, the very idea of artificial intelligence has given philosophers and psychologists much to ponder.

4.2 Three Issues at the Intersection of Philosophy and Artificial Intelligence

Each of the three quotations from the movie *AI* given at the beginning of the chapter highlights one of the three issues that lie at the intersection of philosophy and AI. The first issue falls within a subarea of philosophy called **philosophy of mind**. This specialty within philosophy is interested primarily in understanding the mind—what it is and what it does. AI has proven to be a fertile source for new ideas on this topic. Can a computer have a mind? If so, what does that tell us about the nature of the mind and its relationship to the body? If not, why not—what feature of "mindedness" does a computer lack? Various philosophers have answered these questions in different ways. In sections 4.4 and 4.5 we shall be looking in detail at these answers and the arguments philosophers have given to support them.

A second issue brought up by the possibility of artificial intelligence questions whether a computer could be a moral person. Virtually every ethical theory says that I have serious moral obligations to other people. I ought not harm them without just cause. In some cases, I also have positive obligations—actions concerning others that I ought not refrain from doing. The chapter on ethics discusses the most popular ethical theories in depth. Each of these theories presupposes that there is some way of distinguishing between persons (those beings to whom I have moral obligations) and everything else. You are a person. I am a person. Steven Spielberg is a person. My coffee cup is not a person. My telephone is not a person. Stanley Kubrick's dead body is not a person. What about a (living) dog, or, better yet, a chimpanzee? Do I have moral obligations to a chimp in the same way that I have moral obligations to Steven Spielberg? It would be wrong of me to harm Spielberg without just cause. It would be wrong of me to kill or maim or steal from him. Would it be wrong to kill a chimp? Suppose AI researchers in the future develop a highly sophisticated computer-based robot that is not only good at chess, but also good at the list of general-purpose tasks mentioned earlier. This hypothetical robot exceeds not only a three-year-old child at these tasks but also the average adult. Would it be wrong of me to destroy that robot without just cause? What if the robot, in addition to all of these capabilities, also exhibited the same reactions to harmful stimuli that I do? When stuck with a pin, it howled in pain and begged not to be hurt any more. Would I be doing anything wrong if I continued to stab it with the pin? These questions and others like them can help ethicists clarify what it means to be a person. The ramifications of defining person one way versus another are quite far-reaching. There have been many cases in history in which members of another society or members of a minority group within a society were judged to be "nonpersons" and persecuted without remorse. Closer to home, there are several contemporary moral issues in our country that have a stake in this debate. For example, many believe that the moral status of abortion hinges on whether the fetus is a person. Similarly, if nonhuman animals are persons, then killing animals in order to eat them may be morally wrong, given that other sources of food are available. As you can see, this is not just a philosopher's question. We will be exploring the issue of personhood in the context of the movie *AI* in section 4.6.

The final philosophical issue brought up by AI also falls within the domain of ethics. While current AI systems are not very advanced relative to humans, that is likely to change. Should AI researchers (and society more generally) be worried about what the world will look like if and when computer-controlled robots surpass their human makers in intelligence? History shows that it is hard to put genies back into bottles. Nuclear weapons are here to stay. There may have been a time when nuclear proliferation could have been avoided, but, that time is passed and now it is too late. Are we at a similar crossroads with regard to AI? What are the likely consequences of the development of intelligent robots—for life on the planet in general and humans in particular? Many futuristic science-fiction movies involving robots depict those robots killing or at least supplanting their makers and taking over the world. (We shall see that the movie *AI* recognizes this concern, but does not present it in the stereotypical way.) Would it be a bad thing if that were to happen? Is that likely to happen? If so, could we prevent it from happening? Do we have a moral obligation to future generations of humans to see to it that it doesn't happen? This last question points to why I said above that this topic belongs within the domain of ethics. Ultimately, it boils down to what we ought to do here and now. We will examine this issue in section 4.7.

4.3 An Overview of the Movie

AI: Artificial Intelligence (2001). Directed by Steven Spielberg. Starring Haley Joel Osment, Jude Law, Frances O'Connor, Sam Robards.

AI is set in the United States at some unspecified time in the future—distant enough in time to make the existence of highly advanced robots credible, yet close enough that current human social roles are easily recognized. Global warming has caused flooding over much of the earth, with a corresponding decrease in the availability of resources. Affluent countries such as the United States have coped by limiting the (human) population. The widespread use of humanoid robots has allowed these countries to maintain their standard of living. Enter David—the first of his kind—a robot "child" whose sole function is to love whatever human he imprints upon.

The family that "adopts" David as a surrogate for their own gravely ill son doesn't give much thought at first to the ramifications of their choice. When their biological son recovers (and David is no longer needed), the question arises as to what to do with him. He is built to be nonrecyclable, so, if they take him back, he will be destroyed. Monica, David's adopted mother, has serious misgivings about this course of action. She decides instead to abandon him in the woods. David's travels after that point show us the underside of this future world—a world in which humans' dependence on robots is set off against their deep-seated hatred of them, because, inevitably, it will be the robots that survive.

The story continues after that point on a fantastical foray, weaving the story of Pinocchio into David's adventures as he travels even farther into the future. The outline of the three philosophical issues described above should be easy to recognize in both the plot and dialogue.

4.4 What Does It Mean to Have a Mind?

Historically, it was assumed that only humans had minds, and all other creatures had either no mind at all or merely protominds. This view had two main sources. One was the theory of mind that equated having a mind with having an (immaterial) soul. In section 3.5, we discussed Cartesian dualism. According to this theory, two distinct types of "stuff" exist. One of these, matter, is the type of stuff that makes up physical objects (my body is made of matter). The second type of stuff is immaterial, it is just as real as matter, but it is nonphysical. My soul is an example of this immaterial stuff. Mental activity, according to René Descartes, is realized in (or by) the soul, just as physical activity is realized by the body. No soul, no mind. So far, though, nothing I have said bears directly on the issue of who (or what) has a mind. For an answer to this question, we must add another of Descartes's assumptions: only humans have souls. This, combined with "no soul, no mind," implies that only humans have minds. Descartes thought it was obvious that humans alone possessed souls. He was so willing to defend this position, no matter how odd its implications, that he assigned all nonhuman animals the status "mere machines"—the equivalent of clocks, noting that they "are not rational, and that nature makes them behave as they do according to the disposition of their organs; just as a clock, composed only of wheels and weights and springs, can count the hours and measure the time more accurately than we can with all our intelligence."[6]

Clearly, anyone who accepts a view like Descartes's will reject the assertion that a robot could possibly have a mind. Thus, David's "pain response" is not an indication that he is experiencing pain. For, lacking a mind, he does not experience pain. Similarly, he does not have beliefs. He does not have wishes. He does not make plans. All of those things that we associate with having a mind are things that David cannot do, no matter how much his externally observable behavior leads us to believe otherwise. We shall return shortly to the soul-based view of the mind. First, though, I want to consider its main competitor.

The difference between humans and all other creatures at certain skills has led some to infer that only humans have minds. Until recently, it was a given that humans were the only animals capable of fashioning and using tools—that is, creating something new by changing or combining things that already exist with the intention of using the newly created object to achieve some goal. The amount of abstract reasoning and planning implicit in tool creation and use is great enough that if humans are the only toolmakers on the earth, we are indeed truly special. It turns out, though, that other animals make and use tools, at least rudimentary ones. Chimps in the wild have been observed fashioning "termite fishing rods" by biting off the side branches on a small, straight branch to make a straight, smooth-sided stick that can be poked in the hole of the termite mound.[7] Admittedly, a branchless stick is not a jet airplane, but, in making the tool, a qualitative boundary has been crossed.

A second major skill often pointed to as separating humans and all other creatures is the use of a complex language. Clearly, animals communicate. My dog's barking is a way of telling me or other dogs in the vicinity that something is up. It is unclear, though, if the dog is communicating anything more than "*Hey!*" when it barks. In order to count as a language, a communication medium must be able to express a minimum number of message types. One or just a few message types isn't good enough. Human languages, because they are founded on a recursive grammar, possess the capacity to express an infinite number of distinct messages. English, for example, includes an infinite number of grammatical sentences. Even if we grant that many of these sentences are indistinguishable in terms of their meaning, still, the number of meanings I can express using English is immense. Dog communication can't do that. Even chimp and gorilla communication appears to lack the richness of the typical human language. There have been attempts to teach chimps and gorillas nonoral languages (for example, American Sign Language or a language based on concatenating symbols by pointing). The correct interpretation of the postlearning primate's behavior has been the object of heated debate.[8] The jury is still out on whether humans are alone in their ability to use a complex language.

Which of these two ways of interpreting "mindedness" strikes us as preferable: the soul-based view or the skills-based view? A major disadvantage of the soul-based view is that the belief that other humans have a mind turns out to be totally unfounded. Recall how the criticism of the same-soul criterion for personal identity went in section 3.5: souls, being immaterial, are not the sorts of things that can be perceived. All I can perceive when I look at someone else is the outside of that individual's body. I cannot see the soul. I must infer, given the external appearance and behavior, that there is a soul "inside." But, if judgments about mindedness are based on nothing but external observables, why bother with positing a soul at all? Why not just say: this individual has a mind because I can observe that this individual possesses these attributes associated with mindedness? In terms of our judgments about who has a mind and who doesn't, souls don't play any role. At least the skills-based view jibes with our everyday practice. We shall see a little later that there are some problems with a strict skills-based view; however, it seems to be on the right track. Throughout the remainder of this and the next section, I shall be assuming that something akin to the skills-based view offers the best way of interpreting what it means to have a mind. We are still a long way from settling the issue, but at least we know now where to look for clues: external behavior.

While our everyday practice in ascribing mentality to individuals is a useful touchstone, we need to guard against taking all such ascriptions literally. Consider the following example. My car breaks down en route to an important meeting, causing me to miss the meeting. In describing what has happened, I say, "The car *knew* I had an important meeting so it *decided* to break down just then, because it *hates* me so much."

We would all agree that I am speaking metaphorically here. I do not literally believe that my car knows, or decides, or hates anything. One sees this sort of metaphorical ascription of mentality quite often. Garry Kasparov, in describing how Deep Blue plays chess, naturally fell into the habit of describing it in mentalistic terms. "The computer played like a human today," he said. "I have to praise the machine for understanding some very deep positions." It is unclear, however, whether Kasparov thought he was speaking metaphorically.

What sorts of attributes lead us to use mentalistic terms literally? Is there some sort of litmus test that could guide us in saying of someone, "That individual has a mind"? Alan Turing (1912–1954), a brilliant mathematician whose work in the theory of computation in the 1930s laid the groundwork for modern computer science, developed a test that, he thought, could justify the claim that an individual that passed the test had a mind.[9] Turing believed that conversational language fluency brought to bear so many skills and so much information that it could serve as the touchstone of mindedness. The test regimen he described formalized that view.

In general terms, the **Turing test** works by testing whether a computer can fool a human communicating with it into thinking it is a human. Turing described the test protocol in greater detail.[10] There were to be two human participants and one computer, and all three subjects were in different rooms. The only means they had for communicating with one another was via a keyboard and monitor. (Think instant messaging.) One of the human subjects was designated as the interviewer. This person would pose various questions to the other two subjects (the second human and the computer). She could ask anything at all. The human interviewee was required to answer all questions honestly. The computer interviewee was supposed to lie as needed. (Obviously, if the computer were required to answer all questions honestly and the interviewer asked the computer. "Are you a computer?" the test would be over very quickly.) The test was to last one hour—long enough, Turing thought, for the interviewer to uncover any "tricks" the computer might be using to fake language competence. At the end of the hour, the interviewer must decide which interviewee was the computer and which was the human. If the computer could fool the interviewer for at least 50 percent of the trials, then the computer "passed."

Clearly, all of the robots depicted in *AI* would pass the Turing test.[11] Even the outmoded robot destroyed at the Flesh Fair showed signs of language competence on a par with that of the surrounding humans. So if we settle on the Turing test as a test for mindedness, all of the robots in *AI* pass; but should we accept the Turing test? A major advantage of the test is that it avoids the pitfalls of the soul-based view of the mind. It has a couple of fairly serious problems, though. One involves its assumption about the centrality of language skills. Turing intended the test to provide *sufficient* conditions for mindedness, but not *necessary* conditions. In other words, if an individual passes the test, that shows that that individual has a mind. Failing the test, though, shows nothing.

(Something with a mind could still fail the test.) Even interpreting the Turing test as providing only a sufficient condition for mindedness is problematic. Humans have bodies. We use those bodies to perceive and interact with the world around us. We learn most of the concepts we possess via such interaction. Turing's test allows a "disembodied" computer—a computer without sense organs or means to manipulate objects in the environment—to count as having a mind. Is it really possible to possess the concept *red* without being able to see? Is it possible to have the concept *pain* without being able to experience pain? Turing's hypothetical computer could talk convincing about seeing red things and being in pain all day long, but its lack of sense organs leaves one wondering whether it really *understands* what it is talking about. The majority of the concepts humans use—the concepts that underlie the meaning of words—are grounded ultimately in our interaction with the world around us. Many philosophers have complained that the Turing test misses an important component of language use: understanding. We will return to this topic in the next section.

A second complaint against the Turing test is that it is too skills-based, too focused on observable behavior (in particular, linguistic behavior) without regard to what is going on inside. Imagine that I wrote a computer program that could take sentences in English typed in at a keyboard as input. My program had access to a very large database of English sentence pairs, handcrafted by me. Now, the way this program works is as follows: a sentence is entered. The program looks up in the database to see if that sentence is among the set of first items in the pairs. If it is, the program displays on the monitor the second item in the pair. If it is not, the program displays "I don't understand." So, for example, one of the pairs of sentences in this database would be: <"How are you today?" || "Very well, thank you."> If the "interviewer" types in the question "How are you today?" the computer looks up the appropriate response in the database. In order for the computer to come anywhere close to producing natural-seeming conversation, this database would have to be immense. So, it would be really hard to create, but not, in theory, impossible. Would you say that a computer that managed to pass the Turing test using canned responses in the way outlined above should count as having a mind? If you are thinking that such a computer program could never fool anyone, think again. What I've outlined above is similar to a program called Eliza that was written to mimic the sorts of responses that a Rogerian psychotherapist gives.[12] (This form of psychotherapy basically throws back in the form of a question whatever a patient says. So, if the patient says "I hate my mother," the therapist would respond with "Why do you hate your mother?") Eliza was a little more complicated than this simple lookup table program, but not by much. Yet Eliza was famous for fooling people into divulging intimate secrets, unaware that they were communicating with a computer.

The example of Eliza, a decidedly mindless program, points to a serious deficit in the Turing test, or, indeed, any 100 percent skills-based test for mindedness. What is going on inside does matter. In his original paper describing the Turing test, Turing considered this criticism and rejected it. He argued when you look at me, you don't see what is happening on the inside. All you see are skills as manifested in my observable behavior. You judge that I have a mind based solely on that criterion. It is (unfairly) stacking the cards against a computer to change the basis for judgment, suddenly requiring that a skill be implemented in the "right" way in order to say that it gives evidence of a mind.

So, should we count Eliza as having a mind? It seems that, in this response, Turing was missing a crucial point. We are willing to make judgments concerning the mindedness of other humans based only on observable behavior because we assume that others, being made of the same kinds of bodies as we are, accomplish tasks in roughly the same way. With a computer, this underlying assumption of sameness disappears, and it becomes legitimate to question how the computer is achieving that level of competence. Notice that, in this criticism of Turing's response, I am not saying computers could not get it right on the inside: by "on the inside" I mean "how it solves a problem" not "what it is made of." But, it is justified for the bar to be higher in this regard for nonhumans.

So, where does this leave us? It seems to me that *AI* is implicitly arguing for the view that David has a mind. We might find something useful if we try to make that argument explicit. Clearly, David is a robot, so we need to examine not only *what* he can do, but also *how* he does it (to the extent that that can be inferred). The *what* part is easy: in terms of his skills level, David is indistinguishable from Martin.

But, we also need to examine *how* David implements those skills; in particular, we want to guard against the possibility that David's performance is the result of canned responses of the sort we saw in the Eliza program. (For a robot's behavioral repertoire to be canned would require an enormous database of input/output pairs, where the input part consisted of, not sentences typed in at a keyboard, but data received through the robot's sense apparatuses and the output specified the actions the robot should perform given that input.) We cannot see directly how David works, but we can make some reasonable inferences, given what we do see. What we need to look for are signs that David is crafting and adapting his behavior to suit the various circumstances that he finds himself in—he is not merely responding with rigid, stereotyped behavior patterns.[13]

AI offers us many examples of the fluidity of David's behavioral responses. David can form multistep plans on the fly, judging the preconditions of the various steps so as to perform those steps in the proper order. We see this ability very clearly displayed as David tries to figure out a way to get what he wants: Monica's love. The plan he ultimately develops (with the help of Gigolo Joe) turns out to be quite complicated and includes steps that are the result of learning and experience. David is capable of using the sense data he receives in analyzing the situation—deciding what in the environment is most salient, and forming his short-term plans accordingly. There are many instances of this; for example, his quite accurate sizing up of the situation when the hunters for the Flesh Fair appear. David can deliberate, considering multiple possible

actions and deciding between them based on the available data. He can also reason—
at least when it comes to making commonsense decisions. Indeed, in many situations,
the decision he makes is the same one that you or I would make given those same circumstances. He shows evidence of a highly developed learning facility and an ability to
exploit analogies. He uses the story of Pinocchio in novel ways to fill in some of the
missing steps in his plan to gain Monica's love. All of these signs of adaptability and
many more besides are displayed by both David and Gigolo Joe.

In case we in the audience didn't pick up on this, a couple of the speeches from
Professor Hobby lay it out for us. In the lecture that Hobby gives to his employees,
explaining what he intends to create (at the 2:00 minute mark),[14] he talks about building a robot "with an inner world—of metaphor, of intuition, of self-motivated reasoning, of dreams." Again, toward the end of the film, as David returns to the Cybertronics
home base in Manhattan, Professor Hobby praises David for displaying exactly those
skills (especially self-motivated reasoning) he had originally dreamed of realizing in
this new line of robot.

We can now take a step back and look at the concept of mindedness more broadly.
I warned above that one shouldn't always take mentalistic ascriptions literally. Thus,
even if I say my car *knew* this and *wanted* that, I clearly don't really mean that. Why
not? Because there are better explanations for why my car broke down at that point
in time—explanations that are more robust and more likely to yield useful predictions about the car's behavior in the future. If I really believe that my car broke down
because it knew of the importance of my meeting and wanted me to fail because it
hated me, I might predict that, if I give it a bath and wax job, it will like me again
and not break down. I will then be dumbfounded when it won't start the morning
after I have pampered it. If, on the other hand, I assume that there is a better explanation for its breaking down and I take it to a mechanic, my chances of predicting its
behavior in the future improve dramatically. Mentalistic ascription is literal when
that ascription is part of an explanation that is offered as the best explanation for
what happened. Describing much human behavior in terms of beliefs, desires, plans,
and wishes (in general, describing behavior mentalistically) is justified because this
way of describing the behavior has the greatest predictive and explanatory power.
David's behavior cannot, or can only poorly, be explained in terms of rigid, stereotyped responses to stimuli; however, his behavior is well explained by imputing to
him beliefs, desires, and emotions and all the other things that go along with having
a mind.

Notice that the preceding discussion focused solely on the relationship between the
mind and what an individual does—the mind as viewed from the outside. It may strike
many as strange that, in a section asking the question, What does it mean to have a
mind? there was no mention of *consciousness*—the mind as viewed "from the inside."
This omission was quite deliberate, for this topic deserves a section all its own.

4.5 Consciousness

The word *consciousness* has to be one of the most slippery in the English language. Pinning down what people mean when they use this word is notoriously difficult. Our luck here may be improved if we focus on what the word could mean in the context of the question, Can a computer be conscious? We will still have some disambiguating to do, but at least some possible meanings can be excluded right from the start.[15]

The most basic sense of the word *conscious* (I shall call it "**conscious$_1$**") is easiest to see in contrast with its opposite. What does it mean to say "Jim lay *unconscious* on the ground"? It means that Jim is unresponsive, that Jim is neither sensing the environment nor responding to it. Normal humans lack consciousness$_1$ for a good portion of their lives—sleep is one form of unconsciousness$_1$. The state of unconsciousness$_1$ in sleep persists even through dreams, for, in dreams, the images experienced are not images coming in through the sense organs, as required for consciousness$_1$.

Could a computer be conscious$_1$? Yes. However, in order to do so, the computer must possess sensors and effectors—the computer would have to be a robot. Even present-day AI has produced robots that can sense the environment and act based on the data received. Clearly, all the robots depicted in the film *AI* are conscious$_1$.

The word *consciousness* is sometimes used to refer to a type of internal monitoring or explicit awareness of both one's own sensory state and one's current actions. In many circumstances, a human not only senses and reacts to the environment but also explicitly formulates a description of the environment and his actions to himself. In linguistic creatures such as humans, to be conscious in this sense implies that one can make a verbal report concerning what is being sensed and what is being done. We are all familiar with the experience of absentmindedness. An example of this is driving a car while listening intently to the radio or a book-on-tape. Clearly, we are still sensing the environment and reacting to it, for otherwise we could not explain how we managed to avoid hitting all of the other vehicles. You can't drive a car blindfolded. So, we are conscious$_1$. However, something is missing—an explicit awareness of what we are sensing and what we are doing. That awareness is what is meant by **consciousness$_2$**.

Can a computer possess the sort of internal monitoring required for consciousness$_2$? Here again, the answer is yes. There is no reason why a computer program could not be produced that not only did everything required for consciousness$_1$ but always included some high-level process that monitored what was happening at lower levels. Assuming this hypothetical computer program also had linguistic competence, there is no obvious barrier to using the high-level monitor to generate a verbal report of internal events. David's ability to articulate his beliefs, desires, and current emotional state show that he is assumed to have an internal monitor sufficient for consciousness$_2$.

We are working our way up to consciousness$_3$—the sense of the word usually intended when asking about the possibility of computer consciousness. Here, *AI* provides us early on with a wonderful exposition of consciousness in this sense. In Professor Hobby's lecture to his employees (MM 2:00), he offers a demonstration involving the current model of robot—a mecha named "Sheila." He stabs Sheila in the hand. She shrieks. He then moves as if to stab it again. Sheila withdraws noticeably. Even though, as Hobby points out, her superficial response is humanlike, there is something missing.

> **Professor Hobby:** How did that make you feel?—Angry? Shocked?
> **Sheila:** I don't understand.
> **Professor Hobby:** What did I do to your feelings?
> **Sheila:** You did it to my hand.

Later on in his interview with Sheila, the extent of her difference from normal humans is brought into even sharper focus:

> **Professor Hobby:** Tell me, what is love?
> **Sheila:** Love is first widening my eyes a little bit and quickening my breathing a
>   little and warming my skin and touching . . .
> **Professor Hobby:** And so on. Exactly so. Thank you, Sheila.

Hobby describes Sheila and other mechas like her as "sensuality simulators." The subjective character of her experiences (both sensory experiences of the environment and the inner sense that the internal monitor associated with consciousness$_2$ makes possible) is radically different from ours. What is it like to *be* Sheila? Is it like anything at all? When Professor Hobby stabs her with the knife, does she really feel pain, or is her response the result of some sort of harm-avoidance system—the robot equivalent of an automatic reflex? The "ouchiness" of pain, the "greenness" of early spring grass, the "flashiness" of a bolt of lightening, the "rumbly-ness" of distant thunder—these are among the items included in **consciousness**$_3$. Emotions also have a subjective feel associated with them. There is a particular way it feels to be angry—and it's something more than merely increased heart rate. Could a robot actually experience any of these? Sheila's litany of characteristics associated with love, and, more important, her failure to mention anything about the way it *feels* to be in love, imply that she cannot.

Before you jump to the conclusion that a being made of silicon chips and wire could never possibly experience these "feely" properties associated with sensations, ask yourself how it's possible for humans to experience them. We are made of flesh. Our brains are made of nerve cells. Why should a certain pattern of excitation among nerve cells cause "ouchiness" to suddenly exist? Only when we are able to answer that question will we be in a position to say whether robots could have similar experiences.

While I've been stressing the "feely" properties associated with our external senses (vision, touch, hearing) and our emotions, higher cognitive states sometimes also have "feely" properties. In the introduction to this book, I described something that I assumed everyone has felt at one time or another—the "Aha!" experience—the feeling that accompanies the sudden understanding of an issue or an answer to a question. So, while it might sound strange, there is a feeling associated with understanding—a feeling that is absent when someone is just muddling through an intellectual task.

A widely discussed paper written by the contemporary American philosopher John Searle argues that a computer could never really understand what it is doing. While he does not couch this argument in terms of the "feely" property that goes along with understanding, he implicitly relies upon it. So, I include the argument in this section on consciousness.

Searle's **Chinese room thought experiment** asks you to imagine that you have volunteered to be the subject in a very interesting test involving language competence.[16] You are put into a room alone. The only other items in the room are many blank sheets of paper, some writing implements, and a very thick book. You are told to read the introduction to the book carefully, for it explains how the experiment is to work and provides you with instructions. These instructions request that you look around the room and note the location of two mail slots—one labeled *out* and one labeled *in*. You look, and sure enough, the mail slots are there. Next, you read that, every now a then, a piece of paper will fall in through the *in* slot. Whenever that happens, you are to look at what is written on the paper and continue reading in the set of instructions. So, you wait. Soon, the first piece of paper appears in the *in* slot. You look at it. There is indeed something written on it—but the writing is meaningless squiggles as far as you are concerned. You start up again reading the instructions where you left off earlier. Now, the instructions become quite complicated—it is like a 2,000-step recipe. Each step is very clear, but you must concentrate in order to perform each step correctly. Some of the steps tell you take up a new sheet of clean paper from the stack of unused paper and write a squiggle on it. The shape of the squiggle that you are to draw is given with the instruction, so, you copy the squiggle as accurately as you can. Other steps in the complex process tell you to turn to a particular page in the book and start reading at a specific line. Yet other instructions tell you to look through a list of squiggles and, if any of them match the one that has just been drawn by you on the paper, to draw another squiggle directly under the one that you already drew on the paper. It is incredibly tedious work, but, after many hours, you finally get to a step that says, "Now insert the piece of paper you wrote the most recent squiggle on through the *out* slot, go back to the beginning of the instructions and wait for the next piece of paper to come in through the *in* slot."

The next piece of paper appears at the *in* slot a short time later. Again, the book specifies a highly complicated step-by-step process describing very precisely what to do at each step. This time, you manage to complete the process in about half the time as the first go-round. You take the paper you drew the squiggles on and put it in the *out* slot, just as the instructions specify, and go back to waiting for another piece of paper to arrive in the *in* slot.

This process is repeated many, many times. You do it so often you learn many of the rules specified in the book, so you need to consult it less and less frequently in order to know what to do at a given stage. Indeed, after many years spent in the room following the instructions in the book, you've become so adept, you never need to consult—you've internalized the entire book by now.

Finally, many years later, you are let out of the room and debriefed. It is explained to you that those "meaningless squiggles" you've been manipulating all this time are really Chinese characters. The pieces of paper you've been receiving through the *in* slot have consisted of, first, a short story in Chinese, followed by a series of questions related to that story, again, in Chinese. What you've been producing through the *out* slot have been answers to those questions, again, in Chinese. It is further explained that some native Chinese speakers visiting the lab just before your release were offered the opportunity to write a story and questions about it. This story and set of questions were inserted through the room's *in* slot, as usual. A few minutes later, when you returned the "answers" back through the *out* slot, they were handed over to these Chinese speakers, who marveled at the depth of understanding of the story's metaphors implicit in your responses. You are now shown the piece of paper with the story and the paper with your responses. You recognize them both—not that you can read them, but you remember that pattern of squiggles. The scientist doing the debriefing asks you what is written on the two pieces of paper. You say you have no idea—you don't *understand* Chinese. The scientist asks, "How can that be, given that you are able to produce responses indistinguishable from those that would be produced by a native Chinese speaker?" You respond, "I'm just following the rules given in the book. That's all I'm doing. I don't understand a word of Chinese. Trust me." The scientist now hands you a piece of paper with a story in English written on it, followed by some questions, which you read. Afterward, you say, "Now this I understand. There's a world of difference between my reading this and my looking over a piece of paper with the squiggles on it." The scientist smiles and says: "That's an English translation of the Chinese story." The scientist then hands you another piece of paper with some more English on it. It is explained that this is a translation of the "answers" you gave earlier in Chinese. You are surprised that *you* produced those responses, but you insist that there is a huge difference between what it feels like to read (and understand) English text versus what it feels like to look at (and not understand) a page full of Chinese characters.

Searle grabs this difference and runs with it. When you are in the Chinese room you are the equivalent of a computer running a program. In this case, the program is not written in the form of computer-executable rules, but in the form of concise instructions in English. When you follow the rules in the book, you are, in effect, manually simulating the steps a computer goes through as it executes a program. If you don't understand Chinese as a result of performing this process (as you claim you don't), then a computer doesn't understand anything of what it is doing, either.

What are we to make of Searle's Chinese room thought experiment? Has he shown that computers cannot understand? It is important to recognize that the crux of Searle's argument rests on the fact that he has a subjective feeling of understanding when reading English that he (assumes he) would lack if he were the subject in the Chinese room. (It is because this argument is based on the mind "as viewed from the inside" that I put it in the section on consciousness.) Clearly, there is a difference between understanding and having the feeling of understanding. I can remember many instances in my own life when I felt I understood something, only to discover in retrospect that I did not. The opposite—lacking a feeling of understanding despite truly understanding something—occurs less frequently. But, even here, I can think of instances in my own life that I would categorize this way in retrospect. This dissociation between understanding and the feeling of understanding shows that, to make his point that a computer cannot truly understand, Searle has some more work to do. The argument as it currently stands doesn't prove Searle's claim.

To drive the point home, let's add a coda to Searle's thought experiment. Just before the debriefing session ends the group of native Chinese speakers mentioned earlier returns. The scientist decides to do one more test run. Even though you were really looking forward to finally going home, you acquiesce. The scientist whispers something to one of the Chinese speakers in English, but you can't quite make out what he said. The Chinese speaker smiles and draws some squiggles on a piece of paper. The scientist takes it and hands it to you, then asks: "Do you understand this?" You are getting rather tired of this question, repeated now for the umpteenth time, so you respond, "No, stupid. Like I told you, I don't understand Chinese." The scientist smiles and asks you to please use your knowledge of symbol manipulation gained from the book to write your reply. You agree, but only on the condition that you can leave as soon as you are done. In a few moments you are finished with your response and hand over a page with several squiggles on it. The scientist hands it to the Chinese speaker who had done the translation earlier. He whispers something back to the scientist who then smiles broadly. He asks the translator to tell you in English what was written on the two pieces of paper. The one you were just given contains one single question in Chinese: "Do you understand Chinese?" The paper containing your response contains the Chinese sentence: "Yes, stupid, why are you asking me such an idiotic question?" Which response should we believe, the one in English or the one in Chinese?

In the final analysis, what is our answer to the question Can a computer be conscious? The answer is pretty clearly yes when either conscious$_1$ or conscious$_2$ is the intended sense. For consciousness$_3$, it seems to me that the jury is still out. We don't even know how it arises in humans, so it is difficult to know whether it would arise in a highly advanced AI system. What about David? Does the movie *AI* imply that he is conscious$_3$? The contrast that is set up early on in the movie between David and Sheila (the mecha who described love solely in terms of physiological responses) leads us to believe that David is conscious$_3$; however, because of the purely subjective character of consciousness$_3$, it is hard to know. We cannot see others' minds "from the inside," and that is the only way we could settle the question with certainty. It is interesting to note that we don't need to bring in computers to pose this question. I cannot know whether *you* have "feely" properties accompanying your perceptions. Even if I assume that you do, I cannot know that the "feely" properties you experience when you look at grass in the early spring are the same as the ones I experience. Trying to settle this issue by asking you whether it looks green to you misses the point.

Our answer to the broader question Can a computer have a mind? must also be left without conclusion. Even though current AI systems do not possess the externally observable skills associated with having a mind, there is nothing in theory that precludes them from developing those skills as AI matures. If you assume that consciousness$_3$ is also a necessary prerequisite for having a mind, then we must await an answer to the question: "Can a computer be conscious$_3$?"

4.6 Can Computers Be Moral Persons?

A second issue at the intersection of philosophy and AI involves the moral status of highly advanced AI systems. While robots with the level of sophistication of David and Gigolo Joe are nowhere on the horizon, such systems may at some point in the future become a reality. If and when they do, how ought they be treated? While the question of the moral status of robots is at present of merely hypothetical interest, the issues that this question brings up are not. For several contemporary moral issues, the debate is framed in terms of the moral status of a certain class of individuals. For example, the moral permissibility of abortion is usually seen as boiling down to the moral status of fetuses. Does a fetus have moral rights? In many ways, using robots as a hypothetical test case for examining the issue of moral status is useful, because it allows the participants in the debate to think about the issue without the tincture of prior political commitments that come to the fore when abortion is the focus.

The depiction of the treatment of robots at the Flesh Fair in the movie *AI* demonstrates that, for the humans in that fictional world, robots, even highly advanced ones, are not considered persons. An implicit argument in the film is that this refusal to grant a moral status to robots is incorrect and is based on "speciesism." Just as with its more familiar cousin, racism, speciesism elevates the status of one group at the expense of another. Throughout recorded human history, members of one race have tried to justify discriminating against, enslaving, or even killing members of other racial groups, based on the assumption that members of those other groups have no moral status—their well-being does not need to be considered in moral decision making. Speciesism is analogous, but, in this case it is *species* membership, not *race* membership, that is considered decisive in granting moral status. The main difference between the robots being destroyed at the Flesh Fair and the observers in the bleachers is species membership; the robots are not members of our species. Indeed, being robots, they are not members of any species. (The importance of this *biological* difference in the minds of the inhabitants of *AI*'s fictional world is emphasized repeatedly: robots are "mecha" whereas humans are "orga.") Is the treatment the robots receive at the Flesh Fair morally permissible, or should the highly advanced robots depicted in *AI* be given the same moral status as you or I? Traditionally, philosophers have used the word **person** to pick out the set of individuals whose well-being matters morally. What attributes must an individual have to count as a person in this sense? Are computers necessarily excluded?

I shall begin by formalizing the question somewhat. Consider the following schema:

An individual is a person if and only if that individual has property $P*$.[17]

A theory of personhood tells us what $P*$ is. In particular, it tells us what attributes an individual needs in order for that individual to be a person. The theory of personhood implicit in the actions of the audience members at the Flesh Fair is that property $P*$ is membership in the species *Homo sapiens*. (Actually, since we never see how nonhuman animals are treated, it is unclear whether it is species membership or biological status that is the important factor. In either case, though, robots are necessarily excluded from being persons.) As mentioned above, *AI* implicitly argues that this in incorrect. We, as viewers of the movie, are supposed to be repulsed by the Flesh Fair and by the narrow-minded prejudice against robots exhibited by the attendees. So, the movie's creators want us to think that it is something other than species membership that is decisive in determining moral status. To what extent are we like the attendees at the Flesh Fair? Assuming we decide to reject the species-based theory of personhood, what are the alternatives?

The view that there is something morally special about humans (members of the species *Homo sapiens*) is widespread in contemporary Anglo-America. Enslaving humans is considered morally wrong nowadays, whereas enslaving nonhuman animals (as pets, in zoos, and in the contexts of agriculture and medical experimentation) is not. Cannibalism is considered morally wrong nowadays, whereas eating nonhuman animals is not. Killing large numbers of humans because they are a nuisance is considered morally wrong, whereas killing large numbers of nonhuman animals is not. There are dissenting voices among proponents of animal rights, but by and large this represents the moral views of the average Westerner. And, the list of instances in which we attach diametrically opposed moral evaluations to actions directed at humans versus similar actions directed at nonhuman animals could be multiplied many-fold.

What is responsible for these differences in our moral judgments? Clearly, they are evidence of an underlying difference in the moral status we attach to humans on the one hand and nonhuman animals on the other. We judge humans as persons and non-human animals as nonpersons. Does that mean that we, along with the audience members at the Flesh Fair, equate personhood with species membership? Possibly. However, there are other explanations available in our case. Among philosophers, the most widely held view on personhood equates being a person and being rational. (This corresponds to identifying the property P* with possessing the ability to reason.) This view has its roots in ancient philosophy and has retained its position of preeminence among secular philosophers to the present day. If it turns out that there are no rational nonhuman animals, then our differing ways of treating nonhuman animals on the one hand and humans on the other would be justified. The upshot of this theory of person-hood for the moral status of computers is clear: if a rational computer could be produced, then that computer would count as a person. David and Gigolo Joe—indeed, all the robots depicted in *AI*, even Sheila—show signs of rationality. So, according to the rationality-based theory of personhood, they all count as persons.

There are difficulties in squaring the rationality-based view of personhood with our actual judgments, however. Infants and very small children are not rational; neither is a severely retarded adult human. Nevertheless, killing children and the severely retarded are considered morally wrong. Why? If we were consistently basing our judgments about personhood on the reasoning capacity of the individual, we would judge infanticide as having the same moral status as killing a chimp, or even a dog or cat. But we don't. Why not? The only explanation is that we do not (or, at least, do not consistently) equate personhood with reasoning capacity.

Some philosophers have suggested that both the species-based and rationality-based theories of personhood are mistaken. Rather, they maintain that the property P* that distinguishes persons and nonpersons is the ability to experience pleasure and pain.[18] (I shall call this the *sentience-based theory of personhood*.) According to this view, if a robot could be built that experienced pleasure or pain, then that robot would be a full-fledged person, with the same claim not to be harmed as you or I have. In applying this theory to the film *AI*, it is unclear how we should answer the question Is David a person? The reason has already been addressed in the preceding section on consciousness. Can a robot have a conscious$_3$ experience of pain or pleasure? Recall that we ended section 4.5 without resolving this question.

In a few cases, the sentience-based theory of personhood squares better with our moral judgments. The average Westerner judges torturing animals (harming them for no good reason or for the sadistic pleasure one experiences in seeing another suffer) to be morally wrong—perhaps not as wrong as torturing humans, but wrong nevertheless. On both the species-based and the rationality-based theories, this judgment is left unexplained. However, the implications of the sentience-based theory diverge from the view of the average Westerner on many counts, for, according to the sentience-based theory, the bar is very high for justifying harm to animals. Not only is it morally impermissible to torture animals, it is also impermissible to harm animals in any way, unless there is a greater compensating good produced. So, unless the pleasure experienced at consuming an animal's flesh and wearing its skin is greater than the suffering the animal experiences, eating meat and wearing leather are morally wrong. Similarly, the sentience-based theory allows no qualitative distinction between enslaving animals as pets and enslaving humans. As with the rationality-based theory, the sentience-based theory has problems as a stand-alone theory of personhood.

In trying to capture the theory of personhood implicit in the average Westerner's moral judgments, we might try combining one or more of these theories. One such hybrid theory would use sentience to grant limited moral status to an individual while reserving rationality as a requirement for full-blown personhood. Obviously, this view needs to be fleshed out. What does "limited moral status" mean? What rights, if any, accrue to individuals with limited moral status? Under what conditions could these rights be denied in favor of the rights of fully realized persons? Despite its vagueness, this hybrid view should give you an idea of how the three theories of personhood discussed above could be combined to produce something that meshed better with the average Westerner's moral judgments.

Should philosophers care about producing a theory of personhood that comports with Western common sense? Is the question of how well one theory versus another meshes with what the average Westerner would say an appropriate one to ask in the first place? Can philosophers afford to trust that contemporary Western society is not just as deluded as Western society five hundred years ago—a society that routinely excluded all non-Europeans from the class of persons? While interesting, these questions take us outside the scope of this section.

4.7 Science-Fiction Dystopias and Reasonable Prudence

Movies about futuristic science-fiction dystopias constitute a well-developed genre in American cinema. In the usual case, movies in this genre depict humans fighting for their lives to save the species from annihilation at the hands of their now uncontrollable robot creations. *AI*, while an instance of the science-fiction dystopia genre, is atypical in that it is the robots—not the humans—who are shown being wronged. In some ways, it is as if the movie *AI* covers a period of time prior to the one in which the standard futuristic science-fiction dystopia is set. The humans can see what is coming, yet they feel powerless to prevent it. That is what is driving them to attend and even enjoy an event as grotesque as the Flesh Fair. Gigolo Joe tries to explain this to David (MM 92:00), saying, "They made us too smart, too quick, and too many. We are suffering for the mistakes that they made. Because, when the end comes, all that will be left is us. That's why they hate us." Humans are afraid that the robots will eventually become more intelligent than they are and will begin to treat them the way that humans have treated their less-intelligent animal cousins for millennia. For these super intelligent robots—just around the corner, given the state of development of AI depicted in the movie—humans will be seen as at best slaves, at worst a mere nuisance that may justifiably be eradicated from the face of the earth. It is an interesting twist of fate that what the humans in *AI* are afraid of is being treated the way they have themselves been treating members of other animal species.

As emphasized in section 4.1, we in the early twenty-first century are far removed from the day when robots will challenge us for dominance; however, the possibility of this scenario if we press forward with AI research does bring up an interesting series of questions. Do we have a moral obligation to persons living in the distant future? How ought we to proceed in developing a technology that may harm those in the future? In the specific case of AI, is the scenario sketched above likely to occur? Is there some way to prevent its occurrence short of banning all AI research?

The first two questions are quite general and find application in many technology domains. One strand in the current debate over human cloning questions the long-term consequences of engaging in this form of tinkering with the human gene pool. Similarly, many debates within environmental ethics bring up these issues. One of these, the effects that increased carbon dioxide emissions are likely to have on future generations, is touched on in *AI*. There is still some controversy among present-day scientists, but the predicted negative consequences, the "greenhouse effect" and associated global warming and massive coastal flooding, are not expected for many years. The people who might be seriously harmed have not even been born yet. Another example from within the realm of environmental ethics: Should we be engaging in activities that produce very dangerous radioactive waste? We have the technology to store it (relatively) safely in the near term. Unfortunately, some of this material remains radioactive (and, hence, highly dangerous) for thousands of years.[19] We do not currently possess the ability to safely and reliably store this material for that length of time. Are we doing something morally wrong when we persist in producing this material, given that, by doing so, we are putting future generations at serious risk?

The ethical issue we are addressing here is the nature of our relationship to future generations: Do we have any moral obligations to them? If so, are these obligations the same as obligations we have to present-day persons? A simple thought experiment should convince you that we do indeed have a moral obligation not to harm future persons without just cause. Suppose I plant a time bomb with a 150-year "fuse." That bomb goes off right on time, killing hundreds of people. In planting the bomb, am I doing anything wrong? I assume that we all agree that the act of creating and planting the bomb is morally wrong, even though those harmed do not exist at the time that the act is performed.

The case involving the morality of AI research is not so straightforward. For one thing, current AI researchers cannot predict the consequences of the future development of AI with the same accuracy with which I could predict the outcome of planting the bomb. The "bad" scenario (the one in which robots enslave or kill off their human creators) is only one of many scenarios that might come to pass, as far as we know. Furthermore, AI research holds out the possibility of producing great benefits to humankind, whereas planting the bomb helps no one. (In this respect, AI research is more like the carbon dioxide emissions case. There is a trade-off: the short term good consequences for many humans brought about by the high standard of living made possible by fossil fuels versus the long-term possibility of catastrophe.) A further respect in which the AI case is not so straightforward involves how we should evaluation the "bad" scenario. If these future robots are themselves persons, then *their* future thriving needs to be added into the mix. Thus, while future *humans* may be harmed by robot dominance, other future persons (namely, highly advanced *robots*) may be benefited. As discussed in section 4.6, many consider it unjustified speciesism for us to focus solely on members of our species in making moral evaluations. In the long process of evolution, the ancestors of humans have achieved dominance over their competitors. No one believes that there is anything wrong when one species supplants another. Why should the dominance of robots be thought of any differently?

But, maybe we humans can have our cake and eat it, too. Is there some way that we can receive the benefits of AI research while avoiding the "bad" scenario? *AI* hints that a potential driving force to the "bad" scenario is the role that robots had been given in that society: they are the cognitive equal of humans in many respects, yet they are accorded even less status than the higher animals. One sees a similar line of reasoning in Mary Shelley's *Frankenstein*: the monster becomes a monster only when it is shunned by human society. Certainly, this novel was intended as a cautionary tale about the dangers of technology; however, the caution may be less "don't go there" than "if you are going to go there, think very carefully about how to proceed."

Discussion Questions

1. Can a computer be conscious$_3$?
2. Can a computer have a mind?
3. What did you make of *AI*'s focusing on the emotion of love? Can mindedness be "bootstrapped" using love, as Professor Hobby implies?

4. What attributes does an individual need to be a person? What does that view imply about the moral status of abortion? Vegetarianism?

5. Do you think personhood is an all-or-none attribute or something that admits of degrees? If the latter, what does that imply about ethics?

6. Is robot dominance of the world something we should fear?

Annotated List of Film Titles Relevant to Philosophy and Artificial Intelligence

Bicentennial Man (1999). Directed by Chris Columbus. Starring Robin Williams, Sam Neill, Wendy Crewson.

Addresses both the question of mindedness and personhood for highly advanced robots.

Terminator and *Terminator II* (1984 and 1991). Directed by James Cameron. Starring Arnold Schwarzenegger, Linda Hamilton.

These two films depict the standard futuristic science-fiction dystopia.

Blade Runner (1982). Directed by Ridley Scott. Starring Harrison Ford, Rutger Hauer, Sean Young.

The arrival of four rogue replicants (biologically engineered humanoids) on earth in 2019 bring Rick Deckard, replicant-destroyer extraordinaire, out of retirement. The end of the film leaves one wondering who are the good guys and who are the bad guys in a world in which very little separates humans and highly advanced artificial creatures.

Annotated List of Book Titles Relevant to Philosophy and Artificial Intelligence

Jack Copeland, *Artificial Intelligence: A Philosophical Introduction* (Oxford: Blackwell, 1993). This very readable book discusses the history of artificial intelligence and the most important issues at the intersection of philosophy and AI.

Margaret Bodon, ed., *Philosophy of Artificial Intelligence* (Oxford: Oxford University Press, 1990). This collection contains the most important essays on philosophy and AI. Some of the articles are quite accessible, including Alan Turing's original paper in which he describes the Turing test. Other papers are more advanced.

Douglas Hofstadter and Daniel Dennett, eds., *The Mind's I*, first published 1981 (reissued New York: Basic Books, 2001).

Daniel Crevier, *AI: The Tumultuous History of the Search for Artificial Intelligence* (New York: Basic Books, 1994). Crevier covers the history of AI from its beginnings up to the early 1990s.

Rodney Brooks, *Cambrian Intelligence: The Early History of the New AI* (Cambridge, MA: MIT Press, 1999). Brooks, head of MIT's AI lab, has argued for years that the top-down approach of traditional AI will go nowhere: this book is a collection of his papers.

Hans Moravec, *Robot: Mere Machine to Transcendent Mind* (Oxford: Oxford University Press, 2000). Moravec, a principal researcher in robotics at Carnegie-Mellon University, enjoys speculating about how AI research (and, along with it, the human race) will develop in the future.

Annotated List of Relevant Resources on the Web

MIT AI lab (for humanoid robotics): <http://www.ai.mit.edu/projects/humanoid-robotics-group/>.

IBM site describing Deep Blue: <http://www.research.ibm.com/deepblue/home/html/b.html>.

Relevant Entries in the *Internet Encyclopedia of Philosophy*

Artificial intelligence: <http://www.utm.edu/research/iep/a/artintel.htm>.

Searle's Chinese room argument: <http://www.utm.edu/research/iep/c/chineser.htm>.

Personhood: <http://www.utm.edu/research/iep/p/personho.htm>.

PART III

Ethics and Moral Responsibility

5

Ethics

Crimes and Misdemeanors (1988)

Aunt May: For those who want morality, there's morality.

Halley: No matter how elaborate a philosophical system you work out, in the end, it's gotta be incomplete.

—from Crimes and Misdemeanors

What distinguishes morally right action from morally wrong action? This is the primary question posed within ethics. It is also one of the questions posed within *Crimes and Misdemeanors*. In this film we meet characters who "represent," either by word or deed, many of the ethical theories philosophers have developed in answer to this question. Seeing these theories "made flesh" is useful in discussing the pros and cons of each. As always, the first few sections of this chapter provide a general introduction to the topic—one that does not require previous acquaintance with the movie. My advice is to read up through section 5.3, watch *Crimes and Misdemeanors*, then pick up reading again with section 5.4.

5.1 What Is Ethics?

Of all the subareas of philosophy, moral philosophy (also known as "ethics") is the one that is most familiar to nonphilosophers. We are all used to the idea of making moral evaluations of the actions of ourselves and others—judging some actions as morally right and others as morally wrong. But let's step back for a moment and ask, What is going on when we make moral evaluations? In chapter 2, I introduced a distinction between value judgments and nonvalue judgments. The examples I used by way of illustration were:

S1: Some of Hitler's actions indirectly caused the death of millions of people.
S2: Some of Hitler's actions were morally wrong.

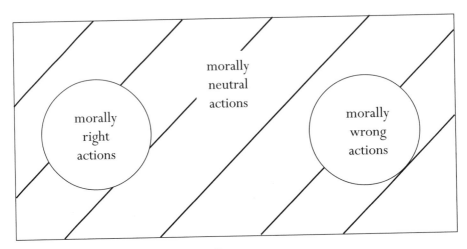

Figure 5.1

S2 is a value judgment: it is judging the value or worth of Hitler's actions. In particular, it is stating that some of Hitler's actions fall toward the "bad" end of the moral spectrum. *S1*, on the other hand, is a nonvalue judgment. It is not making any sort of evaluation of Hitler's actions. We, on being confronted with *S1*, are likely to infer moral condemnation of some of Hitler's actions, but that move on our part is an inference: it is not included explicitly in *S1* itself. This difference is important. To generate *S2* from *S1*, *we* must supply an additional premise, such as:

> Moral Principle 1: Any action that indirectly causes the death of millions of people is morally wrong.

Now the question becomes: Where did Moral Principle 1 come from? Is it in turn an inference from some more general moral principle? Or, is it something that is just a brute moral fact? Ethics is the field of inquiry that looks at these sorts of questions.

First and foremost, moral philosophy is concerned with figuring out what distinguishes morally right actions from morally wrong ones. To see what this means, consider the diagram in figure 5.1. The rectangle-shaped figure of this Venn diagram represents the set of all possible human actions. (Throughout this chapter, we shall be confining ourselves to moral evaluation of *human* action.) The two circles within the rectangle represent the set of morally right and morally wrong actions, respectively. The area within the rectangle not falling within one of the two circles represents the set of morally neutral actions. I assume that many actions are morally neutral: they have no moral status either way. For example, my tying my left shoe, then my right one is neither morally right nor morally wrong. Many actions, perhaps *most* actions, are of this sort.

Of those actions that *do* have a moral status, what features of the action determine whether it is morally right or morally wrong? This is the central question within moral philosophy. Using this diagram in figure 5.1, this question boils down to, What is special about the set of morally right actions that sets them apart as morally right? Finding the answer to this question is the first step toward determining, for any given action, whether it is right or wrong.

Different ethical theories propose different answers to this question. Some theories view the *consequences* that arise from an action as decisive in determining the moral status of that action. Thus, an action that produces overall good consequences is morally preferable to an action that produces overall poor consequences. Other ethical theories ignore consequences altogether and focus instead on the *intentions* of the actor—what he was trying to do when he performed that action. If an actor had good intentions when he performed the action, then the action is morally good—never mind that horrendous consequences may have accidentally been produced.

Obviously, the above sketch is just a sketch. Philosophers owe us much more detail in fleshing out the individual theories. For example, what constitutes *good* consequences? How does one figure out what the relevant consequences of an action are? In the case of theories that focus on intentions, what are *good* intentions? As we shall see in section 5.4, the major ethical theories do specify these things in detail. For now, I shall hold off an examination of the individual ethical theories and discuss them in the context of their depiction in *Crimes and Misdemeanors*.

I should warn the reader that, while my presentation of ethics is fairly standard, there are some dissenting voices in the history of ethics that I must omit for space reasons. The way that contemporary philosophers understand ethics would have seemed quite foreign to ancient philosophers such as Plato and Aristotle. While the current standard is to treat ethics as dealing primarily with moral evaluation of *actions*, the ancients viewed ethics as concerned primarily with evaluation of *whole persons*—in particular, ethics in classical Greece was concerned first and foremost with evaluating character traits that made an individual good. Some modern ethicists (e.g., Alisdair MacIntyre) have called for a return to the classical understanding of the proper domain of ethics.

5.2 *Moral Objectivism versus Moral Relativism*

In chapter 2, we considered cognitive relativism, the claim that the truth of all judgments is relative to some set of background assumptions. These background assumptions were usually understood to be a conceptual framework that an individual uses in making sense of the world. I noted in section 2.1 that there are other, more circumscribed versions of relativism. One such theory is **moral relativism**, according to which there are no objective moral facts: the truth of all moral evaluations is relative either to individual or cultural moral standards. Moral relativism is contrasted with **moral objectivism**, the view that there *are* moral facts—facts about what is morally right and morally wrong, facts that do not depend on what anyone or any group of people happens to think. Like cognitive relativism, moral relativism has achieved some support among both intellectuals and the general population. Much of this support is the result of increasing contact over the past century between Western (in particular, mainstream Anglo-American) society and far-flung cultures. Some of these other cultures have very different ideas about which sorts of practices are acceptable and which are not. While cultural anthropology and television have brought the peoples of the world into our living room, contact between cultures is nothing new. Herodotus, the principle historian of the classical era, notes that, even in ancient times, differences between social norms of different cultures were apparent. There was no single set of practices that all people everywhere held in common. To many, the diversity of social norms shows that there are no objective moral facts. This line of reasoning resembles the main empirical argument for cognitive relativism discussed in section 2.3. We will consider it further below.

A second line of argument for moral relativism can also be traced out in classical sources. Thrasymachus, one of the characters in Plato's dialogue *The Republic*, puts forward the position that can be roughly summarized as "might makes right." What Thrasymachus meant was that moral standards are determined by the politically dominant group in a culture and are aimed at preserving that group's political power.

Before looking at some of the arguments pro and con, I would like to describe moral relativism in greater detail. Moral relativism further subdivides into two distinct theories, depending on which individual or set of individuals the truth of moral judgments is assumed to be relative to. **Moral subjectivism** is the view that moral judgments are true or false relative to an individual's moral standards. Thus, if *I believe* that eating meat is morally permissible, then it is morally permissible for me to eat meat. Others may disagree as to the moral status of eating meat, but that is irrelevant, because the only arbiter of morality is the individual engaging in the action and her own moral code.[1] **Cultural moral relativism** is the view that moral judgments are true or false relative to the actor's culture's moral standards. If I live in a culture in which eating meat is considered acceptable, then it is morally permissible for me to eat meat.[2] If, on the other hand, I live in a culture in which eating meat is looked down upon, then it would be morally wrong of me to eat meat. According to cultural moral relativism, it is possible for an individual's moral judgments to be false. This occurs when the individual's moral standards are at odds with those of his culture. Thus, there is a court of appeals of sorts (that is, one's culture's standards) for moral judgments within cultural moral relativism. We are still within the realm of relativism, however, since even cultural moral relativism claims there is no objective fact about what is morally right and what is morally wrong. There is a third view within ethics that, while not a version of relativism, shares much in common with it. That view, **moral nihilism**, holds that moral statements are meaningless. According to moral nihilists, the very notion of evaluating actions on moral grounds makes no sense. While moral nihilism does not have many followers among current philosophers, it has had followers in the past. Emotivism, the view that moral statements are really expressions of emotional responses to certain events, was popular early in the twentieth century. According to emotivism, the statement "Some of Hitler's actions were morally wrong" is equivalent to "Some of Hitler's actions—*yuck!*" I will return to a discussion of moral nihilism in later sections. For the rest of this section, however, I shall concentrate on the two versions of moral relativism defined above.

What sorts of arguments can be given in favor of moral relativism? Let's consider cultural moral relativism first. One line of argument begins with the observation that different cultures vary widely in their moral standards. In some cultures, eating meat is uniformly frowned upon; in others, it is not. In some cultures, it is uniformly frowned upon to walk around with one's genitals exposed; in others, it is not. We are all familiar with these differences in moral standards across cultures. Indeed, no one (not even the most ardent moral objectivist) would deny the claim that there is a great deal of diversity in the world regarding which types of actions are considered to be morally acceptable and which are not. The cultural moral relativist uses this diversity in moral standards as evidence for the total relativity of moral truth. If there really were objective moral values, so the argument goes, one would expect to see all cultures adopt roughly the same set of moral standards. Since one sees diversity of moral values across cultures instead of uniformity, moral relativism is supported. The general intracultural uniformity of moral standards tips the tide of reason in favor of cultural moral relativism.

Yet is the argument outlined in the preceding paragraph a good argument? Does (1) intercultural moral standard diversity plus (2) intracultural moral standard uniformity imply cultural moral relativism? I think not.[3] There are two ways of criticizing this argument. The first route attacks the argument on the grounds that it is structurally unsound.[4] According to this criticism, (1) intercultural moral standard diversity and (2) intracultural moral standard uniformity *do not* logically entail that cultural moral relativism is correct. To see this, the moral objectivist considers a related argument that highlights the original argument's flaw.[5] The related argument runs something like this: Different cultures have different views on whether the earth is flat or not. In general, the degree of intracultural agreement on this point of geography is quite high. (That is, the members of a culture either uniformly believe the earth is flat or uniformly disbelieve it). However, (1) intercultural diversity and (2) intracultural uniformity on the question of the earth's shape do not entail that there is no objective fact of the matter about whether the earth is flat or not. Some cultures (namely, those cultures in which the flat-earth hypothesis is widespread) are just mistaken on this point. Similarly, the moral objectivist would say that some cultures have adopted incorrect moral standards. Mere difference of opinion does not constitute evidence in favor of relativism, whether cognitive or moral.

A second way of criticizing the argument given in support of cultural moral relativism attacks the truth of the premise that states there is a high degree of intercultural diversity in moral standards. Some have argued that the differences we see in cultural moral standards are fairly superficial, the protestations of cultural anthropologists notwithstanding. At a deeper level, cultures' moral standards *must* have many aspects in common. The reason this is so, argues the moral objectivist, is that there are certain norms of behavior that all viable cultures must respect, lest the culture cease to exist. For example, a culture in which care for infants and small children was not a norm would be a culture that wouldn't survive past the current generation. It is not too difficult to come up with other moral principles of this sort—that is, principles that constitute minimum requirements in order for a group of people to form a cohesive and viable culture.

Perhaps the relativist can salvage some form of moral relativism by retrenching to moral subjectivism. While there is a high degree of uniformity of moral beliefs among members of the same culture, this agreement is not absolute. Abortion, euthanasia, and capital punishment should all be familiar examples to Anglo-Americans of actions whose moral status is highly controversial. Maybe the cultural moral relativist got it wrong. Maybe it is the *individual*, not the culture, whose moral standards are the ultimate arbiter of morality—and intracultural moral controversy proves it. Here again I think the moral objectivist can counter that mere difference of opinion does not imply relativism. Without compelling argument to the contrary, the objectivist can claim that some people are just mistaken in various of their moral beliefs.[6]

The preceding argument and counterargument has left us at a stalemate. The moral relativist's main arguments are seen to be seriously flawed. However, merely pointing out flaws in an argument does not by itself show that the conclusion of that argument is false. So, moral relativism is still a straw afloat. Are there any reasons that can be given against moral relativism? I think there are. To see them, we must revisit the tolerance-based argument discussed in section 2.8.

Recall that one benefit cited in favor of relativism is its apparent connection with tolerance. Moral relativism teaches that there is no such thing as the objectively correct answer to the question, Is X morally right? If I am a consistent cultural moral relativist, I will not—indeed, I *cannot*—criticize the norms of other societies as incorrect. While this may strike you as a reasonable position when it comes to many norms (for example, eating practices), the consistent moral relativist's "tolerance" must also encompass other practices, such as slavery, the subjection of women, and genocide. Thus, the persecution of the Jews during the Nazi era was morally permissible, so long as that persecution was in line with the social norms current in the German Reich during the late 1930s and early 1940s. Similarly, consistent moral subjectivists cannot criticize on moral grounds the practices of others, either those within their own culture or those without.

Even stranger, moral relativism implies that moral progress (that is, the replacement of a set of cultural norms by a *better* set) is an impossibility. The overthrow of current moral standards is always morally wrong at the time the overthrow is occurring. For example, the actions constituting the civil rights struggle in the United States during the 1950s and 1960s must be judged by the consistent cultural moral relativist as morally wrong, for the actions were contrary to the then current norms. And, according to them, anything contrary to a culture's norms is ipso facto morally wrong.

These implications of moral relativism are highly counterintuitive—they are so contrary to our normal understanding of what ethics is about that they demonstrate that moral relativism is not a tenable theory.

5.3 An Overview of the Movie

CRIMES AND MISDEMEANORS (1988). DIRECTED BY WOODY ALLEN.
STARRING MARTIN LANDAU, WOODY ALLEN, MIA FARROW, ALAN ALDA,
ANGELICA HUSTON, SAM WATERSTON.

With a nod to Fyodor Dostoevksy and his great novel *Crime and Punishment*, Woody Allen's *Crimes and Misdemeanors* poses the question, What happens to ethics in a world in which the wheels of justice are not set right in the end, either by an omnipotent god or the evil-doer himself? Many believe that *Crimes and Misdemeanors* is Allen's greatest film, combining comedy, drama, and philosophy (and some fine acting, too) with more deftness than any of his efforts before or since. The film weaves together two subplots. In one, Judah Rosenthal, a successful physician, loving family man, and all-round pillar of the community, is the protagonist. We only learn later that he has a secret. His way of dealing with the problems generated by this secret form one subplot. Clifford Stern is the movie's second protagonist. Cliff is a ne'er-do-well filmmaker whose current pet project is a documentary on the philosopher Louis Levy. Cliff's wife has other ideas. She convinces Cliff to work on a documentary about her successful TV-producer brother, Lester. While working on this documentary, Cliff meets and falls in love with the documentary's producer, Halley Reed. Cliff's travails in his work and romance with Halley form the movie's second subplot. The character that links the two subplots together is the rabbi Ben, who is both Cliff's brother-in-law and Judah's patient. The two subplots finally intersect at a wedding reception for Ben's daughter at the end of the film.

The viewer needn't know anything about ethical theory to recognize the cleverness of Allen's screenplay, but appreciation for Allen's wit and creativity grow with even a passing knowledge of ethics. In *Crimes and Misdemeanors* Allen has managed to bring several ethical debates to life, and he has developed the main characters so that the major ethical theories are "represented" by someone in the film. *Crimes and Misdemeanors* also poses various existentialist questions, so it will be one of the two focus films in chapter 8, on existentialism.

5.4 *Ethical Theories in* Crimes and Misdemeanors

Even if one assumes that moral objectivism provides the correct interpretation of ethics, there are still many questions yet to be answered. What makes an action morally praiseworthy? What makes an action morally blameworthy? These are very abstract questions that are hard to get a handle on. Consider something more concrete: the scene in which Judah calls up his brother Jack to make arrangements for the hit man to kill Delores, beginning at the 43:00 minute mark.[7] I assume that, when you watched this scene in *Crimes and Misdemeanors*, your immediate response to Judah's action was moral condemnation—Judah's action was morally wrong. Why? What was it about Judah's action that made it morally wrong? Can you glean any useful generalizations from this concrete example that would be helpful in answering the two questions posed earlier in the paragraph?

This exercise points to a broad distinction made between ethical theories. **Consequentialism** is the view that what sets morally right actions apart from morally wrong ones has to do with the consequences that result from the action: morally right actions produce good consequences while morally wrong actions produce bad consequences. **Nonconsequentialism**, on the other hand, is the view that it is something other than consequences that is important in distinguishing right from wrong. Consider again Judah's action described above. Which of the following explanations comes closest to your way of viewing this example?

Consequentialist interpretation: Judah's action is morally wrong because of several factors. For one, he harms Delores in taking away the rest of her life. Also, unless her death occurred without any foreknowledge or pain on her part, the psychological and physical suffering Delores experienced right before her death must also be considered. Although we are not told anything about Delores's family, friends, and others who would be affected by her death, it is possible that these people also suffer as a result of Delores's death. In contrast, there appears to be relatively little positive that comes out of Delores's death that might compensate for the suffering she and others experienced.[8] This combined suffering is what made Judah's action morally wrong.

Non-consequentialist interpretation: Judah's action is morally wrong because, in so acting, he fails to recognize Delores's intrinsic moral worth as a person. In ordering her death, he treats her as a mere object that can be used in whatever way he sees fit. In an earlier conversation with Ben (MM 13:15), Judah even admits that he had been merely using Delores throughout their relationship. Ordering her death by the hit man is only the last in a series of wrong actions involving her. Even if Judah's action (the *ordering* of the killing) had failed in its ultimate goal because the hit man did not follow through with it, Judah's action in ordering the killing would have been just as wrong.

Even though both competing interpretations come to the same conclusion (that is, Judah's action is morally wrong), the line of reasoning that leads to these conclusions is importantly different.

Let's consider the consequentialist interpretation of events first. Judah's action is wrong because it produced bad consequences. With this observation we are pushed back to a further question: What is it about the consequences of Judah's action that makes them bad? In attempting to answer these questions, the English philosopher **John Stuart Mill** (1806–1873) looked for guidance to human psychology. What sorts of things do all humans desire? To this Mill answered, "Pleasure and freedom from pain are the only things desirable as ends; . . . all desirable things [i.e., particular objects of desire] . . . are desirable either for pleasure inherent in themselves or as means to the promotion of pleasure and the prevention of pain."[9] What Mill meant was, looking as hard as you will, the only thing you will find humans really care about is pleasure (and freedom from pain). Particular things humans might want (for example, a fancy car, a good reputation, or a loving family) are desirable only insofar as they bring about pleasure for someone. According to this view, something (an object or an action) that was neither itself inherently pleasurable nor the means to the production of pleasure would not be desirable.

Once this principle about human psychology was accepted, Mill believed, the upshot for ethics was clear. Actions are morally right to the extent that they produce good consequences. Good consequences are consequences that result in lots of pleasure. So, actions are morally right to the extent that they produce lots of pleasure. Mill captured this inference in the principle (variously known as "the principle of utility" and "the greatest happiness principle"), which claimed "Actions are right in proportion as they tend to promote happiness, wrong as they tend to produce the reverse of happiness."[10]

Since Mill equated *happiness* with *pleasure*, the greatest happiness principle is the equivalent to the claim that actions are morally right to the extent that they produce lots of pleasure.

Interestingly, Mill did not think that all pleasures were created equal. He was not calling for everyone to adopt the life of the glutton, seeking sensual pleasure at every possible opportunity. Even if someone could manage to satisfy all of his sensual desires—the proverbial happy pig—his life would not be as pleasurable as that of someone engaged in intellectual pursuits. According to Mill, "It's better to be a human being dissatisfied than a pig satisfied; better to be Socrates dissatisfied than a fool satisfied."[11] It's not that Mill thought sensual pleasures bad; quite the contrary—all pleasures, he felt, are good. It's just that sensual pleasures are not as deeply satisfying as other types of pleasures (for example, the pleasure an individual receives from intellectual pursuits or the "warm, fuzzy feelings" one receives from helping others).

Many contemporary followers of Mill have formalized his views in an ethical theory called **act utilitarianism**. According to this theory, acting in a morally right fashion is a matter of: (i) figuring which action will maximize overall happiness and (ii) choosing that action. Ethical decision making starts with a choice. A person has various options; which of several alternative actions is the person going to choose? The process for making morally correct decisions according to act utilitarianism can be boiled down to a three-step process:

1. Enumerate all the alternative actions from which the actor has to choose.
2. For each alternative, figure out the total amount of happiness that would result if that alternative were chosen. (This sum total is referred to as the alternative's **utility**.)
3. The alternative with the greatest utility is the morally right thing to do under the circumstances. Any alternative with less than maximal utility is morally wrong.

Let's apply this process in analyzing Judah's decision to ask his brother Jack to arrange for a hit man to kill Delores. Prior to the actual choice, Judah has various options open to him. He could have confessed his infidelity to his wife, as Ben had suggested. He could have "done nothing"—continued on trying to hide the affair and the embezzlement while not taking steps to silence Delores. He could have arranged for the hit man. (This is what Judah ends up choosing.) There are in fact many things Judah *could have* done, many different actions he *could have* chosen. All of these possible actions are what is meant in step 1 by "the alternatives."

Each of these alternatives has ramifications for the (un)happiness that various people would experience. The first alternative (confessing to his wife) would result in some unhappiness on his wife's part when she learns that her presumed-faithful husband is in fact not faithful. This knowledge will have ramifications for Judah and his happiness level. (Perhaps his wife will divorce him or perhaps their marriage will suffer in other ways.) While Ben suggests that this new honesty in their marriage will be a blessing in disguise, this is by no means guaranteed. There may be other people affected were Judah to choose this option. Among them are Judah's friends, relatives, neighbors, and patients. The list of affected people could grow to be quite large. Admittedly, most of the people on the list would be only marginally affected by this choice, but, if we want to follow through in applying the step 2 of the process, we need to consider them as well.

What about the second alternative—the "do nothing" alternative? Who would be affected, and to what extent would they be affected in terms of their (un)happiness? Here again, there is a relatively small set of directly affected people (Judah, his wife, Delores); however, the list of marginally affected people may be quite large.

Finally, what about the alternative that Judah actually chose in the movie? What is the utility associated with that alternative? Obviously, Delores suffers. Death is not bad in and of itself within utilitarianism; however, since life is a prerequisite for experiencing happiness, actions that cause the death of persons generally turn out to be morally wrong according to act utilitarianism. Furthermore, if Delores's death caused her pain and suffering just before she died, that fact would tend to make this alternative all the worse. But, we cannot end the analysis there. Even though *we* may focus on the consequences for the murder victim when judging a homicide to be morally wrong, act utilitarianism requires that we consider *everybody* affected and that we take the *overall* amount of (un)happiness resulting from an action as the final measure in determining its moral status. The action's effect on Judah, his wife, his family, and his friends must also be taken into account. We learn in the closing conversation of the movie (MM 93:30) that Judah and his family have prospered because of Judah's choice. While the short-run consequences for Judah's state of happiness are bad (pangs of guilt so severe he seriously contemplated turning himself in to the authorities), in the long run, he and everyone he cares about prospered. Does this mean that, according to act utilitarianism, Judah did the right thing in choosing to have Delores killed? No—or at least not necessarily. That would depend on many things that we, as viewers of the movie, were given little information about: Did Delores have close friends and family who would have suffered greatly at learning of her murder? Was Delores generally a happy person, who could be expected to produce a lot of happiness during the remainder of her life, had she not been killed? Did the person who was convicted of Delores's murder suffer as a result of being falsely accused? (We are given some information that the answer to this question is no—he had already committed a string of murders sufficient to get him a life sentence, anyway.) Would Judah ultimately be found out, contrary to his expectations, so that, in the *very* long run, he and those around him would have their prosperity broken? A strange feature of act utilitarianism is that, if the circumstances (and corresponding consequences) turn out just so, even homicide will be judged as morally right. We shall return to this feature of act utilitarianism later.

This exercise highlights several interesting attributes of act utilitarianism. First, the theory is egalitarian, which means that everyone's happiness needs to be considered.

Everyone is treated equally: the actor making the choice doesn't count as any more important than anyone else. Each person's contribution to the overall utility is a function not of his position in society but only of the total amount of happiness he experiences if that alternative is chosen. The powerful don't count as any more important than the powerless; the rich don't count as any more important than the poor; the "innocent" don't count as any more important than the "guilty."

Utilitarianism also assumes there is some way to measure the happiness that people experience, so that the happiness level experienced by person A can be meaningful added to the happiness level experienced by person B. (This assumption is built into step 2 of the process.) Finally, utilitarianism is a general ethical theory; it tells us in general what properties distinguish morally right actions from morally wrong actions. According to act utilitarianism, an action is morally right if it produces at least as much total happiness as any other action an actor could have performed. The theory can be used either after the fact (that is, after a decision has already been made) to assign moral praise or moral blame, or prior to a decision to figure out which among several alternatives is the morally right thing to do.

Act utilitarianism is only one theory within the utilitarian family of theories (that is, theories that base evaluations of moral worth on an action's *consequences*.) Another version of utilitarianism is a theory called **moral egoism**. According to this theory, the only person whose happiness matters in determining the moral status of an action is the actor.[12] Thus, if my happiness is maximized when I perform action X, then action X is the morally right thing to do. The extent to which others are affected by one choice over another is not relevant in determining the moral status of an action. Keep in mind, as with act utilitarianism, that moral egoism focuses on long-run happiness. It is possible that the morally right thing to do according to moral egoism is an action that only bears fruit after many months or years. Furthermore, it may turn out that the way to maximize my own level of happiness is by helping others, either because helping others makes me feel good or because helping others increases the likelihood that others will help me in the future. While moral egoism has its problems (as we shall see in the next section), one shouldn't turn it into the straw man theory that implies that it is morally right for me to satisfy my every whim.

The character in *Crimes and Misdemeanors* that most clearly embodies moral egoism is Judah: in both word and deed, he shows that his sole concern in making decisions is how an action is going to affect himself. At the end of the movie, everything points to his success in having maximized his self-interest.

But, is it really the case that the consequences of an action are the correct thing to focus on in making judgments about an action's moral status? Recall that above I distinguished between two possible reactions to the question, Was Judah's action in arranging for the hit man to kill Delores morally right? The first reaction embodied the consequentialist view of ethics: Judah's action was wrong because it produced worse consequences than some other action he could have chosen. Many philosophers reject this way of doing ethics; however, they disagree among themselves as to what the correct theory is.

Among philosophers, the ethical theory that is the most popular alternative to consequentialism is Kant's ethical theory, named after the German philosopher **Immanuel Kant** (1724–1804).[13] According to Kant, the consequences of an action are totally irrelevant in determining the moral status of an action. Rather, it is the actor's intention (that is, the motive that was driving the actor when she performed the action) that is the sole determiner of the action's moral status. It is hard to formulate Kant's view in a single sentence; one can, however, think of Kant's ethical theory as a set of nested descriptions that, when taken together, specify what it means for an action to be morally right. First, as we have already seen, an action is morally right if the actor's intention in performing that action was good. There is only one kind of good intention—the intention to do one's duty. One's duty is to act according to those general principles that one can will others to also act according to. (This latter sentence may strike some readers as a rough paraphrase of the golden rule, "Do unto others as you would have them do unto you." Kant rejected identifying his view with the golden rule; however, for our purposes here, this is probably close enough.) So, putting it all together, **Kant's ethical theory** states that an act is morally right if the general principle the actor is following in performing that action is a principle that the actor can and does will others to act in accordance with.

Let's reconsider Judah's action in arranging for the hit man to kill Delores in light of Kant's ethical theory. The first item of business is determining what general principle Judah was following when he performed that action. This is a tricky issue, because the way we describe this general principle will make a huge difference in whether the principle is universalizable. If we make the principle too specific (so that it is applicable only in this one case), it will not really be universalizable. For example, if the "general" principle Judah is following is, "Whenever a person has a mistress who is threatening to reveal both his affair and possible embezzlement, then that person will call his brother who has connections to the mob to arrange for a hit man to kill said mistress," this principle is not general enough to really capture what is driving Judah in arranging for the hit man. What is motivating him is the desire to protect himself against the threat that Delores poses to his well-being. That the particular thing he is being threatened with is exposure of his affair and financial improprieties is mere detail. Thus, the correct way to describe the general principle that Judah is acting based on is, "Whenever a person threatens my well-being, I will kill that person." Is *this* principle something that Judah can and would will others to also act in accordance with? No—because he will certainly at some point pose a threat to others. However, he would not desire that the person he threatens kills him. Judah makes his rejection of the universalization of this principle clear a little later in the movie when, wracked by guilt, he confides to his brother Jack that he is considering confessing his crime to the police (MM 80:00). This act constitutes a threat to Jack, and Jack makes very clear that he won't stand for Judah following through with it. Judah's reaction shows that he is quite unwilling to be killed now that the tables are turned and he is the one threatening rather than the one being threatened. So, the principle that Judah is following when he arranges for the hit man to kill Delores is not something that he is willing to universalize; thus, he is acting wrongly when he acts based on that principle.

Kant had a second way of formulating his ethical theory. This second approach is easier to understand and apply in many cases: "[Act so] as to treat humanity, whether in [your] own person or in that of any other, in every case as an end, . . . never as a means only."[14] The point Kant is making here is that it is always wrong to treat a fellow rational agent (that is, a member of "humanity") merely as an instrument to achieve one's own goals, without concern for that person as an autonomous agent with his or her own goals, desires, capacity for decision making, and so on. In formulating his ethical theory in this way, Kant meant to be describing the same theory in different words—all actions that turn out morally right according to the first formulation also turn out right according to the second, and vice versa. Indeed, Judah's action is also shown to be morally wrong according to this second formulation, since in this case as in others (by his own admission), he is merely using Delores to achieve his own ends.

So far, our discussion of ethical theories has focused on Judah. In many ways, though, it is the supporting characters in *Crimes and Misdemeanors* whose actions and statements are most useful in examining ethical theory. The two characters who are portrayed as deeply religious men, Ben (the rabbi) and Sol (Judah's father), present two different ethical theories that share in common a theistic base.

Sol represents an ethical theory called **divine command theory**, which holds that an action is morally right if that action is in accordance with God's will.[15] According to this theory, I act rightly when I do what God wants me to do; contrariwise, I act wrongly when I fail to do what God wants me to do. For an orthodox Jew like Sol, God's will is revealed to humans through Scripture. Obviously, divine command theory is not a single theory, but a family of theories, one for each religious tradition, because different faiths present different views of what God (or the gods) wills.

Divine command theory is not alone among theories that ground ethics in a transcendent being (God). Ben presents an interesting alternative. In the first conversation between Ben and Judah, when Judah tells Ben of his affair and Delores's threat to expose it, Ben suggests that Judah confess to his wife (Miriam), with the hope that she will understand. Ben even sees this as a possible source of enrichment for Judah and Miriam's marriage as they work through the ramifications of Judah's infidelity. Judah scoffs at this idea. Then Ben responds, "[I]t's a fundamental difference in the way we view the world. You see it as harsh and empty of values and pitiless. And I couldn't go on if I didn't feel with all my heart that there's a moral structure—with real meaning—with forgiveness and some kind of higher power. Otherwise, there's no basis to know how to live . . ." (MM 13:50).

The theory that Ben is summarizing above is called **theistic natural law theory**. Its key features are that right and wrong are grounded in the natural order of things (what Ben calls "the moral structure"), which is ultimately grounded in God's purposes. You may be asking what the difference is between this theory and divine command theory. The answer is that, for theistic natural law theory, there is a conceptual layer separating ethics and God's will, whereas for divine command theory, ethics is defined directly in terms of God's will. According to theistic natural law theory, everything has a purpose or function, one that God had in mind and that led God to create it. This purpose or function is something that rational creatures like us can glean by examining how nature is "put together." Thus, unlike with divine command theory, we don't need explicit revelation from God to figure out whether an action is right or wrong. Indeed, according to this theory, the theist has no special access to moral knowledge because all that is required to discern right from wrong is human reason.

Natural law theory also comes in a nontheistic flavor. This theory, appropriately called **nontheistic natural law theory**, grounds right and wrong in natural purposes and functions, but explains these purposes and functions without invoking God as creator. Rather, the concept of a "natural purpose" or "natural function" would be cashed out by the theory of evolution and other laws of nature.

What about other ethical theories that are represented in *Crimes and Misdemeanors*? The most colorful character from the movie has to be Judah's aunt May, who we meet during Judah's reminiscence of a Passover seder from his youth (MM 69:50). Sol labels her a "nihilist"; although, it is unclear that she is best described as a moral nihilist. If anything, Aunt May represents cultural moral relativism. In particular, her statement "might makes right" is the watchword for one way of understanding that theory. At the least, it is clear that she is no moral objectivist, as seen in the following exchange:

Seder Guest: What are you saying, May? There's no morality in the whole world?
May: For those who want morality, there's morality. Nothing is handed down in stone.

Before ending this section on ethical theories, it may be useful to offer a condensed description of all the ethical theories we have discussed, so that they can be understood in relation to one another.

Table 5.1   Ethical Theories.

MORAL RELATIVISM

- **Moral nihilism**[16]—all moral statements are meaningless
- **Moral subjectivism**—the individual is the final arbiter of morality
- **Cultural moral relativism**—the culture is the final arbiter of morality

MORAL OBJECTIVISM

- **Consequentialism**

    (1) **Moral egoism**—an action is right if it maximizes the actor's happiness
    (2) **Act utilitarianism**—an action is right if it maximizes overall happiness

- **Nonconsequentialism**

    (1) **Kant's ethical theory**—an action is right based on the actor's intentions
    (2) **Natural law theory**—an action is right if it accords with "nature"
          (a) **theistic**—"nature" is fleshed out in terms of God's purposes
          (b) **nontheistic**—"nature" is fleshed out without mentioning God
    (3) **Divine command theory**—an action is right if it accords with God's will

5.5 Evaluating Ethical Theories

I hope you agree with me that *Crimes and Misdemeanors* is a rich source for introducing various ethical theories. The movie, however, does more than just introduce the theories, it also offers implicit arguments for and against the various theories.

One such argument has already been hinted at above. How would a utilitarian analyze Judah's action in arranging for the hit man to kill Delores? First, one must consider the amount of happiness produced by the action and compare it with the amount of happiness produced by the other alternative actions that Judah could have chosen under the circumstances. If it turns out that Judah's choice produces the most happiness, then it is morally right. But, our moral intuitions tell us that any ethical theory worth its salt had better judge Judah's action as morally wrong. If it doesn't, that is reason enough to reject the theory as unacceptable. Unfortunately for utilitarianism, depending on what happens in the future, Judah's action may well be judged by that theory as the morally right thing for Judah to have done. Indeed, the movie hinted that this was the case. Delores appeared to be a loner who wasn't very happy, anyway, so neither she nor those close to her would suffer greatly by her death. Judah and his family, on the other hand, prospered because he made this choice, they prospered in a way that was *only* possible *because* he made this choice. Even the person who was falsely accused of the murder was not harmed, since, as a multiple killer, his jail time would not have increased because of his conviction for this crime. It is hard to point to someone apart from Delores who was harmed by her death, while it is easy to find those who profited (in terms of their happiness level) because of it. And even for Delores, if she died quickly and painlessly, the nature of her harm is limited to the happiness she would have experienced had she continued living. The movie suggests that she was not a particularly happy person. Thus, this loss may be more than compensated for by the increase in happiness experienced because of her death by Judah and his family. This analysis points to one of the most serious problems for utilitarianism sometimes referred to as the **problem of rights**: utilitarianism doesn't recognize the notion of a right—for example, the right not to be killed. For this ethical theory, there is nothing in and of itself wrong with killing someone, so long as that killing produces more happiness than not killing.

Also, for the classical version of utilitarianism (e.g., act utilitarianism as described in section 5.4), there is no requirement that happiness be equitably distributed. Thus, causing a few innocent people to suffer for the sake of producing benefits for the many may turn out to be the morally right thing to do according to act utilitarianism, so long as the benefits to the many taken together outweigh the suffering of the few and there was no other way to achieve those benefits apart from sacrificing the few. (An example often used to illustrate this **problem of injustice** with act utilitarianism is the use of involuntary human research subjects harmed in the course of medical experimentation.)

How would an act utilitarian respond? She might say, "This analysis is incorrect in implying that Judah's action would turn out right according to act utilitarianism. It is based on several false assumptions. First, it's unlikely that Delores had so little happiness in her life that she didn't miss out on much by being killed. Anyway, the analysis offered above misses the point: act utilitarianism is concerned with the long-run happiness produced, whereas the above analysis focused too much on the short-term consequences of Judah's action."

Neither of these responses succeeds in thwarting the criticism. Whether Delores was a generally happy person or not isn't really the issue—the criticism points to a very basic assumption within utilitarianism that the ends justify the means. All *Crimes and Misdemeanors* is doing is pointing out that this assumption raises the specter of highly counterintuitive results. (The theory implies Judah's action was morally right, whereas our moral intuitions insist that Judah's act was morally wrong.) Indeed, our moral intuitions *demand* that the type of action Judah performed (that is, killing someone under those circumstances) be judged wrong based solely on the type of action that it was. Our moral intuitions tell us we needn't know anything about the future (short run or long run) to know that what he did was morally wrong.

The act utilitarian's concern that we look to the long run when calculating the utility associated with an alternative brings up a third problem for the theory: in order to actually follow through with this calculation, we need to know *a lot* about how the future of the world is affected by choosing one alternative versus another. As such, the theory isn't of much practical use in moral decision making. This problem is referred to in the literature as the **problem of omniscience**.

Despite all these problems, act utilitarianism continues to be a popular theory among philosophers. Even for nonphilosophers, its focus on consequences captures an important facet of our moral reasoning: in our everyday decision making, we look to what the likely outcome will be of acting one way versus another in deciding what we ought to do. But, in the words of the character Halley, "No matter how elaborate a philosophical system you work out, in the end, it's gotta be incomplete." As an all-encompassing ethical theory, act utilitarianism is seriously incomplete.

Does *Crimes and Misdemeanors* offer a better suggestion? Yes and no. One of the major themes in the movie is questioning the relationship between theism and ethics. This theme is relevant not only to the adequacy of utilitarianism but also to the adequacy of Kant's ethical theory and nontheistic natural law theory. Are those theories missing a necessary ingredient, namely, God?

The best entry point for this discussion is a revisitation of moral objectivism. Utilitarianism, Kant's ethical theory, natural law theory (both theistic and nontheistic) and divine command theory all claim to be objectivist ethical theories. Where does the *ought* come from within these theories? For example, why, according to the utilitarian, *ought* someone maximize happiness? Certainly, the following two statements say different things:

S: Action A maximizes overall happiness.

S': Action A is morally right.

Why, according to the act utilitarian, does S' follow from S? The utilitarian, following Mill, grounds *ought* in a fact about human psychology—the only thing that is desirable in-and-of-itself is happiness (in Mill's words, "pleasure and freedom from pain").

This question about where the "ought" comes from is not just a question for the utilitarian. One can equally well ask the Kantian, Why *ought* someone act only with an eye to following universalizable principles? Kant grounds *ought* in the assumption that "[n]othing can possibly be conceived in the world . . . which can be called good without qualification, except a Good Will,"[17] and in our existence as rational beings.

A line of argument that runs through *Crimes and Misdemeanors* disparages both of these responses as qualitatively inadequate. There are three conversations that are relevant here. The first is one we have already considered: the first conversation between Ben and Judah in Judah's office (MM 13:50). The second occurs in Judah's head as he is deciding whether to take Jack up on his offer to "get rid of" Delores (MM 40:50). It begins with a replay of parts of the conversation mentioned above but continues on with a new ending:

Ben: Without the law, it's all darkness.
Judah: You sound like my father. What good is the law to me if I can't get justice?

This "conversation" ends when Judah goes to call Jack. The third conversation is the one that links together the subplots of the movie—one involving Cliff and his travails, the other involving Judah and his murder. It occurs at the wedding reception for Ben's daughter. (The conversation stretches from MM 93:30 to MM 99:30.) In it, Judah informs us of what his life has been like since Delores was killed, by describing it to Cliff as a plot for a murder mystery. He repeats what we have already seen earlier in the film—that he was wracked by guilt just after the murder took place to such an extent that he contemplated turning himself in. The world, previously viewed by him as empty of values, is now seen as very much full of values—and his act is a major violation. The eyes of God are watching his every move. But then, Judah reports, something changed. Gradually, these feelings of guilt and the fear of being found out faded away. The murder was pinned on a serial killer, so he seemed to be totally off the hook. Occasionally, little pangs of guilt would surface, but, as time went on, they were less frequent and less disturbing. Several months later, he was back to his comfortable life of wealth and privilege, as if nothing had happened.

This latter conversation contains implicit reference to Dostoevsky's *Crime and Punishment*, the story of a man (Raskolnikov) who murders a neighborhood pawnbroker. A glaring difference between subsequent events in this novel and those in Woody Allen's movie is that Raskolnikov's guilt increases without abatement until finally, in order to find some sort of relief, he turns himself in to the police. Cliff cannot stand the idea that the murderer got away in Judah's "story." The killer is not even plagued with a persistently guilty conscience. This lack of ultimate punishment (either via incarceration or pangs of guilt) is what makes Judah's "story" so chilling.

While many theists would agree, the unsettlingness of a world without ultimate punishment is a special theme of Christian apologists, those who present arguments with an aim toward convincing others of the truth of Christianity. The character of Sol is proof that this tendency also appears within Judaism.

Yet, what's so bad about a world without ultimate punishment? Earlier I stressed the difference between a value judgment and a nonvalue judgment. Moral evaluations are instances of the former. But moral evaluations are more than that. Moral evaluations also include an implicit imperative or command. When you see someone about to do something that you believe is wrong and you say to them, "It would be wrong of you to do that," implicit in that sentence is the imperative, "Don't do that!" While issuing a command (whether implicit or explicit) about a past action doesn't make much sense, still, the shadow of the implicit imperative is there when you judge as morally wrong an action that has already been performed. Earlier, I posed the question, Where does the 'ought' come from within various ethical theories? We saw what Mill and Kant had to say about their respective theories. Do their answers explain this implicit imperative in moral evaluations? If not, what could? Many apologists answer the first question with a no—the only thing that could serve to explain where the imperative comes from is the stick that God holds over everyone's head, ready to strike down evildoers, either here on earth or in the afterlife:

> If life ends at the grave, then it makes no difference whether one has lived as a Stalin or as a saint. Since one's destiny is ultimately unrelated to one's behavior, you may as well just live as you please. As Dostoevsky put it: 'If there is no immortality then all things are permitted.' On such a basis, . . . sacrifice for another person would be stupid. Kai Nielsen, an atheist philosopher who attempts to defend the viability of ethics without God, in the end admits, 'We have not been able to show that reason requires the moral point of view, or that all really rational persons, unhoodwinked by myth or ideology, need not be individual egoists or classical amoralists. Reason doesn't decide here. . . . Pure practical reason, even with a good knowledge of the facts, will not take you to morality.'[18] If there is no God, then there can be no objective standards of right and wrong. All we are confronted with is, in Jean-Paul Sartre's words, the bare valueless fact of existence.[19]

This "bare valueless fact of existence" is what Ben means when he said "Without the law, it's all darkness," and, "You [Judah, the atheist] see [the world] as harsh and empty of values and pitiless. And I couldn't go on if I didn't feel with all my heart that there's a moral structure—with real meaning—with forgiveness and some kind of higher power. Otherwise there's no basis to know how to live." Morality doesn't exist unless there is some transcendent being (God) who can invest the world with values "from without."

For what ethical theory does *Crimes and Misdemeanors* argue? It is interesting to note that the film doesn't end with Cliff and Judah's conversation and the implicit argument for some theist-based ethical theory, but rather gives the last word to a voice-over from Professor Levy:

> We're all faced throughout our lives with agonizing decisions . . . moral choices. Some are on a grand scale, most of these choices are on lesser points. But, we define ourselves by the choices we have made. We are, in fact, the sum total of our choices. Events unfold so unpredictably, so unfairly. Human happiness does not seem to have

been included in the design of creation. It is only we, with our capacity to love, that give meaning to an indifferent universe. And yet, most human beings seem to have the ability to keep trying and find joy from simple things—from their family, their work, and from the hope that future generations might understand more.

Levy admits that we live in an objectively "indifferent [i.e., valueless] universe," but he thinks that isn't such a bad thing. I will leave you to ponder the significance of his suicide—of his own personal inability "to keep trying and find joy from the simple things."

Discussion Questions

1. Should counterintuitive implications count against an ethical theory? What does that say about ethics if they are counted? If they are not counted?
2. Which ethical theory does Cliff represent? What about Lester? Delores?
3. What is the significance of Louis Levy's suicide?
4. What is the significance of Ben's going blind?
5. Does ethics presuppose the existence of a god (or some means to set the wheels of justice right in the end)? Is atheism a "dangerous idea"? Do you agree with Judah that the "movie plot" he describes to Cliff at the wedding reception is "a chilling story"?
6. Do you think *Crimes and Misdemeanors* is implicitly arguing in favor of an ethical theory? If so, which one? What hints do you see in the movie of a preferred theory?
7. Is it really a *fact* about human psychology that the only thing desirable in and of itself is pleasure and freedom from pain?

Annotated List of Film Titles Relevant to Ethics

FILMS THAT CONTAIN IMPLICIT ARGUMENTS AGAINST ACT UTILITARIANISM

Extreme Measures (1996). Directed by Michael Apted. Starring Hugh Grant, Gene Hackman.
   A movie that explores whether the ends always justify the means.
Run, Lola, Run (1999). Directed by Tom Twyker. Starring Franka Potente, Moritz Bleibtreu.
   This movie brings up the problem of omniscience.

OTHER FILMS RELEVANT TO MORAL PHILOSOPHY

Schindler's List (1993). Directed by Steven Spielberg. Starring Liam Neeson, Ralph Fiennes.

At the beginning of the movie, the protagonist Oskar Schindler is a self-starting businessman and wheeler-dealer who sees the Second World War as an incredible opportunity for making money. But his attitude starts to change when he witnesses the suffering experienced by the Jews.

Crime and Punishment (1935). Directed by Josef von Sternberg. Starring Peter Lorre, Edward Arnold.

For those who'd rather watch an adaptation of Dostoevsky's novel rather than read it, here's your chance.

Annotated List of Book Titles Relevant to Ethics

"Classics" in the History of Moral Philosophy

Aristotle

Nichomachean Ethics. This book was written by Aristotle during his tenure as teacher and leader at the Lyceum (a precursor of the modern university) in Athens, 334–323 B.C.E. Aristotle's writing style makes the work somewhat difficult reading. Indeed, many scholars believe that *Nichomachean Ethics* was actually Aristotle's lecture notes, and was never meant for publication. The translation by Terence Irwin, published by Hackett in 1985 is highly recommended. The *Ethics* is also available in its entirety online at <http://classics. mit.edu/Aristotle/nicomachaen.html>.

Thomas Aquinas

Summa Theologica, completed in 1273. The source for natural law theory. Still very influential on Christian (especially Roman Catholic) doctrine. The *Summa Theologica* is also available in its entirety online at <http://www.ccel.org/a/aquinas/summa/home.html>.

Immanuel Kant

Fundamental Principles of the Metaphysic of Morals (sometimes translated as *Groundwork of the Metaphysic of Morals*). First published in German in 1785, this one-hundred-page book is the main source for Kant's ethical theory. The *Groundwork* is also available in its entirety online at <http://www.vt.edu/vt98/academics/books/kant/pr_moral>.

John Stuart Mill

Utilitarianism. Originally published in 1861, this very readable little book presents the most thorough and influential defense of utilitarian theory. Quotations here are from the Hackett edition published in 1979. *Utilitarianism* is also available in its entirety online at <http://www.utilitarianism.com/mill1.htm> and <http://www.la.utexas.edu/research/poltheory/mill/util/index.html>.

W. D. Ross

The Right and the Good (Oxford: Oxford University Press, 1930). Ross argues that ethical theories need not be one-dimensional. This book has been very influential in shaping recent moral philosophy.

John Rawls

A Theory of Justice (Cambridge, MA: Harvard University Press, 1971). This book tries to combine a reinterpretation of Kant's ethical theory with a social contract theory of justice.

Collections of Essays and Single Author Books on Moral Philosophy

James Rachels, *The Elements of Moral Philosophy*, 3rd ed. (New York: McGraw-Hill, 1999). An excellent introduction to ethics.

Daniel Bonavec, *Today's Moral Issues*, 4th ed. (New York: McGraw-Hill, 2002). This book marries ethical theory and applied ethics.

Kai Nielson, *Ethics without God* (London: Pemberton Press, 1973). This book examines the question, Does objectivist ethics presuppose the existence of God?

Jack Meiland and Michael Krausz, eds., *Relativism: Cognitive and Moral* (Notre Dame, IN: Notre Dame University Press, 1982). This book examines the pros and cons of moral relativism.

Related Works

Alisdair MacIntyre, *After Virtue* (Notre Dame, IN: University of Notre Dame Press, 1981). MacIntyre argues for a return to virtue-based ethics.

The History of Herodotus, first published in 440 B.C.E. Herodotus is the greatest historian of the classical period; his *History* is a useful early source for fodder for the cultural moral relativist's argument.

Fyodor Dostoevsky, *Crime and Punishment*, first published in 1865. An understanding of *Crimes and Misdemeanors* is enhanced with knowledge of this work. *Crime and Punishment* is available in its entirety online at <http://www.online-literature.com/dostoevsky/crimeandpunishment/>.

6

Free Will, Determinism, and Moral Responsibility

Gattaca (1997) and *Memento* (2000)

For Jerome, selection was virtually guaranteed at birth. He's blessed with all the gifts required for such an undertaking. A genetic quotient second to none. No, there is truly nothing remarkable about the progress of Jerome Morrow, except that I am not Jerome Morrow.

You are the authority on what is not possible.

—from *Gattaca*

To what extent are the choices we make truly free? At least at first glance, there is a problem squaring the existence of human free will with the fact that we have (or we *are*) physical bodies that are subject to the laws of biology, chemistry, and physics. Perhaps freedom is just an illusion. Perhaps the trajectory of my life is just as predictable and unalterable as the trajectory of a stone that has been hurled through the air— outside forces such as gravity and air resistance will affect its flight path, but there is nothing that *it* can do to change its movement. What is the relationship between determinism and freedom of the will? If determinism is true, does that imply that none of my "choices" are free? If so, what does that say about moral responsibility? How can I be held morally (or legally) responsible for actions that I could not possibly avoid doing? Maybe determinism is false. Maybe at least some of my decisions could have turned out otherwise. Is *that* what is meant by "freedom of the will"? This topic is broken up as follows. Section 6.1 will examine what scientists and philosophers mean by the word "determinism." After a brief overview of the two focus films, we move on to look at the relationships among determinism, freedom of the will, and moral responsibility, using *Gattaca* and *Memento* as a source of ideas and illustrations.

6.1 What Is Determinism?

In our everyday dealings with the things around us (including other people), when something happens, we usually assume that there is something that *caused* that thing to happen. For example, if I walk out to my car after work and discover that the windshield has been shattered, I would start asking myself, What was responsible for its breaking? Did someone shatter it on purpose, perhaps in an attempt to break into the car? Maybe it was broken by a large overhanging limb that fell from the tree nearby. Or maybe there was some defect in the windshield such that, under exactly those conditions (for example, the light hitting it in a certain way), it shattered. These are all alternative explanations for what caused the windshield's breaking. This sort of reasoning should strike you as so mundane it hardly bears remarking upon. I mention it to draw attention to a point that might otherwise slip by unnoticed. There is one possibility that I would *not* entertain: I would not consider the possibility that the windshield just broke for no reason at all. I may decide that I am unable to find the cause, but this claim of ignorance is far different than the claim that there was no cause. Things don't *just happen* like that. An assumption built into my reasoning is that when something happens, there must be a *cause* for its happening.

Universal determinism is the thesis that every event has a cause that fully determines it. In other words, for everything that happens, there are antecedent conditions, whether known or unknown, such that that event could not be other than it was. The modifier universal tells us that this thesis is intended to apply to *all* events—those at the level of elementary particles and those at the level of visible objects—those involving inanimate objects and those involving animate objects (including humans). Universal determinism makes a very bold claim about the way the world is. If universal determinism is true, there never has been and never will be an event that was not fully determined by events that preceded it.

The implications of this view are far-reaching. To drive the point home, the French astronomer and mathematician Pierre Laplace (1749–1827) described a hypothetical entity, since named Laplace's demon, which, with complete knowledge of the *deterministic* causal laws, a description of the complete state of the universe at a time, and unlimited calculating ability, would be able to predict with perfect accuracy everything that would happen thereafter. As Laplace notes, "We ought then to regard the present state of the universe as the effect of its [preceding] state and as the cause of the one which is to follow. Given for one instant an intelligence which could comprehend all the forces by which nature is animated and the respective situation of the beings who compose it—an intelligence sufficiently vast to submit these data to analysis—it would embrace in the same formula the movements of the greatest bodies of the universe and those of the lightest atom; for it, nothing would be uncertain and the future, as the past, would be present to its eyes."[1] In this passage, Laplace puts his finger on a useful way of understanding what universal determinism is claiming. Normally, we recognize an important difference between the past and the future—a temporal asymmetry. Events in the past are determined and fixed; we may regret that something happened, be angry that it happened, or prefer that it hadn't happened, but we cannot choose that it did not happen. There is nothing we can do now to influence the past one iota. The future is different—at least we talk as if it is. Our use of such terms as *choice*, *options*, and *alternatives* makes it appear as though the future is not fixed in the same way that the past is. What Laplace is saying in this passage is that, if universal determinism is true, the future is just as determinate and fixed as the past. For this imagined superintelligence with full knowledge of the deterministic causal laws governing the evolution of the universe, "the future, as the past, would be present to its eyes."

We shall return to a discussion of Laplace's demon later to examine its implications for another form of determinism. First, though, I want to consider universal determinism in more detail. Right from the start, some criticisms of universal determinism spring to mind. Unless the history of the universe extends infinitely far back into the past, there must be at least one event (namely, the creation of the universe), that was not caused by antecedent events. This is true whether the creation is assumed to involve a divine creator or not. A second criticism questions the truth of determinism as applied to events involving subatomic particles. Most contemporary physicists believe that there are some events that are not fully determined by antecedent events. It is not just that we do not yet know the causes of these events; rather, they are truly uncaused.[2] The best that science can do, even in theory, is describe the relevant probabilities of an event's occurrence—what is the likelihood that X will happen in the next five seconds, for example. While this view is the most popular among physicists today, it was initially derided by some prominent scientists in the early twentieth century. The most famous of these was Albert Einstein, who wrote in a letter to Max Born, a leading proponent of the indeterministic interpretation of quantum theory, "You believe in [a] God who plays dice, and I in complete law and order in a world which objectively exists."[3] In the world of contemporary physics, Einstein's view has lost out. I shall therefore assume that universal determinism is false.[4] Does that mean that the line of reasoning illustrated in the example of the shattered windshield is illegitimate? Is it possible that the windshield's shattering was uncaused after all? The answer is no. The indeterminacy that physics posits at the level of subatomic particles has no practical bearing on events that happen in the world of (relatively) large objects, and any object I can see, even with the aid of an optical microscope, counts as a large object.

This view seems paradoxical. Aren't large objects just conglomerations of subatomic particles? If many of the events at the microlevel are indeterministic, mustn't this indeterminacy "percolate up" to the level of large objects? No—because it is possible for the indeterminism of a huge number of events at the subatomic level to cancel out. This canceling out is not a foregone conclusion, but it is at least a serious possibility. So, we still need to ask the question, "For the sorts of events we care about in our everyday lives (namely, events involving directly perceivable objects), is determinism true?"

I'd like to focus the question even further, for this chapter is primarily concerned with whether one particular kind of object, humankind, is subject to determinism.

The thesis of **human determinism** states that all human actions are fully determined by preceding events—some of those events are internal to the human, some are external. If human determinism is true, then, given my current makeup and my current circumstances, there is only one thing that I can do. I may feel as though I could choose something else under those circumstances; however, this feeling is an illusion. The opposite of this thesis is **human indeterminism**, according to which at least some human actions are not fully determined by preceding events.

It is important to keep in mind what human determinism is *not* claiming; it is not claiming that, had circumstances been different, or had I been physically or psychologically different, I would have done the same thing. Thus, human determinism is not the same as human fatalism. Although, as we shall see in section 6.7, if one thinks through the implications of human determinism and universal determinism confined to the domain of (relatively) large objects, the upshot for humans is the same.

While Laplace described his "demon" within the context of a world in which universal determinism is true, we can reuse his example in considering the implications of human determinism. If human determinism is true, then there are deterministic laws that govern all human actions. For many of the activities that humans engage in— digestion, perspiration, reflex responses—there is no special difficulty in granting that they occur deterministically. One needn't posit Laplace's demon with its unlimited calculating power to infer that, when I exert myself in a hot environment, I will perspire. Even for events over which I have some self-regulating ability (for example, the timing of a sneeze or my breathing rate), these still seem more like things that happen to me than things I do, and, therefore, are not problematic cases of deterministic events. Problems arise only for a special class of events, so-called **voluntary actions**, characterized by a prior decision process and the subjective feeling that several different choices are available. Here's a little experiment you can perform that demonstrates what is meant by *voluntary action*. Continue reading until you reach the section of the page with the line across it. When you reach the line, you should close the book and wait a few seconds before opening the book again and continuing to read. This pause can be as long as you like: fifteen seconds, twenty seconds. Whenever you decide the pause has been long enough, start reading again. So, here we go.

What just happened? You closed the book, waited a little bit, and opened it again. Did you feel compelled to open it again at exactly the moment you opened it? No. If you are like me, it felt as if you could have easily waited a few seconds longer before opening it again, had you chosen to do this. The exact timing of the movements your hands and arms undertook to reopen the book could have been delayed by a few seconds, even if everything else about the world had remained unchanged. *This* is something that human determinism denies. If by *choice* one means the ability to do something different under exactly the same circumstances, then the human determinist denies that you have choices. The subjective feeling that you could have opened the book a few seconds later than you actually did is an illusion.

Obviously, the example involving when to reopen a book is not of any great import. However, other instances of voluntary action are: your decision to buy this book (your decision to buy *anything*, for that matter); your decision to propose marriage; your decision to go to college; your decision to go to the particular college you chose; your decision to write *onions* on your grocery list; your decision to strike your classmate when you were six years old. All of these count as voluntary actions, and, according to human determinism, they are all fully determined by preceding events. The calculations required for the prediction would be more complex than the calculations required to predict that when put in a hot environment, you will perspire, but they are not qualitatively different.

Is there any evidence against human determinism? There is no direct evidence. If you think about it for a moment, it should be obvious why not. The only thing that would constitute direct evidence against human determinism is a case in which someone did A and then, under *exactly* the circumstances, did B (where B ≠ A). But the circumstances could not be exactly the same in the two cases, for in the latter case, the individual had just done A, whereas in the former case, the individual hadn't. Nevertheless, the fact that the same individual makes one choice under a set of circumstances and a different choice under *very similar* circumstances is some evidence against human determinism. For example, every morning I eat a bowl of cold cereal with milk for breakfast. I generally have several varieties on hand on any given day. One morning I pour myself raisin bran. The next morning, I pour myself corn flakes. There is no discernible difference *in the environment* on those two occasions that would explain why one morning I picked raisin bran and the next I picked corn flakes. Similarly, my difference in choice of cereal from one morning to the next was, as far as I can tell, not governed by some change *in me*. This is getting very close to evidence that, under the same circumstances, there are several different things that I am able to do. Even though my choice of breakfast cereal is unimportant in the overall scheme of things, this sort of example should not be dismissed by philosophers in sorting out the question of whether human determinism is true.

A second bit of evidence against human determinism can be gleaned from the little experiment with reopening the book. As you were opening the book, it felt as though you could have easily waited a few seconds longer before opening it. (At least, it felt that way to me.) This subjective feeling that alternative possibilities are open is what leads most people to reject human determinism. The view of our own decision making "from the inside" can be very persuasive.

Neither the case of acting differently under very similar circumstances nor the view "from the inside" provides proof for human indeterminism, so we need to look at the evidence on the other side. Is there any evidence in favor of human determinism? There are three pieces of evidence often mentioned in this context. First, the success of the physical, biological, and psychosocial sciences in predicting what our body will do is some evidence for human determinism. The jury, though, is still out, since there continue to be areas of human voluntary action beyond science's current reach. Furthermore, many of the laws in the psychosocial sciences have as effects, not types of actions, but tendencies to act one way versus another. It is possible that these scientific disciplines will continue to develop in the direction of probabilistic, rather than deterministic, laws.

Two further bits of evidence for human determinism work by undercutting the main reason cited by many in favor of human indeterminism: their trust in the subjective feeling that alternative possibilities are open at any given choice point. In a well-worn stage show, a subject is hypnotized, then given a posthypnotic suggestion—for example, that he will be offered his choice of a cola or a root beer after the show is over and he is to pick the root beer. The audience members react with increasing laughter when the subject, as requested, chooses the root beer a few minutes later and looks around dumbfounded as people in the audience start to laugh. If asked, the subject reports that this choice was no different than other previous beverage choices—sometimes he drinks cola, sometime root beer. Right then, he picked root beer. The audience members' reaction is based on their belief that something *is* different this time: because of the posthypnotic suggestion, the subject's feeling that there are alternative possibilities is an illusion. There is no reason to believe, though, that the subjects in such cases are misreporting how things feel "from the inside." If the subject can be mistaken in this case, how do we know that we are not likewise mistaken when we claim that we have alternative possibilities open before us, any of which we could choose?

The final bit of evidence in favor of human determinism again works by undercutting our trust in the view "from the inside," but it is a little bit more complicated than the case of posthypnotic suggestion. In a famous series of experiments,[5] researchers have shown that there is a characteristic pattern of brain activity that precedes the physical movement associated with voluntary action occuring at time *t* by approximately 550 milliseconds (that is roughly one-half second). This pattern can be detected by means of a simple EEG—a noninvasive device for measuring the electrical activity present in all functioning brains.[6] The fact that there is identifiable brain activity preceding the movement is not surprising, since muscle movement is caused by signals from the brain. (Even human indeterminists grant this.) What is surprising, though, is the amount of time by which this characteristic EEG pattern precedes the actual movement. The researchers could predict on average one-half second before the voluntary movement that it would occur.[7] More surprising still is that the subjects reported the forming of the conscious intention to act only 200 milliseconds (roughly one-fifth of a second) before the actual movement. The picture that emerges looks like that in figure 6.1.

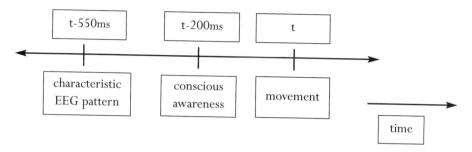

Figure 6.1   Timing of events related to voluntary finger movement.

If the view of voluntary action "from the inside" is correct, the conscious intention to act should occur *before* the characteristic EEG pattern that precedes the movement. But, according to these researchers, it occurs *after*. Researcher Benjamin Libet interpreted this data as showing that "the brain 'decides' to initiate or, at least, to prepare to initiate the act before there is any reportable subjective awareness that such a decision has taken place."[8]

If Libet's conclusion is correct, then we have serious reason to question the accuracy of the view of voluntary action "from the inside." But, it was this view that was driving many people (both philosophers and nonphilosophers alike) in the direction of human indeterminism. In the book reopening experiment described earlier, it feels as though the conscious choice "I'm going to reopen it *now*" is the initial driving force to your arm and hand movements; however, if Libet is correct, this view is mistaken—initiation of the action begins a third of a second *before* the conscious "choice" is made.

We leave the debate over determinism unresolved. Ultimately, the question Is (human) determinism true? is not a question for philosophy to decide. Rather, in the rest of this chapter, we will be focusing on a topic that does lie within philosophy's purview: What are the conceptual relationships among human determinism, free will, and moral responsibility? Does human determinism imply that humans have no free will? Does a lack of free will imply that humans are not morally responsible for what they do? As we shall see, even if human determinism is granted, there are still many questions to answer.

6.2 An Overview of the Movies

GATTACA (1997). DIRECTED BY ANDREW NICCOL.
STARRING ETHAN HAWKE, UMA THURMAN, JUDE LAW.

In the not-too-distant future, widespread genetic testing in the reproductive process has allowed humanity to create near-perfect humans. Not only are those with severe birth defects or a propensity to develop a lethal disease weeded out at conception, but even individuals with fairly common shortcomings (both physical and mental) are screened out. In the brave new world that results, the few humans conceived and born in the "old-fashioned" way face discrimination at every turn. One such love child named Vincent refuses to accept his position in society. More importantly, he refuses to accept the nearly universal belief that, because of his genetic makeup, it is simply not physically *possible* for him to succeed.

Vincent assumes the genetic identity of Jerome, a man with a "genetic quotient second to none," in order to achieve his dream of becoming an astronaut. But there are still huge hurdles separating him from his goal. Will he be able to prove the geneticists wrong? Do humans really have the ability to defy the laws of nature?

There are several strands running through *Gattaca*: Is genetic testing (and the use of screening based on genetics in the human reproductive process) a good idea, or will it lead to a dystopia in which those who do not fit within tightly controlled norms are discriminated against? To what extent is *biology* destiny? Do humans have free will? It is this later strand that we shall be focusing on here.

MEMENTO (2000). DIRECTED BY CHRISTOPHER NOLAN. STARRING GUY PEARCE, CARRIE-ANNE MOSS, JOE PANTOLIANO.

This is the second time around for *Memento*, which also served as one of the focus films in chapter 3. It is included here primarily for the issues it brings up surrounding the relationships among free will, personhood, and moral responsibility. Do Leonard's physical injuries (and resulting mental impairment) prevent him from acting freely? If so, does he escape moral responsibility for his actions? The use of the insanity defense in challenging a defendant's *legal* responsibility for some action shares aspects in common with issues surrounding moral responsibility. Should Leonard be held legally responsible for the multiple homicides he commits? Sometimes, examining nonstandard cases of voluntary action allows us to notice things we would not otherwise see. Leonard, because of his severe anterograde amnesia, is missing several attributes that seem relevant to the free will/moral responsibility link.

6.3 *Two Interpretations of "Freedom of the Will"*

What does it mean to have freedom of the will? Is free will only possible if human determinism is false? Different philosophers working on the free-will debate answer these questions in different ways. Before examining these differences, let's look at what they have in common. In what follows, I will particularize the issue; rather than looking at the question What is freedom of the will (in general)? I will be looking at What does it mean for an individual action to be free?

As a first pass, an action is free if the actor could have chosen otherwise—could have done something other than the action that was in fact performed. While this definition still contains much ambiguity, it does automatically rule out some actions as being unfree. Consider the following example. Suppose you and a friend are waiting in a line to purchase movie tickets. Your friend receives a very strong shove from behind that causes her to bump into you. Your friend's bumping into you is an unfree act. (Indeed, because of her passive involvement, one even questions whether referring to the bumping as an "act" is appropriate in this case.) It was unfree because once she received the shove, there was nothing she could do to prevent bumping into you.

Suppose that once you and your friend get up to the ticket counter, your friend offers to pay for both movie tickets. Is this offer on her part a free act? Here, philosophers' intuitions start to diverge. According to one view, called **incompatibilism**, an act is free if and only if the actor could have done something different *under exactly the same circumstances.* So your friend's action was free only if at that moment there were at least two possible alternatives open to her—even if nothing else in the world changed (either in the environment or in herself), it was possible for her to have chosen one of those alternatives. The reason why this interpretation of the concept of freedom is called incompatibilism is because, on this view, free will is *incompatible* with human determinism. (Recall that, if human determinism is true, your friend's act was the only possible act she could have performed under those circumstances.)

Incompatibilism is not a view about whether humans have free will, it is a view about what it means to have free will. Some incompatibilists, the **hard determinists,** claim that humans lack free will. They base this on: (1) their incompatibilist interpretation of "free will" and (2) their view that human determinism is true. Other incompatibilists, the **indeterminists** (also known as **libertarians**), claim that humans do have free will. While they share with hard determinism the interpretation of "freedom" as being able to do something else under the same circumstances, they reject human determinism. Libertarians would say that your friend's act in offering to buy both tickets was free, because she could have chosen not to offer to buy the tickets, even if everything else about the situation remained unchanged.

Not all philosophers accept the claim that human determinism is incompatible with free will. **Compatibilism** is the view that it is conceptually possible that both human determinism is true and humans have free will (determinism is *compatible* with free will). Obviously, in order for this to work, the compatibilist must offer a different interpretation of the concept of freedom from that offered by the incompatibilist. While different compatibilists would offer slightly differently nuanced definitions of "freedom," what they all share in common is recognizing an important distinction in models of human behavior. Some human actions are the result of external force or compulsion. (The example of your friend's bumping you after being shoved is an instance of this.) Other actions are the result of deliberate decisions. Presumably, your friend's offer to buy both tickets is of this sort. Prior to making the offer, she thought about it, then decided in favor of it. This decision is influenced by her beliefs (about how much money she has, about what will make you happy, etc.) and her desires (a desire to make you happy, for example). Indeed, as far as the compatibilist is concerned, these beliefs and desires may causally *determine* her action. It may be that, given those beliefs and desires, there was nothing she could do but offer to buy both tickets. What is important for the compatibilist is that the action is not caused against her wishes by something external to her.

According to the incompatibilist, there is a conceptual relationship between free will and determinism. The truth of one implies the falsity of the other. For the compatibilist, though, "free will" is defined in such a way that humans' possession of it is independent of debates over whether human determinism is true. While there are two possible versions of incompatibilism (hard determinism and libertarianism) there are four conceptually possible versions of compatibilism corresponding to the four possible combinations of the assertion or denial of human determinism and human free will, respectively. In practice, though, only one of these four possibilities finds support among philosophers. This view, called **soft determinism**, holds that human determinism is true (hence, soft *determinism*) and at least some human actions are free (in the compatibilist sense of "free"). Figure 6.2 reviews the positions discussed thus far.

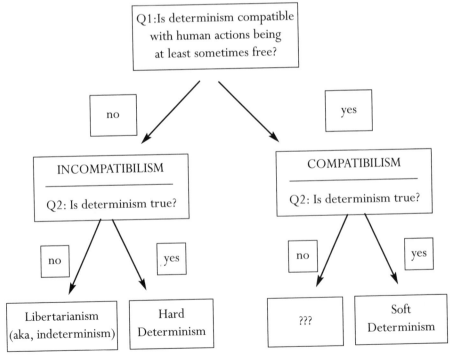

Figure 6.2   The free will and determinism debate.

As we shall see in subsequent sections, there are two main considerations drawing philosophers in the direction of one or the other interpretation of "free will." One of these involves the relationship between free will and the dignity and meaning of human life. Some philosophers (especially the libertarians) reject the compatibilist version of free will on these grounds. In order for free will to be worth having, they argue, it must raise humans above the level of being "mere machines," capable of nothing but powerlessly following the laws of nature. Free will must make humans the equivalent of "unmoved movers," able to cause things to happen without our own behavior being, in turn, caused. It is only in this context that human life has any real significance in the world. The movie *Gattaca* represents this view of freedom: Vincent, by sheer strength of will, molds himself into his ideal. He does this despite its being impossible, according to the laws of nature (as presented within the context of the movie's fictional world). What makes this feat especially significant is that he initially recognizes its impossibility, but he does it anyway. Both as a child and as an adult he is reminded of his physical limitations. It is not just Irene; *everybody* around him is an "authority on what is not possible." We will examine libertarianism in greater detail in the next section.

The importance of free will to standard conceptions of moral responsibility has guided many philosophers to support one or the other view on free will. In section 6.5 we will examine an oft-cited complaint against hard determinism that it does not allow for moral responsibility. There is less agreement on which (if either) of the two remaining views can do any better. Soft determinists complain that libertarian freedom amounts to nothing more than random events that happen to the actor—not the sort of thing that can ground moral responsibility for actions. Libertarians complain in turn that the distinction between *internally caused* and *externally caused* dissolves as soon as the soft determinist tries to specify it in any sort of detail.

Each of the three views is subject to quite severe criticism. One conclusion that some contemporary philosophers have come to is that progress on this issue over the past centuries has been slow-to-negligible because the issue has been improperly framed. Other philosophers do not so much reject the framework as merely lament philosophy's inability to make any headway. An example of the latter is Robert Nozick, who writes, "over the years I have spent more time thinking about the problem of free will—it felt like banging my head against it—than about any other philosophical topic. . . . Fresh ideas would come frequently, soon afterwards to curdle. . . . [The problem of free will] is the most frustrating and unyielding of problems."[9]

6.4 Libertarianism

Libertarianism, also known as indeterminism, is the view that humans have free will— a sort of free will that they could not have if human determinism were true. This view has found adherents among both philosophers and nonphilosophers. One of its earliest formulations within the Western tradition of philosophy is found in the ancient world among the Epicureans. The Epicureans believed that everything (the mind included) was composed of tiny atoms that, for the most part, obeyed rigid deterministic laws. Sometimes, though, an atom would "swerve." It was in these swerves that the source for human indeterminism could be found. As Lucretius (ca. 99–55 B.C.E.) asked, "[I]f all movement is always interconnected, the new arising from the old in a determinate order—if the atoms never swerve so as to originate some new movement that will snap the bonds of fate, the everlasting sequence of cause and effect—what is the source of free will possessed by living things throughout the earth?"[10]

Some contemporary philosophers and physicists have attempted to find the source for human indeterminism in similar ways. Now, however, instead of "swerving atoms," mention is made of quantum mechanical indeterminacy magnified to the macrolevel by certain structural elements in brain cells.

In either case, a problem arises in making sense of this indeterminacy. Where does it occur along the process of performing a voluntary action? If it occurs late in the process (for example, between the decision and the bodily movement), then actors would lack the requisite control over their own actions to ground moral responsibility. Try to imagine what it would be like to be in this situation. You deliberate among several alternatives and decide in favor of one. You will your body to carry out that decision. However, your body does not carry out that decision; instead, it does something else. You watch powerlessly as your body fails to act as you commanded it to. This sounds like a nightmare, not like the exercise of free will. Furthermore, placing the indeterminacy here absolves *me* of any moral responsibility for the actions that my body performs. Why should I be held accountable for something that happened despite my doing everything in my power to act otherwise? But similar problems arise if we conjecture that the indeterminacy occurs earlier on in the process. If we place it just prior to the decision, allowing that once the decision is made everything after that is determined, we are again left explaining how *I* can be held accountable for making that decision. I can deliberate for as long as I want, but my deliberations will be ineffectual.

Difficulties in making sense of libertarianism at the level of event-chains has led some philosophers to reject this version of libertarianism in favor of an account that imports the agent-as-cause as a primitive concept. On this version of libertarianism, most often referred to as **agent causation**, *I* as a freely acting agent have the ability to terminate causal chains. I can also start up new causal chains whose initiating event is itself uncaused. This power I possess is reminiscent of the old adage "the buck stops here." In this case, though, the buck is causal power. There is a chain of causal interactions flowing from the past that stop cold with my intervention. There is also a chain of events flowing from me into the future, that, but for my intervention, would not have occurred.

Historically, agent causation has been the most widely held version of libertarian-ism among philosophers. One finds it espoused by those at opposite ends of the West-ern philosophical spectrum. The notion of a radical choice, through which an individual can create his own future out of nothing, plays a major role in the philoso-phy of Jean-Paul Sartre (1905–1980), one of the leaders of the existentialist move-ment. As he describes it, a free agent is "a being who can realize a nihilating rupture with the world and with himself."[11] This ability to make choices unconstrained by deterministic laws is also, so Sartre argues, a necessary prerequisite for life's mean-ingfulness and a sense of self-honor and self-worth. This latter sentiment is echoed by some contemporary philosophers in the Anglo-American tradition, as seen in the following passage from Saul Smilansky:

> Even after admitting the compatibilist claim that on one level we have, say, reason to
> be morally proud of ourselves because we are honest (after all, we chose to be), when
> we reflect on life as a whole, it matters when we realize that we lack libertarian free
> will. We begin to see ourselves in a new light: what we choose . . . is the unfolding of
> what we are, the choices result from that which is not under our control (and ulti-
> mately is luck). . . . [Determinism is] extremely damaging to our view of ourselves,
> to our sense of achievement, worth, and self-respect. . . . [I]f any virtue that one has
> exhibited, if all that one has achieved, was "in the cards," just an unfolding of what
> one has been made out to be, one's view of oneself (or important others) cannot stay
> the same.[12]

Something like agent causation seems to be lurking in the background in the movie *Gattaca* in explaining both how Vincent's achievements were possible and why we should view them as especially worthy of respect. The voice over that occurs early on and sets up the telling of Vincent's story in flashback (at the 8:30 minute mark),[13] while enigmatic given its location early on in the movie, leads us down the garden path of genetic-based human determinism, only to take it all back in the last clause:

> For Jerome, selection was virtually guaranteed at birth. He's blessed with all the
> gifts required for such an undertaking. A genetic quotient second to none. No, there
> is truly nothing remarkable about the progress of Jerome Morrow, *except that I am
> not Jerome Morrow.*

While agent causation has its appeal, it also has some serious problems as a philo-sophical position. For one, how does it make sense of the limitations that we all clearly have? Vincent can achieve his goal of becoming an astronaut, but he cannot jump over the moon. Why not? If it really is the case that agents, by sheer dint of will, can break the laws of nature, why are there no limits? Can the supporter of agent causation give a principled answer as to why action A is possible but action B is not, when both A and B involve transgressing physical laws? A second difficulty involves the concept of agent causation itself. Is this a new type of causation—something totally distinct from the sort of causation we see in other contexts? If so, we are justified in requiring a more thorough analysis of this type of causation than has been offered to date. Many nonlibertarians accuse libertarianism in general and agent causation in particular as involving "panicky metaphysics." (This is a philosopher's way of saying "there's something fishy here.") Finally, recent advances in our understanding of the brain have tended to undercut the main source of support for libertarianism—the view of voluntary action "from the inside." Libertarians have been slow to respond to this data, leading some to believe that they have no serious response.

6.5 Hard Determinism and Moral Responsibility

Recall that hard determinism is the view that humans lack free will, because human determinism is true. It is the incompatibilist position that opts in favor of human determinism. Throughout the history of Western philosophy, hard determinism has found relatively few adherents. The primary reason for its lack of popularity has been the nearly universal fear that, if hard determinism is true, then no one is morally responsible for what they do. (Indeed, some philosophers build this into the very definition of "hard determinism." They define "incompatibilism" as the view that human determinism is incompatible with *the sort of freedom needed to ground moral responsibility*.) To give up on the notion of moral responsibility, both moral praise and moral blame, is to give up on a large part of the picture of who we are as humans. Before simply dismissing hard determinism as a live option on these grounds, it would be wise to look into the connection between it and moral responsibility in more detail. Here is the argument formalized:

1. If an actor is morally responsible for an action, then the actor must have performed the action freely.
2. If an actor performed an action freely, then it must have been possible for the actor to have done something other than what she in fact did.
3. It is never possible for an actor to have done something other than what she in fact did.
4. Therefore, an actor never performs an action freely.
5. Therefore, an actor is never morally responsible for an action.

The first statement follows directly from what it means for someone to be *morally responsible* for an action. This view of moral responsibility is independent of hard determinism—the libertarian and soft determinist would both assent to it. The second and third statements formulate hard determinism. In particular, the second statement formulates the incompatibilist interpretation of "freedom," while the third statement formulates human determinism. The fourth statement is an implication of the second and third statements, while the fifth statement, the conclusion of the argument, is an implication of the first and fourth statements. Apart from giving up hard determinism, there seems to be no way to evade this conclusion.

But, is the conclusion really so bad? In both our moral and legal evaluations of others' actions, we take into account the extent to which the actor performed that action freely. If I discover that a vicious murderer's behavior is the result of severe abuse as a child, that information tends to lessen my moral condemnation of the murderer. I still condemn the behavior, but I hold the actor individually as less liable for it. The law, likewise, treats evidence that a defendant was unable to control his or her behavior as exculpatory. The insanity defense has traditionally been understood this way. If a mental illness prevents me from being able to control my behavior, I am not *legally* responsible for that behavior and may not justifiably be punished for it, even if my behavior involves breaking a law.[14] I am not "let off the hook," though, for the state then claims justification for putting me in a mental institution—perhaps for a longer period of time than I would have served in a penitentiary had I been found guilty of the crime. While moral and legal responsibility are related, they do not necessarily coincide. (Indeed, legal responsibility varies from one jurisdiction to another; presumably, moral responsibility does not.) Does hard determinism imply that all punishment is unjustified?[15] Is that why so many philosophers and nonphilosophers alike shun this view? No, at least not if "punishment" is understood broadly. Society justifies punishing lawbreakers in order to achieve several distinct goals; only one of these would be affected if we no longer held people as responsible for their behavior. The other reasons we inflict punishment (in particular, incarceration)—to protect society from future harm by this individual, to discourage the lawbreaker from engaging in that behavior again upon release, to deter others who may commit crimes—are still valid. Human determinism is not the view that all people are incorrigible. As we shall see in the next section, human determinism does not specify whether genetic endowment or past learning plays the dominant role in determining behavior. Assuming the hard determinist opts for a position somewhere toward the middle of the nature-versus-nurture debate (see section 6.6) behavioral patterns can be altered by a judicious use of rewards and punishments, both actual and threatened. This is as true of criminal behavior as any other. Hard determinism, then, does not imply that the criminal justice system should be dismantled.

Memento raises some interesting questions surrounding the relationship between moral responsibility and punishment in cases of insanity or other mental incapacity. In chapter 3, I argued that the best way of describing what is happening in Leonard's case is that, prior to the incident that left him with anterograde amnesia, there was a single person who was Leonard Shelby. After the accident, Leonard's amnesia results in the isolation of the later selves associated with his body. Each of these persons lasts for no more than a day (the time between when Leonard wakes up and the next time he goes to sleep.) These persons are isolated in the sense that they are not identical to Leonard before the incident, nor are they identical to one another. Even Leonard, by some of his actions, shows that this is also how he sees things, at least in regard to his relationship with future "occupants" of his body. He could easily kill Teddy at the warehouse just after he kills Jimmy. Instead, Leonard sets one of his future selves up to kill Teddy by writing down Teddy's license plate number and saying to himself, "You'll be my John G" (MM 107:00). Later in fictional time (but earlier in the movie), Leonard's future self performs this task, just as Leonard intended. If Leonard as he writes Teddy's license number is a distinct person from Leonard as he kills Teddy, which of the two is morally responsible for killing Teddy? Are both morally responsible? What about "occupants" of Leonard's body after the homicide? Are they also morally responsible for killing Teddy?

I did not discuss it in either chapters 3, 4, or 5, but the concept of a person that crops up within ethics is supposed to be the same concept as used in discussions of personal identity. I can be held morally responsible now for something that I did in the past because I am identical to the person who did that thing in the past. In Leonard's case, though, the notion of moral responsibility falls apart, not because of hard determinism, but because there is no person in the present to hold morally responsible. The person who killed Teddy has ceased to exist. What should be done with Leonard if he is eventually caught for Teddy's or Jimmy's murder? Would the state be justified in putting him in prison? He is clearly a serious danger to others. He even recognizes his own dangerousness when he infers that the gun he finds is not his, because people like him would not be allowed to have a gun. Because of the danger he poses, the state's justification in incarcerating Leonard would not depend on whether Leonard is morally responsible.

If a lack of moral responsibility does not imply that punishment is illegitimate, why, then, is hard determinism so unpopular? The contemporary American philosopher Daniel Dennett has hypothesized that many people find any form of determinism repulsive because they mistake it for something it is not. In his book *Elbow Room*, Dennett describes several "bugbears" that are mistakenly assumed to follow from an acceptance of determinism. In *Gattaca*, one of these bugbears is represented by the character Irene. Like Vincent, Irene also wants to be an astronaut. However, because of her paltry genetic makeup, this desire can never be realized—it is simply physically impossible for her to realize her desires. One is left wondering whether her acceptance of these predictions about her future turn those predictions into a self-fulfilling prophecy. Similarly, Dennett considers whether acceptance of determinism (and, in particular, hard determinism) would have this sort of pernicious effect. "But [the acceptance of determinism] would be awful, it seems, for wouldn't it lead to a truly pernicious and self-destructive resignation and apathy? Think, for instance, of the obscene resignation of those who see nuclear war as utterly inevitable and hence not worth trying to prevent. Shouldn't we deplore the promulgation of any claim (even if it is true—perhaps especially if it is true) that encourages this sort of attitude?"[16] Dennett denies that determinism implies our powerlessness as agents. He also denies that accepting determinism would lead us to see ourselves as powerless. Determinism is true or false quite independent of us. However, the issue with which Dennett is concerned here is not determinism's truth, but our acceptance of it.

Let's consider another example—one that brings out the powerlessness angle in sharper contrast. Imagine what it would be like to be completely paralyzed, wanting desperately to move but unable to. When Western science first learned of the existence of curare, it was unclear how the substance worked. On the surface, it appears to cause unconsciousness; if given in too large a dose, it causes death. In reality, curare does not cause unconsciousness; rather, it arrests the action of the nerve cells that enervate the muscles (but, interestingly, not the heart muscle). An individual to whom it is given is still 100 percent aware of what is going on, is capable of feeling pain, but is incapable of moving at all. Try to imagine what it would be like if curare were used in place of an anesthetic during surgery;[17] this is the stuff of nightmares. Maybe *that* is what acceptance of hard determinism would "feel" like—we would discover the horrible truth, just as the pathetic surgery patient did, that we are utterly powerless. Embracing hard determinism would shatter the image of ourselves as potent agents and force us to see that we cannot even control our own bodies.

Dennett was right to dismiss this as a picture of the world according to determinism, whether the hard or the soft variety. Determinism does not mean that we are puppets, forced to do things "against our will" by the laws of nature. (A useful contrasting analogy here can be drawn from the movie *Being John Malkovich*. Craig turned Malkovich into his puppet, such that Malkovich lost control of his own body and was aware of that loss of control.) Rather, there is only one agent "in here." All determinism says is that our mental and physical states—our beliefs, desires, emotions, physical abilities, and current physical state—determine what we will do. There is only one course of action truly open to us. Luckily, though, it is the course of action that we choose. Both the Malkovich example and the example involving paralysis are based on the mistaken assumption that determinism implies that there is a radical disconnect between what we want and what our bodies end up doing. Once this assumption is rejected, human determinism loses some, if not all, of its repugnance. A way then opens for the soft determinist to find a place for moral responsibility within the context of a compatibilist interpretation of "free will." We shall examine soft determinism in greater detail in section 6.7.

6.6 *The Irrelevance of "Nature-versus-Nurture"*

A debate has been raging for decades between those who espouse the claim that an individual's behavioral dispositions are determined by that individual's genetic inheritance and those who claim that it is not genetics, but environmental factors (in particular, learning) that impart the greatest effect in shaping individual humans. This disagreement is most often referred to as the nature-versus-nurture debate. (The "naturists" argue for the preeminence of genetics, while the "nurturists" argue for the preeminence of environmental factors.) Even before the discovery of the genetic basis of heritable characteristics, the nature-versus-nurture debate has played itself out in education, psychology, sociology, and political science. The ramifications of this debate extend well beyond theory to some very important public policy decisions.

The movie *Gattaca* presents a somewhat crude version of the naturist position. Within the context of the fictional world it creates, the genetic endowment a human receives at conception determines not only that individual's sex, eye color, and hair color, but a whole host of other characteristics both physical and mental. Genetic testing and screening in the reproductive process allow the society to select only individuals judged most fit or most likely to contribute to the society. (The movie leaves unspecified the exact goal of the selection criteria.)

While the nature-versus-nurture debate has far-reaching implications for public policy, it does not make a difference to any of the core issues in the controversy over free will, determinism, and moral responsibility. Both sides of the debate assume that human determinism (or something very close to it) is true. So, they are not distinguishable on that account. Similarly, neither naturism nor nurturism dictates whether the compatibilist or incompatibilist interpretation of free will is preferable. Even the issue of moral responsibility is not affected by the debate. As we shall see in section 6.7, many philosophers believe that the question of whether human determinism allows for moral responsibility boils down to whether one is a *soft* or a *hard* determinist—the source of human determinism, whether genetics or environmental influences (in combination with innate learning mechanisms), has no bearing on this distinction.

The nature-versus-nurture debate does have one point of contact with the discussion in section 6.5. If the extreme naturist view is true, then, short of some sort of genetic manipulation or other biological intervention humans are incorrigible. If I have behavioral dispositions that incline me to break certain laws, attempts at rehabilitation will be ineffectual at changing my criminal behavior. This has ramifications for the justifiability of punishment. Incarceration can still be justified as a way to protect society from me, but it can no longer be justified based on its rehabilitative effect.

6.7 The Soft Determinist Compromise?

The view that hard determinism implies that no one is morally responsible for his actions has led many philosophers to reject it. Some have responded by embracing libertarian freedom in the hopes of regaining a basis for moral responsibility. Others have felt that the evidence for human determinism was just too great. For this latter group, a way out of the hard determinist's dilemma can be achieved by rejecting the incompatibilist interpretation of freedom. For these philosophers, the soft determinists, free will is compatible with human determinism.

The compatibilist interpretation of free will is grounded in a distinction that we all recognize. Some of my behavior is compelled by external forces, whereas other of my behavior is the result of my own volitions and desires. According to the soft determinist, an action of mine is free provided that nothing prevents me from acting according to my desires, nor constrains me to act contrary to my desires. My action is still 100 percent determined by my current state, but at least *I* am the author of that action.

Because of this emphasis on *my role* in causing a free action, the soft determinist maintains that I can be held morally responsible for that action. The task then becomes to distinguish between internally caused and externally compelled actions. A problem for the soft determinist arises when one considers various classes of actions that lie in the gray area between free and unfree. Suppose that you are walking down the street and a robber jumps out of the bushes, points a gun at you, and says "your money or your life!" You very much desire to continue living—more than you desire to keep the fifty dollars you have in your pocket, so you "choose" to give the robber the money. Would the soft determinist consider your action in that case free? In one respect, the action was caused by your desires—foremost among these, your desire to continue living. In another respect, though, your choice was coerced. Had the robber not pointed the gun at you, you would not have given up your money. It runs very much contrary to common usage to say that you gave up your money *freely* under such circumstances.

Is the robbery case exceptional?[18] While I've never been robbed at gunpoint, I do quite often make a decision under the threat of bad consequences happening if I choose one way versus another. Sometimes, when I am running late for an appointment, I consider speeding in order to arrive at the appointment on time. I opt against speeding, though, because I fear being pulled over by a police officer and being fined. Is my choice not to speed a free one? Is this case qualitatively different from the robbery case? If not, it appears that many, perhaps most, of my actions will turn out to be externally compelled (hence, unfree, according to the compatibilist), because my ultimate choice is based on a desire I have to avoid various sorts of bad consequences.

Another type of gray area case involves compulsive and addictive behaviors. How will the soft determinist classify them—are they free or are they unfree? The contemporary

American philosopher Harry Frankfurt has written extensively about how the soft determinist should deal with these types of behaviors.[19] Frankfurt distinguishes between first- and second-order desires. First-order desires are those for particular things or states of affairs—for example, a desire for vanilla ice cream, a desire for fame, a desire for world peace. A second-order desire is a desire to have a particular desire. In some cases, especially in cases involving addictive behavior, an individual has a strong desire *not* to have a particular desire. Frankfurt illustrates this using the example of an unwilling heroin addict who has a second-order desire—a desire *not* to have a desire to use heroin. For Frankfurt, an action is free if the individual is performing it based on a desire that the individual desires to have. The unwilling addict is acting unfreely because the desire that is driving the drug use is a desire that is *not* desired. While Frankfurt's analysis of "free" is useful in some cases, it falls short of offering us a robust method for distinguishing between free and unfree actions in the general case.[20]

In addition to worries about describing in detail what separates internally caused and externally caused actions, soft determinism suffers from an even deeper problem. Recall that soft determinists are human determinists. They disagree with hard determinists only in the analysis they provide of free will. Being human determinists, they hold that all of an individual's desires are caused by antecedent events, which are themselves caused by antecedent events, and so on. This chain of events thus extends back into the past to a time even before the individual was born. What sense, then, can be made of the distinction between internally and externally caused actions? One is left with the sinking feeling that soft determinism is based on a distinction that does not really exist.

What lessons can we take from this chapter? All of the three traditional positions within the free will and determinism debate have serious unanswered questions. I mentioned in Section 6.3 that philosophy's seeming inability to make headway on this issue has led some in the field to think that the framework within which the debate is taking place is seriously flawed. To date, though, no real alternatives have gained more than marginal support.

Discussion Questions

1. Is addictive behavior free? What does your answer tell you about where you stand on the compatibilism/incompatibilism controversy?
2. Do you see any difficulties in squaring the existence of free will with God's presumed perfect foreknowledge? Does your answer to this question depend on whether you adopt the incompatibilist or the compatibilist interpretation of free will?
3. Should Leonard in *Memento* be held morally responsible for the homicides he commits? Should he be held legally responsible? Why or why not?

4. Would the accomplishments that you and others achieve be less worthy if human determinism were true? How does luck fit into the picture? Does it make sense to praise someone for being lucky?

5. Can you think of a way of interpreting the example involving posthypnotic suggestion that does not undercut libertarianism?

6. Can you think of a way of interpreting Libet's experiment about the predictability of voluntary action that does not undercut libertarianism?

Annotated List of Book Titles Relevant to Free Will and Determinism

"CLASSICS" IN THE HISTORY OF THE FREE WILL DEBATE

Aristotle

Nicomachean Ethics. In this book (see especially book 3), Aristotle defends the view that individuals are responsible for their behavior, and hence, are justifiably punished when they do wrong. The *Ethics* is also available in its entirety online at <http://classics.mit.edu/Aristotle/nicomachaen.html>.

Thomas Hobbes

The Questions concerning Liberty, Necessity, and Chance. In a chapter entitled "Of Liberty and Necessity," the seventeenth-century philosopher Thomas Hobbes argues for the compatibilist view of free will and moral responsibility: "Liberty is the absence of all the impediments to action that are not contained in the nature and intrinsical quality of the agent." This book is volume 5 in *The English Works of Thomas Hobbes* (London: J. Bohn, 1839).

David Hume

A Treatise of Human Nature, 1740. In book 2 of this work Hume lays out his theory of human psychology. The scholarly standard for this work is the 2nd edition, put out by Oxford University Press in 1978. The *Treatise* is also available in its entirety online at <http://socserv2.socsci.mcmaster.ca/~econ/ugcm/3ll3/hume/treat.html>.

Immanuel Kant

Religion within the Bounds of Reason Alone, first published in 1793, and *Fundamental Principles of the Metaphysics of Morals,* first published in 1785. In these two books, Kant makes the case for a libertarian interpretation of *free will.* The *Fundamental Principles* is also available in its entirety online at <http://www.vt.edu/vt98/academics/books/kant/pr_moral>. *Religion within the Bounds* is also available online in its entirety at <http://www.hkbu.edu.hk/~ppp/rbbr/toc.html>.

CONTEMPORARY WORKS ON THE FREE WILL DEBATE

Daniel Dennett, *Elbow Room* (Cambridge, MA: MIT Press, 1984). Dennett's lively and engaging writing style makes this book fun to read.

Laura Ekstrom, *Free Will* (Boulder: Westview Press, 2000). Ekstrom argues that a coherent analysis of agent causation is possible that saves both moral responsibility and our sense of self-worth.

Dirk Pereboom, *Living without Free Will* (Cambridge: Cambridge University Press, 2001). Pereboom attempts to undercut the traditional argument against hard determinism.

Gary Watson, ed. *Free Will* (Oxford: Oxford University Press, 1982). A collection of the most important papers on the free will debate in the latter half of the twentieth century.

PART IV

Philosophy, Religion, and the Meaning of Life

7

The Problem of Evil

The Seventh Seal (1957) and *The Rapture* (1991)

Faith is a torment, did you know that? It is like loving someone who is out there in the darkness but never appears, no matter how loudly you call.

—from *The Seventh Seal*

Why should I thank [God] for a life with so much suffering?

—from *The Rapture*

One of the most difficult intellectual problems facing those who believe in an all-powerful, wholly good God is reconciling that belief with the existence of so much pain and suffering in the world. This problem is known as the problem of evil. If God really does exist and cares deeply about creation, then God should want to get rid of unnecessary suffering in the world. Why doesn't God get rid of it? Some people interpret the existence of pain and suffering as proof that God does not exist; for, if God did exist, there wouldn't be any unnecessary suffering. Defenders of religion have tried various approaches to circumventing the problem of evil. In this chapter, we will examine these approaches and ask, for each one, whether it is successful.

The problem of evil has been recognized as a serious difficulty for religion for millennia. One can find formulations of it among the writings of ancient Greek philosophers.[1] Clearly, then, it did not just spring up with the advance of Western monotheism into Europe. While the existence of evil (both human-caused and nature-caused) is a problem within many religious traditions, it has a particularly severe variant within apocalyptic Christianity. The material in most of this chapter is relevant to any religious tradition that posits the existence of an all-powerful and wholly good God (or gods); however, the material in section 7.3 focuses on the particular difficulties of reconciling the existence of God with what God has in store for the world, as foretold in the last book of the Christian Bible (the Book of Revelation). While *The Rapture* and *The Seventh Seal* both come out of the Christian tradition, they are broad enough to serve as useful tools for examining the problem of evil in general.

As always, the material in the early sections of this chapter (up through section 7.2) can be read before watching the two films. Material beginning with section 7.3

makes heavy reference to *The Seventh Seal* and *The Rapture*, and is best read only after viewing them.

7.1   The Two Faces of the Problem of Evil

The way philosophers approach any topic (including religion) is to sort through the relevant evidence and make a judgment based on that evidence. In many cases, there is evidence on two sides; then the philosopher's job is to judge which side has the best evidence overall. This approach is similar to the approach a jury uses in trying to decide who to believe—the defendant or the prosecutor. Here, the two "sides" correspond to theism (the view that God exists) and atheism (the view that God does not exist). We shall return shortly to reformulate these positions more precisely. Ultimately, the philosopher of religion will look at the evidence (primarily in the form of arguments) in favor of theism and against theism, and decide which makes the best case.

Theologians have put forward many arguments in favor of theism. The most intuitive of these is the **first-cause argument**,[2] which states that God must exist, because it is only the existence of an eternal, powerful creator (God) that can explain why there is a world at all. Someone (or something) must have performed the original act of creation that got the ball rolling. That entity could not be a part of the world. That entity must have been God. Therefore, God exists.

A second popular argument for God's existence is the **argument from design**,[3] which states that the world and everything in it shows evidence of being the product of intelligence design and creation, much as a car shows evidence of the existence of its designer. Cars are complicated objects, with parts that fit together in a way that allows a car to perform a useful function. It is highly unlikely that a car would coalesce as a product of the chance operation of natural forces—the level of complexity is just too great. Rather, the relationship between the car's complexity and the function that it performs gives evidence that cars are designed. If something is designed, there must be a designer. This should not come as a shock—we all know of the existence of these hypothesized designers: they are called automotive engineers. According to the argument from design, the world is like a car, only much more so. Even the simplest one-celled organisms are incredibly complex. It is hard to believe that these organisms (much less something like a human being, or a whole ecosystem) could be the product of the chance operation of natural forces. According to the argument from design, the only entity that could be the "engineer" of the world is God; thus, God-as-creator exists. There are other arguments for God's existence, but these two should give you a feel for the sort of evidence supporting theism.

The problem of evil is the main argument on the other side. Its influence in driving people away from theism is hard to overestimate. Thus, even for those theists not terribly bothered by it, the problem of evil needs to be taken seriously (and looked at from within a reason-based framework), if for no other purpose than engaging with atheists and trying to convince them to come over to the other side.

Not all religions are subject to the problem of evil, but the three main Western religions (Islam, Judaism, and Christianity) are. The problem of evil can only arise in the context of a religion in which the divine being (or beings) is assumed to be: (1) omniscient (all-knowing), (2) omnipotent (all-powerful), and (3) wholly good. A further requirement—one that is implicit in (1) and (2) above—is that the divine being could continue to be involved with the world, changing the course of events at will. With this as background, the **problem of evil** can be formalized as follows:

1. If God exists, then God, being omniscient, knows of the existence of unnecessary pain and suffering in the world.
2. If God exists, then God, being omnipotent, can get rid of all unnecessary pain and suffering.
3. If God exists, then God, being wholly good, would get rid of all unnecessary pain and suffering.
4. If God exists, then there would be no unnecessary pain and suffering.
5. There is unnecessary pain and suffering in the world.
6. Therefore, God does not exist.

Steps 1 through 5 entail the conclusion: theism is false. For a theist to deny this conclusion, at least one of the first five premises must be denied. At first glance, though, they all seem very reasonable. Premises 1 through 3 are merely making explicit what it means for an entity to be omniscient, omnipotent, and wholly good. Admittedly, a theist may opt to deny one of them, but at the cost of denying Western religious orthodoxy. In several places in this chapter we shall examine the implications of denying God's absolute goodness. I think the sincere theist will agree that this attempt at circumventing the problem of evil undercuts the very religious attitude she wants to foster. Likewise, denying steps 1 or 2 undercuts the religious attitude. There is a reason why orthodoxy within Judaism, Islam, and Christianity has settled on these attributes for God—they are part of a worldview in which praise, love, and worship of God is the appropriate attitude. (There are two other attributes that are part of Western religious orthodoxy: God is eternal, existing outside of space and time, and God is responsible for the creation of the world. These attributes are only mentioned in passing, since they do not bear directly on the problem of evil.)

For the remainder of this chapter, I shall use the term **theism** to refer to the orthodox view within the three main Western religions: an entity exists that is omniscient, omnipotent, and wholly good. A theist is someone who believes that theism is true. **Atheism** is the view that no entity exists with all of those properties, and an atheist is someone who believes that atheism is true. Thus, an atheist would say that the name God is like the name Santa Claus—it is associated with a cluster of attributes but does not refer to something that actually exists. A third take on the theism/atheism debate is unlike those mentioned above in being, not yet another alternative view, but rather an attitude toward the theism/atheism debate as a whole; this is called **agnosticism**. An agnostic is someone who is undecided between theism and atheism. Such an individual suspends judgment, neither believing nor disbelieving in the existence of God.

Let's return to the formalization of the problem of evil from above. If steps 1 through 3 are off limits in terms of what the orthodox theist can deny, that leaves only steps 4 and 5. But the theist cannot deny step 4, since that follows logically from the first three. (Logical consistency does not allow one to deny something that is implied by one's other beliefs. If the theist believes steps 1 through 3, then the theist is stuck with believing step 4 or being inconsistent.) That leaves only one premise left for the theist to deny in an attempt to thwart this argument: the theist must deny that there is unnecessary pain and suffering in the world. This could be done in one of two ways, either by denying the existence of pain and suffering or by claiming that all the pain and suffering that exists is necessary. The first approach would be a rather difficult view to argue, as there seems to be an abundance of suffering of all sorts. The second avenue is the approach adopted within Western religious orthodoxy.

But how could a theist hope to accomplish this? Certainly, the theist cannot go one by one through all the instances of pain and suffering, arguing that each, contrary perhaps to first impression, was really necessary. There are just too many instances to consider. What the theist must do is argue in general that pain and suffering are necessary and at least hint at how this might be applied in particular cases. A **theodicy** is an attempt to do just that—it is a description of divine policy that explains why, from God's point of view, pain and suffering are necessary for the accomplishment of some greater good. In order to be successful at countering step 5, above, a theodicy must satisfy three criteria. First, it must demonstrate the necessity of pain and suffering that is caused both by humans (for example, murder) and by nature (for example, harm done by hurricanes). Second, the theodicy must do this in a way that makes the amount of pain and suffering more than compensated for by the good that results. Third, it must show how that good could only be accomplished by that amount of pain and suffering (that is, the good could not have been achieved in some way that involved less pain and suffering).

In case this is all a little too abstract, let me explain with an analogy from the domestic sphere. There are some similarities between the relationship parents bear their children and the relationship that God, according to the theist, bears to creation. For one, parents are responsible for watching over their small children, making sure that the children learn not to dart in front of moving cars. Often, the reasoning capacity of a small child is such that explanations of possible consequences (that is, being run over by the car) are not very effective at convincing the child not to engage in some behavior—a small child is not mentally developed enough to understand many of these possible consequences. The only way to teach the child not to dart in front of moving cars is via punishment. From the child's point of view, this punishment (even if it takes the form of a light reprimand) constitutes pain and suffering. Reprimands are effective because they are viewed by the child as punishment. Now, if all we paid attention to was the child's point of view, this punishment would be unnecessary pain and suffering. Why? Because the child cannot see the greater good that it will bring about. We, though, perceive this greater good. We are like God in that respect, because our perspective of things is less limited than the child's. The pain and suffering we inflict on the child in this context is thus necessary if it achieves a greater good (the child's not being hit by a car), and if that greater good could not have been achieved with less pain and suffering. Returning to the problem of evil, a theodicy has succeeded in showing that all the pain and suffering in the world is necessary if it succeeds in dealing with both broad classes of pain and suffering (human-caused and nature-caused), and in showing them to be required in order to achieve some greater good. In section 7.5 we will examine the two most popular theodicies: the free will defense and the ultimate harmony defense.

Before leaving this section, I want to consider a variant of the problem of evil. The traditional problem of evil questions God's existence. The **modified problem of evil** questions God's praiseworthiness. The way I defined *theism* above, someone who denies God's perfect goodness would count as an atheist, even if that person thinks that a divine being exists that created and continues to intervene in the world. This goes against standard usage of the term *atheism*, so I shall refer to such an individual as a "modified theist." Notice that the modified theist, by denying step 3 of the formalization of the problem of evil, has sidestepped the conclusion without having to worry about whether all the pain and suffering in the world is necessary. But *modified* theism does not come without a price, for it replaces concerns about God's existence with concerns about the appropriate attitude for humans to adopt toward this less-than-wholly-good deity. Would love and worship of this God be warranted? Bertrand Russell argues, "Worship of God is selective, since it depends upon God's goodness."[4] If your experience of pain and suffering in the world convinces you that God is not wholly good, then the reverence toward God associated with the orthodox religious attitude is likely to be replaced either by indifference or even loathing. We shall see exactly this response in Sharon, the protagonist in the movie *The Rapture*.

7.2 An Overview of the Movies

THE SEVENTH SEAL (1957). DIRECTED BY INGMAR BERGMAN.
STARRING MAX VON SYDOW, GUNNAR BJÖRNSTRAND, BIBI ANDERSSON.
(IN SWEDISH.)

How could there be a book entitled *Philosophy through Film* that didn't include at least one film by Ingmar Bergman? Even though it came early in his long career, *The Seventh*

Seal is considered by many to be Bergman's greatest film. It is set in fourteenth-century Sweden—a time during which the Black Death is running rampant throughout all of Europe. Religious zealotry is at an all-time high as the people seek to understand why God is inflicting the plague on them. The film's protagonist is the knight Antonius Block, who, along with his squire Jöns, has just returned to his plague-ravaged homeland after many years' service in the Crusades. The knight is visited by Death, who informs him that his time is up. Reluctant to die without knowing why he and his fellow creatures have had to endure so much suffering, Block challenges Death to a game of chess. If Block wins, he goes free. If Death wins, Block must submit. But, in either case, Block has the interim time to satisfy his desire to know what it has all been for.

THE RAPTURE (1991). DIRECTED BY MICHAEL TOLKIN.
STARRING MIMI ROGERS, DAVID DUCHOVNY.

The Rapture is one of the few Hollywood movies to take religion seriously. As the film opens, Sharon is a telephone operator whose humdrum life on the job is in sharp contrast to her after-hours life as a "swinger." Right from the start, however, the viewer gets the impression that Sharon is less than satisfied with her rather shallow existence. She eventually joins an apocalyptic Christian church, marries, has a child, and seems poised for a very boring, suburban life. Then, everything is turned upside-down when her husband is killed and she starts receiving messages from God—there is something He wants her to do. Sharon responds to God's call as a faithful servant. *The Rapture* lays the groundwork for a modified version of the problem of evil: even if God does exist, is a God who would allow such suffering worthy of praise and adoration? Sharon's final act shows that she, at least, does not think so. Whether you consider yourself religious or not, *The Rapture* is a very thought-provoking film. (I mentioned above that the film is a rare Hollywood export in that it takes religious issues seriously. To see what I mean, ask yourself how you would have responded if one more scene had been inserted at the end—a scene in which Sharon wakes up.)

7.3 The Christian Apocalyptic Tradition as a Special Case

The very titles of *The Seventh Seal* and *The Rapture* show the influence of the Christian apocalyptic tradition, that branch of Christianity which takes the last book of the Christian Bible, the Revelation to John (usually just abbreviated as Revelation) as a literal description of the end of the world. The reference to "the seventh seal" comes from Revelation. In it, the author tells of a vision he has received concerning the end of the world—a vision that God commands him to make known to others as a warning of what is to come. The opening of the seventh seal signifies the last thing to happen before God commences with the total destruction of the world:

When the Lamb opened the seventh seal, there was silence in heaven for about half an hour. Then I saw the seven angels who stand before God, and seven trumpets were given to them. . . . Now the seven angels who had the seven trumpets made ready to blow them. The first angel blew his trumpet, and there followed hail and fire, mixed with blood, which fell on the earth; and a third of the earth was burnt up. . . . The second angel blew his trumpet, and something like a great mountain, burning with fire, was thrown into the sea. . . . The third angel blew his trumpet, and a great star fell from heaven, blazing like a torch, and it fell on a third of the rivers and on the fountains of water. The name of the star is Wormwood. . . . The fourth angel blew his trumpet, and a third of the sun was struck, and a third of the moon, and a third of the stars. . . . Then I looked, and I heard an eagle crying . . . "Woe, woe, woe to those who dwell on the earth, at the blasts of the other trumpets, which the three angels are about to blow!" And the fifth angel blew his trumpet, and I saw a star fallen from heaven to earth, and he was given the key of the shaft of the bottomless pit, and from the shaft rose smoke like the smoke of a great furnace, and the sun and the air were darkened with the smoke from the shaft. Then from the smoke came locusts on the earth, and they were given power like the power of scorpions of the earth; they were told not to harm the grass of the earth or any green growth or any tree, but only those of mankind who have not the seal of God upon their foreheads; they were allowed to torture them for five months, but not to kill them. . . . And in those days men will seek death and will not find it: they will long to die, and death will fly from them.[5]

And this was only the first of the three "woes." Once the destruction of the world is completed, God sets about creating a "new heaven and a new earth":

Then I saw a new heaven and a new earth; for the first heaven and the first earth had passed away, and the sea was no more. And I saw the holy city, new Jerusalem, coming down out of heaven from God, prepared as a bride adorned for her husband; and I heard a great voice from the throne saying, "Behold, the dwelling of God is with men. He will dwell with them, and they shall be his people, and God himself will be with them; he will wipe away every tear from their eyes, and death shall be no more, neither shall there be mourning nor crying nor pain any more, for the former things have passed away."[6]

The first passage (the one dealing with the seventh seal) should sound familiar: in the film the opening several sentences of that passage are read by Karin (the knight's wife) as the knight and his company were eating. It is also read in voice-over during the film's opening scene. *The Rapture* also draws heavily from Revelation as a source, especially in the final part of the movie beginning at minute mark 87:30.[7] Chapter 6 of Revelation (prior to the passage describing the breaking of the seventh seal) tells of strange occurrences involving horses, similar to what is depicted near the end of *The Rapture*. Just after that, the rapture occurs. (The rapture within the Christian apocalyptic tradition refers to events depicted in chapter 7 of Revelation, in which God's chosen ones are transported off the earth into heaven just before the world is destroyed.)

It is debatable as to whether the apocalyptic tradition should be counted as Christian orthodoxy. Many Christians either dismiss the Book of Revelation or take it as merely symbolic. However, for those who hold that it offers a literal description of God's intentions for the end of the world, a particularly severe variant of the problem of evil arises, for, within this tradition, it is not only the pain and suffering here and now that a theodicy must deal with but also the pain and suffering depicted in Revelation. One could dismiss the cataclysmic destruction of the earth as not adding anything to the traditional problem of evil, or as being justified as punishment for the evildoers who were not among the chosen. This won't work, though, because the pain and suffering is explicitly caused by God and God knew from the beginning of the world that this would be how it all would end.[8] Furthermore, God has the power to create a world free from pain and suffering. That's exactly what God creates with the new Jerusalem. You see what an uphill battle the theist has if this story must also be accommodated within a theodicy: God creates a world (namely, ours) knowing not only that some people will be guilty, but knowing, right from the beginning, who those guilty people will be. God knows what is going to happen, and has the power to have created a different world—one that is free from any pain and suffering, one that is presumably just as full of that "greater good" for which God is willing to sacrifice human happiness. So, why didn't God skip our world and go straight to the new Jerusalem? Wouldn't a wholly good God have preferred that course of action?

There is a second variant of the problem of evil that is particular not to apocalyptic Christianity but Christianity more generally. Jesus' suffering has special significance for most Christians. One sees this emphasis manifested in the ubiquity of the cross in Christian iconography. Bergman brings his audience's attention to this in *The Seventh Seal* in several scenes. Just before the scene at the confessional, the knight prays in a small alcove of the church while looking at a wood sculpture of the crucified Jesus: "Christ's face is turned upward, His mouth open as if in a cry of anguish."[9] A little later, Jof and Mia's performance is interrupted by a parade of monks and flagellants. The procession stops and the wood sculpture of Jesus crucified is lifted up. Here again it is the suffering Jesus, with his hands hammered to the cross, his face convulsed in pain and the fear of having been abandoned in his moment of need. The emotional impact of these depictions of Jesus' suffering on the average Christian can be quite profound: "God loves you so much, He was willing to do this for *you*, so that you might be saved." (This interpretation is particularly prominent in contemporary popular Protestantism.) The problem with this way of interpreting Jesus' suffering is that Jesus' suffering isn't that much different from what many unfortunate humans must endure. Why should we have sympathy for Jesus when God inflicts the same thing on us? This is exactly the point that Jöns is making in his final speech (MM 93:00) when he says, "In the darkness where You are supposed to be, where all of us probably are. . . . In the darkness You will find no one to listen to Your cries or be touched by Your sufferings. Wash Your tears and mirror Yourself in Your indifference."

Who is Jöns addressing? Not the knight (although, without the capitalized pronouns, he would appear to be the intended recipient, and in some ways he *is* but not because he is the one being addressed). This is Jöns's "prayer" to a nonexistent God. It is full of bitterness and defiance, in sharp contrast to the sincere prayer just uttered by the knight ("From our darkness, we call out to Thee, Lord. Have mercy on us because we are small and frightened and ignorant"). Implicitly, what Jöns is doing is pointing out the inconsistency of the average Christian who is, on the one hand, deeply moved by the suffering Christ while on the other willing to let God "off the hook" for all of the pain and suffering in the world.

One sees something similar going on in Sharon's final act of defiance in *The Rapture*. In order for God to forgive her for her sins, she must say that she loves God. But, she asks rhetorically, "Who forgives God?" Sharon has been absolutely faithful, sacrificing everything she values to a supremely demanding God. By the end of film, however, she reflects that God was deserving neither of her sacrifices nor her love. Sharon's bitterness and sense of outrage at God's trifling attitude toward the world is at such an extreme that she is willing to forgo heaven.

7.4 The Silence of God

Some religious writers will disagree with the context in which I have framed the question of God's existence in this chapter. Religious belief, they say, is a matter of faith, not a matter of rational justification.[10] If you want to learn about theism, they will suggest that you look not to philosophers for answers but to prayer. If you are sincere and you ask God for guidance, God will answer.

But, does God answer, or is God silent? The knight is the epitome of the sincere seeker, but God does not answer his prayers. God's silence is so complete that the knight is willing to seek out the devil in the hope of hearing back something—anything. The way that the knight explains his dilemma is interesting. The most important scene in this regard is the confessional scene in which the knight pours out his heart to a priest, only to learn later that he has been tricked—he has given his confession to Death (MM 19:00):

Knight: I want knowledge.

Death: You want guarantees?

Knight: Call it whatever you like. Is it so cruelly inconceivable to grasp God with the senses? Why should He hide Himself in a mist of half-spoken promises and unseen miracles?

Death is silent.

Knight: I want knowledge, not faith, not suppositions, but knowledge. I want God to stretch out His hand toward me, reveal Himself and speak to me.

Death: But He remains silent.

Knight: I call out to Him in the dark but no one seems to be there.

Death: Perhaps no one is there.

Humans have a natural inclination to believe the report of their senses: "seeing is believing." We seem to be wired that way. The knight's question—"Is it so cruelly inconceivable to grasp God with the senses?"—poses a serious problem for the theist. The orthodox response to this problem has an important parallel with the orthodox response to the problem of evil: "God will not give a guarantee that would annihilate man's freedom."[11] So, it's not that God is unable to provide the sort of proof the knight is seeking, but that God is unwilling to do so because a belief in God that is based on incontrovertible evidence is not as good as a belief that is made without (or, perhaps even, despite) evidence.

There is, though, one character in *The Seventh Seal* who "grasps God with the senses"—namely, Jof. He often receives visions of the divine. (He was also the only one, apart from the knight himself, who could see Death as he interacted with the knight.) We shall return to a discussion of Jof and his visions in the next section.

What about *The Rapture*? Here, at least initially, the advice "pray, and God will answer" bears fruit. At the depths of despair, just after Sharon tries (and fails) to commit suicide with the gun she stole from Tommy, the talkative hitchhiker from Ver-Mont, she receives her first vision of the pearl. We are led to believe that, over the next several years, this conversation with God through prayer continues. However, even for her, things break down in the end. The way that they break down shows some similarity to one of the knight's complaints in *The Seventh Seal*. The story of Sharon's trip to the desert and killing of her only child is patterned on Abraham's near-sacrifice of his son, Isaac, as described in Genesis 22:1–18. In Abraham's case, though, God's command is never carried out, because Abraham is stopped just as he is about to slay his son. The theist, though, is unwilling to follow the parallel of these two cases to their logical conclusion: if Abraham does the right thing in being willing to give up what he cared about most in the world (namely, his son), then so does Sharon. The difference in the two cases, the theist will say, is that, in Abraham's case, it is *God* who commands Isaac's killing, but in Sharon's case, Sharon has made some sort of error, either misinterpreting what God *really* wants her to do, or allowing her own will rather than God's to influence her actions. God's refusal to offer open, unambiguous instructions, requiring believers to do a lot of guesswork—reading various events as symbolic messages from God—leaves the theist in an awkward position. How can someone tell the difference between a genuine message from God versus a spurious interpretation of some chance happening, or even a misinterpretation of something that really was a message from God? The knight's requirement that "God . . . stretch out His hand toward me, reveal Himself and speak to me" doesn't seem overly demanding, after all.

7.5 The Free Will Defense and the Ultimate Harmony Defense

The theist has rather a lot of work to do to counter the problem of evil. The two most oft-cited approaches to reconciling the existence of pain and suffering with theism are the free will defense and the ultimate harmony defense. They both share in common the assumption that pain and suffering are necessary components in the production of some greater good—a good that more than compensates for the pain and suffering. Thus, they both are attempts to undercut step 5 in the formal version of the problem of evil presented earlier.

Let's look first at the theodicy that has become the orthodox defense against the problem of evil—the free will defense. There are a few concepts that will prove helpful in describing this theodicy.[12] Good$_1$ is pleasure and happiness. Bad$_1$ is pain and suffering. Good$_2$ is the second order good that arises as a result of the development and use of character traits such as compassion, courage, forgiveness, and fortitude. Bad$_2$ is the second order bad that arises as a result of the development and use of character traits such as malice, jealousy, and greed. With these concepts in hand, the **free will defense** is easy to state. Good$_2$ requires the existence of bad$_1$. (One cannot have compassion unless someone is suffering; one cannot be courageous unless one is at least threatened with serious harm; and so on for the other traits associated with good$_2$.) In order, then, to have good$_2$, God has to create a world with some bad$_1$. But, there's more. Good$_2$ requires that humans have free will—the power to choose compassion or hardness of heart; the power to choose to be courageous or to run away. So, in order to get good$_2$, God must not only create a world with some bad$_1$ in it, but must also create a world with at least some creatures with free will. Yet, once God gives those creatures (humans) free will, God leaves open the door that that free will is misused, resulting in bad$_2$. God values good$_2$ so highly that God is willing to put up with bad$_1$ and the possibility of bad$_2$ in order to get it. That is why God chose to create this world, even with its flaws.

Another way to explain the free will defense is by comparing our world (the one God created) with worlds God *could have* created but didn't. Prior to creation, God considered the various possible worlds that could be created. In one of these worlds, there were no sentient creatures; hence, no pain and suffering. In another world, there were sentient creatures, but the world was designed such that there was no pain and suffering. Without pain and suffering, there was no $good_2$. A third world (our world—the one God decided in favor of) had both pain and suffering and some creatures with free will, so it also had some $good_2$ (and the possibility of bad_2). God values $good_2$ so highly that God is willing to put up with both the pain and suffering and the occasional misuse of free will. It was impossible for God to create a world with $good_2$ in it but without pain and suffering. This is the one that God judged to be the best of all possible worlds, so this is the one that God created. And here we are.

Is the free will defense successful as a theodicy? Let's review the criteria that must be satisfied:

1. Does the theodicy handle both human-caused suffering and nature-caused suffering satisfactorily?
2. Does the theodicy explain how it is that the good produced more than compensates for the pain and suffering?
3. Does the theodicy explain why *this amount* of pain and suffering was necessary to achieve the good?

The free will defense was developed primarily to deal with human-caused suffering: Why did God create creatures like us, knowing that we had the potential to be an Adolph Hitler, a Joseph Stalin, or a Pol Pot? Answer: because by doing so, God also created humans with the potential to be a Mother Teresa or a Saint Francis. This theodicy doesn't, though, have much to say by way of explaining the amount of nature-caused suffering in the world. Did we really need the Black Death in order to develop our compassion? Couldn't I develop my sense of compassion just as well by feeling sympathy for someone who had stubbed her toe as by feeling sympathy for someone suffering through an agonizing death? How does the free will defender answer this charge? It is unclear. One route that is not going to work is to say that God allows so much suffering in order to boost up the amount of $good_2$. If this were the case, then Sharon would be right: God is trifling with creation; hence, God is not wholly good. We would never judge someone good who intentionally harmed others and then tried to explain that behavior with "the greater the suffering, the greater the fortitude developed in the person who is suffering." To say that God's goodness makes God an appropriate object of worship and love is to say that God is the supreme exemplar of goodness *as we understand that concept.*

Even in dealing fully with the extent of human-caused pain and suffering, the free will defense shows some weakness. Let's grant that the development and display of the character traits associated with $good_2$ are indeed greater goods capable of compensating for the existence of pain and suffering in the world. Let's also grant that free will is a necessary prerequisite for displaying these character traits. The theist is still left with the question, Why doesn't God intervene in keeping the effects of poor choices from being so disastrous? Consider an example. As Hitler was rising to power in the late 1920s and early '30s, there was a time when the political future in Germany was not yet sealed. Perhaps there was a key speech by Hitler that, if not made, would have kept him from coming to power. Imagine that Hitler is striding up to the podium to deliver that speech. He has made his choice already—if he gains power, he will start an expansionist war against his neighbors and try his darndest to remove groups of people he considers undesirable from the territory Germany controls. The bad_2 is the choice, which has already happened. Now, it is just a matter of following up on that choice. God, being omniscient, sees all this, sees the choice Hitler has already made, and knows what will happen if Hitler is not stopped. So, God gives Hitler temporary laryngitis. God hasn't interfered with the exercise of anyone's free will. Hitler made his choice; God only intervened after the fact. The free will defender needs to explain why this scenario constitutes undue interference.

What is the final assessment of the free will defense? Is it a successful theodicy? Its silence on the amount of nature-caused suffering in the world is a serious problem. As discussed above, it even experiences some difficulties in dealing with human-caused suffering. So, it seems to be unsuccessful—at least as a stand-alone defense against the problem of evil.

There is a second theodicy, the **ultimate harmony defense**, that is often put forward. If the free will defense is the theodicy accepted by religious orthodoxy, the ultimate harmony defense is the preferred theodicy of the average lay theist; it can be summarized as follows: Because of my limited knowledge, I cannot see how the suffering that occurs in the world fits into the overall scheme of things. Mere mortals lack the omniscience to see "the big picture." This theodicy is often described using the metaphor of music, as in an essay by Edward Madden, who writes, "A chord heard in isolation may sound dissonant and ugly, but when heard in context blends into a perfect whole or an ultimate harmony. So it is with evil. What human beings call evil is an event seen out of context, in isolation, and since man has only a fragmentary view of events, this is the only way he can see it. God, however, who has an overall view of events, sees how such events are good in the long run or good from an overall viewpoint."[13]

Presumably, after death God will explain things so that the suffering which individuals have endured will be seen as necessary, or even illusory. In one respect, the place of pain in the overall scheme of things (from God's bird's-eye view of creation) would blunt the problem of evil's claim against the theist. Still, though, there is a problem. In his great novel *The Brothers Karamazov*, Fyodor Dostoevsky presents this problem:

Take the suffering of children, Ivan tells Alyosha; there the point becomes very clear. Here is one example: a Russian general, retired on his great estate, treats his serfs like fools and buffoons. He is a great hunter and has many fine dogs. One day a serf boy of eight throws a stone in play and hurts the paw of the general's favorite dog. The general asks about his dog—what happened? After he is told, he has the boy locked in a shed overnight. Early the next morning the serfs, including the child's mother, are assembled for their edification. The child is stripped naked and told to run. The general sets the hounds after him, shouting "Get him, get him!" The dogs quickly overtake the boy and tear him to pieces in front of his mother's eyes. Did the general deserve to be shot? No doubt, but the atrocity already had been committed. If such an atrocity is needed to manure the soil for some future harmony, Ivan says, then such harmony is not worth the price. Then he asks, if *you* were God, Alyosha, could *you* consent to create a world in which everything turned out well in the end, but to achieve this end you had to see just one child tortured to death, beating its breast in a stinking outhouse, crying to "dear, kind God." No, it is not worth it. No doubt, God sees things differently from men. No doubt, on the day of resurrection, Ivan says, I too will join in the chorus, "Hallelujah, God, thy ways are just!" I too shall sing, as the mother embraces her son's murderer, "Praise God, I see why it had to be!" But, he concludes, I loathe myself now for the very thought of doing that then. I renounce the "higher" morality, the ultimate harmony, altogether, while I still can, while there is still time. For the love of humanity I now renounce it altogether.[14]

One sees exactly this response in Sharon's rejection of salvation at the very end of *The Rapture*. Ultimate harmony or not, the amount of suffering God allows in the world turns religion into a farce. In a similar vein, the knight, Antonius Block, is searching— not so much for proof of God's existence, but proof of God's worthiness. He assumes, at least at death, everything will be explained. But, as Death tells Block that he has lost the chess game, he finds out that even this is too much to expect (MM 84:00):

Knight: And you will divulge your secrets.
Death: I have no secrets.
Knight: So you know nothing.
Death: I have nothing to tell.

There is no ultimate harmony. There is no justification at all for the suffering present in the world. That is what the knight learns. If Death is speaking truthfully, then, irrespective of whether God exists, religion is discredited.

It is interesting to note that the last word in *The Seventh Seal* is given neither to the atheist Jöns nor to the desperate agnostic Block, but to the simple lay theist Jof (MM 94:30). For him, even death is interpreted as a sign of God's beneficence, for with death comes "the rain [that] washes their faces and cleans the salt of the tears from their cheeks." We cannot simply dismiss the view implicit in Jof's inclusion in *The Seventh Seal*. He (perhaps along with Mia) is the only character who has faith. He (again, along with Mia) is the only major character who is not terribly concerned about the problem of evil or God's silence; if asked, he would probably respond to the knight's concerns about the problem of evil in the same way that Mia responds in her conversation with the knight (MM 55:30)—he simply does not understand what the problem is. He is the only character (other than those singled out to die) who can see Death. Even though his life is not trouble-free, he seems perfectly content with things the way they are. What should we make of this? In some ways Jof is the embodiment of Jesus' advice: "whoever does not receive the kingdom of God like a child shall not enter it."[15] His faith is simple. Like a child, he trusts—he does not feel the need to turn that faith into an intellectual puzzle in the way that the knight, and even Jöns, does. Because of that, he seems much happier than the other characters.

As we shall see in the next chapter, theism offers up an easy answer to the question, Is life meaningful? The knight's torment is that on the one hand he wants the answer theism provides to this question while on the other the problem of evil is leading him to reject theism. He cannot have it both ways.

7.6 Other Responses to the Problem of Evil

Recall that the traditional problem of evil is an argument against theism. The argument contends that the amount of pain and suffering present in the world shows that the all-perfect God of Western religious orthodoxy does not exist. We have examined the two main defenses against the problem of evil offered by the theist: the free will defense and the ultimate harmony defense. Both of these are seen to be lacking. What other responses are open to the theist? Do any of those responses work?[16]

One reply to the problem of evil that is often given is that Satan, not God, is responsible for the evil in the world. Hence, the presence of pain and suffering counts neither against God's goodness (the modified problem of evil) nor against the likelihood of God's existence (the traditional problem of evil). This defense has an obvious defect: even if God is not directly responsible for pain and suffering, God is still indirectly responsible for it, since God allows Satan to exist. Remember, in order to be a successful defense of orthodoxy, none of God's perfections can by denied. But this defense denies God's omnipotence, for it leaves open a question as damaging to theism as the original problem of evil: Why doesn't God get rid of Satan?

A second possible response by the theist is that pain and suffering are necessary to serve as a contrast to good. Without that pain and suffering, we could not see good *as* good, much as we cannot see and appreciate health as good until we are sick. The problem here is that the *amount* of pain and suffering experienced by humans is not explained. A slight stomachache will allow me to see the value of health; I don't need a huge amount of pain in order to have that negative serve as a contrast. Why, then, does God allow a huge amount of pain and suffering in the world—far more than is necessary to serve as a contrast to good?

A third possible response is that (the threat of) pain and suffering serves to draw humans towards God: "There are no atheists in foxholes." Here again, there are serious problems with this defense. God has other avenues to drawing humans' attention to religious matters—avenues that are less painful. For example, God could appear to every human individually and say, "Here I am." But God is silent. Indeed, if this really is God's motivation in allowing pain in the world, it seems to have backfired. The problem of evil is probably *the* most important factor in leading people to embrace atheism.

What about the defense that explains pain as the result of natural forces, not the result of God's intentional actions? As with the Satan defense, this defense fails to take God's omnipotence seriously. If God created the world, then God is still responsible for making a world with natural forces that would result in so much pain and suffering.

Perhaps pain and suffering is a way to test humans' faith. Theists often mention the Book of Job in this context, which tells the story of how God allowed Satan to inflict incredible suffering on Job as a way to test his faith. God knew that Job would not reject Him, no matter how much suffering Satan threw his way. And, as predicted, Job remained steadfast. This defense against the problem of evil suggests that Job was not a special case: God regularly uses suffering to see who is worthy and who is not. The difficulty is squaring this defense with God's omniscience. If God already knows the outcome, what is the use of giving the test?[17]

The final defense to consider views suffering as punishment for sin. God is not responsible for the pain and suffering in the world; rather, it is those experiencing the suffering who have brought it upon themselves by their past deeds. While this defense may work in some cases, it is hard to see what the infant born with horrible birth defects has done to deserve that fate.

Many other defenses have been offered in an attempt to thwart the problem of evil. Most of these can be easily rejected as denying one of the attributes (omnipotence, omniscience, and perfect goodness) assigned to God by Western religious orthodoxy.

Where does this leave theism? Recall that we started out the chapter by framing the problem of evil within the context of rational justification for theism—one examines the evidence for theism, examines the evidence against it, and then decides which "side" makes the most convincing case. None of the defenses against the problem of evil discussed above (in both sections 7.5 and 7.6) succeeded, leaving theism with a major unanswered "con" argument. The theist may try some sort of hybrid approach—piecing together two or more theodicies in order to cover the deficiencies of one with patches offered by another. The most likely candidate here is a hybrid of the free will defense and the ultimate harmony defense. I will leave it as an exercise for you to decide whether such a hybrid would succeed in defending theism against the problem of evil.

Another possible approach for the theist is to reject the rationalistic framework in which this debate is taking place. While such a response is unlikely to convince a nonbeliever, it may be the only "answer" to the problem of evil that the theist has to offer.

Discussion Questions

1. Did you ever think about the problem of evil before reading this chapter? If so, what was your response? Do you think that respond was adequate? What is your response now?
2. Is God "silent"?
3. Do you think the apocalyptic tradition within Christianity has a more severe version of the problem of evil? What is happening during the destruction of the world? Is it a sign of God's lack of perfect goodness?
4. Is religion most often based on love of God or fear of God? Which motivation makes the most sense?
5. Were you surprised by the ending of *The Rapture*? If so, what ending were you expecting? What is the significance of the actual ending?
6. Compare Sharon's killing of her daughter in *The Rapture* with Abraham's near-killing of Isaac in the Bible. What are the similarities? Differences? Significance?
7. Why does God require *faith*? That is, why does God require the sort of blind trust that, in all other contexts, would be considered foolhardy?
8. For those who have read chapter 6 on free will and determinism, is God's omniscience (hence, foreknowledge) compatible with the existence of free will? Is God's omnipotence compatible with the existence of free will?

Annotated List of Film Titles Relevant to the Problem of Evil

Virtually any movie that depicts some real-world catastrophe of either human or natural origin can be used to generate the problem of evil.

The Killing Fields (1982). Directed by Roland Joffé. Starring Sam Waterston, Haing S. Ngor, John Malkovich, Julian Sands.
   The Killing Fields is based on a true story and is set in Cambodia during and after the U.S. withdrawal at the end of the Vietnam War. It portrays a period in Cambodia's history that equals or perhaps exceeds the Holocaust in its concentration of cruelty and purposeless suffering.
Schindler's List (1993). Directed by Steven Spielberg. Starring Liam Neeson, Ralph Fiennes.
   Based loosely on the true story of the German war profiteer turned philanthropist Oskar Schindler, *Schindler's List* is set in Nazi-era Poland and Czecho-

slovakia. The movie is relevant to the problem of evil in two respects. First, it depicts a huge amount of suffering. Second, it implicitly argues for the free will defense.

Shadowlands (1993). Directed by Richard Attenborough. Starring Anthony Hopkins, Debra Winger.

Based on a true story about the life of C. S. Lewis, a devout Christian and philosophy professor who specializes in the problem of evil but who lacks a real appreciation for the depths of suffering until he learns this as his "wife" dies of cancer.

AI: Artificial Intelligence (2001). Directed by Steven Spielberg. Starring Haley Joel Osment, Jude Law, Frances O'Connor, Sam Robards.

While *AI* deals primarily with philosophical questions surrounding the creation of intelligent robots, it also weaves in as minor theme a discussion of the problem of evil.

The Apostle (1997). Directed by Robert Duvall. Starring Robert Duvall, Farrah Fawcett.

The Apostle is relevant in presenting a picture of what the perception of an "unsilent" God might be like.

Annotated List of Book Titles Relevant to the Problem of Evil

"CLASSICS" IN THE PROBLEM OF EVIL

Saint Augustine

On Free Choice of the Will, first published in Latin in 395 C.E. Augustine argues for the free will defense against the problem of evil—the theodicy that has since become orthodoxy within Christianity.

David Hume

Dialogues concerning Natural Religion, originally published posthumously in 1777. Offers a very thorough criticism of the standard arguments for theism and a presentation of the problem of evil. The *Dialogues* are also available in their entirety online at <http://www.utm.edu/research/hume/wri/dialogue/dialogue.htm>.

Voltaire

Candide, first published in French in 1759. This novella offers an extended criticism of the ultimate harmony defense. *Candide* is also available in its entirety online at <http://www.vt.edu/vt98/academics/books/voltaire/candide>.

RECENT WORKS DEALING WITH THE PROBLEM OF EVIL
AND PHILOSOPHY OF RELIGION MORE BROADLY

John Perry, *Dialogue on Good, Evil and the Existence of God* (Indianapolis: Hackett, 1999). A useful introduction to the problem of evil and the various theodicies developed by theists to combat it.

Michael Peterson, *God and Evil* (Boulder: Westview Press, 1998). A very thorough treatment of the problem of evil and the major theodicies.

Louis Pojman, ed., *Philosophy of Religion* (Belmont, CA: Wadsworth, 1987). Highly recommended for a thorough treatment of philosophy of religion from all points of view.

Søren Kierkegaard, *Concluding Unscientific Postscript to the Philosophical Fragments*, first published in Danish in 1844. The main source for contemporary fideism (see note 10 for this chapter).

BOOKS ON *THE SEVENTH SEAL*

Ingmar Bergman, *Four Screenplays*, trans. Lars Malmstrom and David Kushner (New York: Simon and Schuster, 1960).

Arthur Gibson, *The Silence of God* (New York: Harper and Row, 1969).

Annotated List of Relevant Web Resources

THE BIBLE

There are many sites offering complete version of the Bible online. One of the best offers the Revised Standard Version along with a very useful special-purpose search engine at <http://etext.virginia.edu/rsv.browse.html>.

Fyodor Dostoevsky, *The Brothers Karamazov*: <http://www.ccel.org/d/dostoevsky/karamozov/karamozov.html>.

8

Existentialism

The Seventh Seal (1957), *Crimes and Misdemeanors* (1988), and *Leaving Las Vegas* (1995)

Knight: I call out to [God] in the dark but no one seems to be there.
Death: Perhaps no one is there.
Knight: Then life is an outrageous horror. No one can live in the face of death, knowing that all is nothingness.
Death: Most people never reflect about either death or the futility of life.
Knight: But one day they will have to stand at that last moment of life and look toward the darkness.
Death: When *that* day comes . . .

—from *The Seventh Seal*

We're all faced throughout our lives with agonizing decisions . . . moral choices. Some are on a grand scale, most of these choices are on lesser points. But, we define ourselves by the choices we have made. We are, in fact, the sum total of our choices. Events unfold so unpredictably, so unfairly. Human happiness does not seem to have been included in the design of creation. It is only we, with our capacity to love, that give meaning to an indifferent universe. And yet, most human beings seem to have the ability to keep trying and find joy from simple things— from their family, their work, and from the hope that future generations might understand more.

—Professor Louis Levy, in *Crimes and Misdemeanors*

Sera: So, Ben, . . . what brings you to Las Vegas?
Ben: I came here to drink myself to death.
Sera: How long's it gonna take to drink yourself to death?
Ben: Oh, I don't know. About four weeks.

—from *Leaving Las Vegas*

Is there any meaning to life? Does it really matter that we (either individually or collectively as a species) ever existed? If you answer yes to these questions, by virtue of what is life meaningful? Is it we ourselves who "give meaning to an indifferent universe" or is there some way to make sense of objective meaning, meaning that does not depend on our individual desires and our individual values? These questions form the central topic of this chapter.

If you are reading the chapters in order, you will note that two of the three focus films for this chapter have served as focus films in previous chapters. There will be a little overlap with discussion in those chapters, but not very much. If you are reading the chapters out of order, it may be useful to refer to the overviews of *The Seventh Seal* and *Crimes and Misdemeanors* from chapters 7 and 5, respectively.

8.1 Is Life Meaningful?

I assume that, at some time in their lives, most people have asked themselves: "What's the point of it all?" The trigger may have been the failure of some important personal project or the death of a loved one. Or maybe the question cropped up out of the blue. Leo Tolstoy, the great nineteenth-century Russian novelist, described in his essay "My Confession" the crisis brought on by his inability to answer this simple question. In his case, the crisis was not spurred by failure or grief. As he describes it, everything in his life was going perfectly. He had wealth and fame from his successful career as a writer. He was held in high esteem as both intelligent and morally upright. He had a loving family, all of whom (including himself) were quite healthy. Everything was going his way. Nevertheless, we read, "I could not attribute a reasonable motive to any single act in my whole life. I was only astonished that I could not have realized this at the very beginning. All this had so long ago been known to me! Illness and death would come . . . to those whom I loved, to myself, and nothing remains but stench and worms. All my acts, whatever I did, would sooner or later be forgotten, and I myself be nowhere. Why, then, busy one's self with anything? . . . It is possible to live only as long as life intoxicates us; as soon as we are sober again we see that it is all a delusion, and a stupid delusion! In this, indeed, there is nothing either ludicrous or amusing; it is only cruel and stupid!"[1] As he reports, this existential crisis reached such depths that he seriously contemplated suicide.

Tolstoy was not unique. Is life meaningful? The question has an import for the individual that is lacking from most of the other questions philosophers ask. I doubt anyone has ever contemplated suicide because of the problem of identity. And skepticism, even though it seems to have far-reaching implications, lacks the personal urgency of this question. The most ardent proponent of skepticism in the modern era, David Hume, even admits that these sorts of topics are of merely intellectual interest— attempts to answer them are games philosophers play. But the question about the meaningfulness of life is different. The twentieth-century writer Albert Camus argues that "the meaning of life is the most urgent of questions"—"[j]udging whether life is or is not worth living" is "the only truly serious philosophical problem."[2]

Before going further, it may be wise to consider what exactly the question is asking. Only then will we be in a position to say what an adequate answer would look like. Is life meaningful? can be interpreted along two different dimensions. The first involves what the word *life* is referring to. At its most particular, this question could be asking, Is *my individual life* meaningful? Or, the question could be asking the more general question: Is the life *of my species* meaningful?—Is there any purpose or meaning to the existence of humanity? More general still, the question could be asking about the meaning of all biological life—is there some purpose or meaning to the existence of living things? Most general of all, the question could be divorced from a literal interpretation of the word *life* to be asking about the meaning of the universe—is there some purpose to the existence of the universe as a whole? We will be focusing here on the first, and, to a lesser extent, the second interpretations of the word *life*.

But, the ambiguity doesn't end there, for there are two competing ways of interpreting what *meaningful* refers to in this context. According to one, in order to be meaningful, life must have **objective meaning**. (The word *objective* as used here means "independent of what anyone or any group of people happen to think.") But how could this be possible, since meaning is, by its very nature, relative to some perspective? In order for life to be *interpreted* as having a purpose, doesn't there have to be an *interpreter*? Yes and no. If one considers only the perspectives of individuals in the world, then objective meaning is an impossibility. However, if God exists, then God's perspective could ground meaning in a way that allows for objectivity. (This use of God as the supplier of objective value should strike the reader as familiar; it is analogous to the pattern seen within the divine command theory of ethics, in which God's will grounds an objectivist ethical theory.) For the theist, *meaningful* can be cashed out in terms of God's plan for the world: my life has objective meaning because God invests the world and everything in it (my life included) with meaning and purpose "from the outside." So, even though my personal accomplishments may be scant, my role in furthering God's plan for the world gives meaning to those accomplishments and to my life as a whole.

There is an alternative to interpreting *meaning* as objective meaning. Many people do not believe that God is the only possible source of meaning and purpose in the world. If I care deeply about something and expend a lot of effort in achieving some goal (for example, in raising my children to be well-adjusted, morally good, competent adults), that should count for something. Even if, as Tolstoy reminds us, "[i]llness and death would come . . . to those whom I loved, to myself, and nothing remains but stench and worms," still, my activities, my life, and my achievements have meant something *to me*. This second framework for interpreting meaningfulness uses **subjective meaning** as the measuring stick. This framework is not necessarily atheistic; it still allows for the possibility that God exists, but denies that God is required to make sense of the meaningfulness of life. For that reason, it is best thought of, not as a nontheistic framework, but as a humanistic framework.

I distinguished above between theism and atheism on the one hand and the two interpretations of *meaning* on the other because they do not go in lockstep. As I have noted, it is possible for a theist to hold that subjective meaning is the proper way to interpret the concept of meaningfulness. It is also possible for someone to long for objective meaning, yet feel that it is unattainable because God does not exist. (We shall meet several characters in *The Seventh Seal* and *Crimes and Misdemeanors* who do just that.) A third option is for someone to hold to the humanistic framework, yet argue that life is meaningless according to that framework. (Again, we shall meet a character in *Crimes and Misdemeanors* who is best described this way.) Thus, while the traditional camps on the proper interpretation of meaningfulness (objective versus subjective) break down neatly into theists on the one side and atheists on the other, other positions are possible.

This distinction between objective and subjective meaning—in particular, reconciling ourselves to the unattainability of objective meaning—was a special concern of Jean-Paul Sartre and Albert Camus, the two most influential members of the intellectual movement known as **existentialism**. This movement had its roots in the latter half of the nineteenth century and blossomed in the 1940s and '50s with the writings of Sartre and Camus (novelists, essayists, and playwrights) and the philosophers Martin Heidegger and Karl Jaspers. While existentialism had many facets and encompassed intellectuals with a wide variety of positions (it is more properly thought of as an antimovement than a movement), I shall be using Camus and Sartre as representatives for the existentialist response to the question: Is life meaningful?

8.2 An Overview of the Movies

THE SEVENTH SEAL (1957). DIRECTED BY INGMAR BERGMAN. STARRING MAX VON SYDOW, GUNNAR BJÖRNSTRAND, BIBI ANDERSSON. (IN SWEDISH.)

We examined *The Seventh Seal* in the previous chapter in the context of the problem of evil. While the silence-of-God problematic is a major preoccupation of this film, it also deals with several existentialist themes. Indeed, it is the only one of the three focus films for this chapter that was actually made during the heyday of existentialism.

I shall assume you are already familiar with the film and don't need a plot overview, so I will cut to the chase. *The Seventh Seal* deals primarily with the question, Is life meaningful if there is no God? As with the silence-of-God problematic, this question runs through several of Bergman's early films. One sees in *The Seventh Seal* how Bergman, the son of a Lutheran minister, struggles with the issue. On the one hand, his reason rejects the theism of his upbringing; on the other, he sees that atheism does not come without a cost—namely, the evaporation of an easy answer to the question of the meaningfulness of life. The knight, Antonius Block, embodies this struggle. What is Block searching for? Is it God, or is it something else—something that could play the same role that God has traditionally played in providing a basis for meaning and purpose?

CRIMES AND MISDEMEANORS (1988). DIRECTED BY WOODY ALLEN. STARRING MARTIN LANDAU, WOODY ALLEN, MIA FARROW, ALAN ALDA, ANGELICA HUSTON, SAM WATERSTON.

It is also the second time around for *Crimes and Misdemeanors*, which was the focus film for the chapter 5 discussion on ethics. Various of the characters in this film represent not just ethical theories but whole worldviews. The theists (Ben and Sol) cannot make sense of the meaningfulness of life outside of a theistic framework. Sol even offers that "[i]f necessary, [he] will always choose God over truth." Professor Louis Levy, on the other hand, presents the humanistic alternative: God does not exist, but humans can nevertheless find real (albeit subjective) meaning in the deeds they perform and in their relationships to others.

LEAVING LAS VEGAS (1995). DIRECTED BY MIKE FIGGIS. STARRING NICOLAS CAGE, ELISABETH SHUE.

Leaving Las Vegas is the story of two profoundly isolated humans whose lives become intertwined over the course of a few weeks. Ben Sanderson is a failed Hollywood screenwriter who has given up on life. He has only one goal left in all the world: to drink himself to death. To accomplish this with minimum fuss, he cuts the few remaining ties to his previous life and moves to Las Vegas. Sera is a prostitute; in her loneliness, she finds something strangely appealing in this pathetic drunk and she clings to Ben. Their relationship, initially based on their mutual need and their acceptance of one another's choices, eventually begins its downward spiral along with Ben's alcoholism.

Leaving Las Vegas shows the complexity of life and human relationships. It remains honest to the end, never sinking into sentimentality nor looking away as the characters' lives follow their necessary trajectories. The characters of Ben and Sera are offered to us with all of life's grit intact. *Leaving Las Vegas* sticks close to the novel of the same name by John O'Brien, on which it is based.

8.3 The Theistic Response in The Seventh Seal and Crimes and Misdemeanors

In section 8.1 I related the personal crisis experienced by Leo Tolstoy. A little later in "My Confession," he describes what happened to him and how he ultimately resolved the crisis. He noticed that he was not alone among his circle of friends and acquaintances in believing that life was meaningless—he was unique only in that he chose to grapple with the issue. However, in looking around at the masses of people outside of his circle, the uneducated laborers who made up the bulk of Russian society, he found very few who believed that life was meaningless. In probing further, Tolstoy discovered that this difference could be traced back to one thing and one thing only: religious faith. He and his circle had jettisoned faith-based justification along with most of the intellectuals during the modern era. Indeed, the distinguishing feature of modernity is belief in the preeminence of the rational approach to understanding the world.

One sees a similar dichotomy depicted in The Seventh Seal. The "simple folk," represented by Jof and Mia, do not share the knight's concerns about the possible meaninglessness of life. Jof in particular possesses a simple, unreflective faith that allows him to "see" the world around him (even death) as all part of God's plan, and consistent with His supreme beneficence. While The Seventh Seal is set in the Middle Ages, the protagonist Antonius Block represents a very modern way of thinking in his refusal to believe in God without adequate reasons. Block would have agreed with twentieth-century philosopher Thomas Nagel, very much in the modern tradition, who described "the idea of God [as] the idea of something that can explain everything else, without having to be explained itself. . . . [T]he belief in God is the belief that the universe is intelligible, but not to us."[3] Faith is, by its very nature, not the product of reason—if not irrational, it is at least arational. But Tolstoy came to believe that God was a necessary prerequisite for meaning. If God didn't exist, there was no purpose to life, for it always ended in nothing but "stench and worms." No, even worse than that—at least stench and worms is something. Without God, life ends in nothing at all. Eventually, the universe as we know it will cease to exist. At that point, my life, the lives of those around me, the whole of humanity, even the universe itself, will have made no difference at all. With God, though, an individual's life has meaning, both because of that individual's role in God's overall plan for the world as well as the importance of an individual's actions during her earthly life in determining how that person will fare for the rest of eternity (in the afterlife). Based on such considerations, Tolstoy was persuaded to become a sincere theist, if for no other reason than to save his sanity. (Notice that this is not an argument for God's existence in the modernist sense. It is not something of the form "X proves that God exists." Tolstoy is not saying that he's found evidence that God exists. Rather, he is saying, "Whether God exists or not is something I cannot know. But I do know that, if I don't believe in God, I feel miserable; whereas, if I do believe in God, I feel good. So, I'll believe in God.")

One sees a degree of similarity between Tolstoy's response and that given by the character Sol in *Crimes and Misdemeanors*. Aunt May, Sol's "nihilist" sister, comes close to the modernist, preconversion Tolstoy in her reaction to Sol and his theism. In the flashback to a Passover seder from his youth at the 69:50 minute mark,[4] Judah depicts Aunt May as the feisty atheist who sees religion and all its trappings as "mumbo jumbo." As far as she is concerned, religion is nothing but superstition for intellectual lightweights: anyone who looks at the real world without blinders on will see that God does not exist. Sol's response is quite interesting. He agrees with May that religion does not ultimately depend on rational belief, but on faith. Furthermore, this faith allows its possessor to have a better life than is attainable for the purely reason-based intellectual (like May).

> **Guest:** And if all your faith is wrong, Sol? Just what if . . . ?
> **Sol:** Then I'll still have a better life than all those who doubt.
> **Guest:** Are you telling me you prefer God to truth?
> **Sol:** If necessary, I will always choose God over truth.

The rabbi Ben also offers theism as the best (or only?) way of making sense of the meaning of life (MM 13:30):

> **Ben:** [I]t's a fundamental difference in the way we view the world. You see it as harsh and empty of values and pitiless. And I couldn't go on if I didn't feel with all my heart that there's a moral structure . . . with real meaning—with forgiveness and some kind of higher power. Otherwise there's no basis to know how to live. . . .
> **Judah:** Now you're talking to me like your congregation.
> **Ben:** That's true. We went from a small infidelity to the meaning of existence.

Ben even suggests that Judah's infidelity may be part of God's plan. The penultimate scene of the movie, the conversation between Judah and Cliff at the wedding reception, offers the final presentation of the theistic framework. This time it is Judah's words that divulge his implicit acceptance of this way of viewing the world, for, it is only the existence of God that could keep the universe from being empty and valueless (MM 93:30). For Judah, as for Tolstoy, the possibility of an "empty" universe is a chilling prospect.

The Seventh Seal offers a more nuanced treatment of the relationship between theism and objective meaning, for the film's protagonist, the knight, Antonius Block, longs desperately for objective meaning even though he is unwilling or unable to abandon reason in favor of faith. As we saw in chapter 7, his reason pushes him in the direction of agnosticism or even atheism; nevertheless, he cannot shake off the interpretation of meaningfulness that requires God's existence. He is left in much the same position as the preconversion Tolstoy—looking for a source for objective meaning but unable to find one. There are three conversations that deal with the tension experienced by the knight. The first relevant scene takes place as he confesses to a monk (later revealed to be Death) in a small church (MM 19:00). There are several motifs running through this conversation between the knight and Death. The knight recognizes that he is trapped within a framework that requires objective meaning, unable because of that to find importance in his relationships to other humans—relationships that could serve as the source for subjective meaning for his life. He is "trapped" because, on the one hand, he requires *knowledge* of God's existence (that is, rationally justified belief). But, as discussed previously in the context of the silence-of-God problematic, God does not provide the evidence needed for this rational justification. Despite the knight's lack of faith, God still retains a major role in his worldview. Subjective meaning, even though it is within his grasp, is (at this point in the conversation) rejected as qualitatively inadequate—the knight wants objective meaning or nothing.

Knight: I want knowledge, not faith, not suppositions, but knowledge. I want God to stretch out His hand toward me, reveal Himself and speak to me.

Death: But He remains silent.

Knight: I call out to Him in the dark but no one seems to be there.

Death: Perhaps no one is there.

Knight: Then life is an outrageous horror. No one can live in the face of death, knowing that all is nothingness.

Death: Most people never reflect about either death or the futility of life.

Knight: But one day they will have to stand at that last moment of life and look toward the darkness.

Death: When *that* day comes . . .

Camus wrote about exactly this phenomenon in *The Myth of Sisyphus*. He referred to the "confrontation of this irrational and . . . wild longing for clarity whose call echoes in the human heart" as the *absurd*.[5] Toward the end of the confessional conversation in *The Seventh Seal* the knight shows that he may be turning a corner in his understanding of meaningfulness—he will use "[his] reprieve for one meaningful deed." (This deed is accomplished later in the film when the knight, by knocking over the chess pieces and thus distracting Death, allows Jof, Mia, and their young son Michael to escape.) The closing line from the knight—"This is my hand . . ."—goes off in yet a third direction, one that is congenial with the ideas of the existentialists Camus and Sartre. For them, either one embraces (objective) meaninglessness with joy, relishing one's freedom to make choices, or one remains stuck in the sulking and depressive existence experienced by the knight up until then.

The knight doesn't continue consistently on this trajectory. As is shown by the conversation with Jöns just before Tyan is burned at the stake, he has reverted back to the framework that demands objective meaning (MM 76:50):

Jöns: Who watches over that child? Is it the angels, or God, or the Devil, or only the emptiness? Emptiness, my lord!
Knight: This cannot be.
Jöns: Look at her eyes, my lord. Her poor brain has just made a discovery. Emptiness under the moon.

"Emptiness under the moon"—that is what you get if you combine a longing for objective meaning and atheism. Both the knight and Jöns are painfully aware of this crushing truth. Jöns's response is to jettison theism and the possibility of objective meaning, replacing it, not with the humanistic framework and a joyful embrace of subjective meaning, but with scorn and, on occasion, bitterness at humanity's fate. He comes closest to the heroic embrace of total meaninglessness as recommended by Sartre and Camus; however, even he wavers from that ideal. As shown by his failure to *act* to try to prevent Tyan's execution, Jöns falls short. Existentialists' highest praise is reserved for those who fight for a lost cause *knowing that it is a lost cause*. The knight becomes the real tragic figure of the story, because, despite his awareness of his predicament, he is unable to extricate himself. *The Seventh Seal* is a tragedy because its hero is fully conscious of his predicament.

The knight remains trapped within this framework until the very end, as his last words attest (MM 92:20):

Knight: From our darkness, we call out to Thee, Lord. Have mercy on us because we are small and frightened and ignorant.
Jöns: [*bitterly*]: In the darkness where You are supposed to be, where all of us probably are. . . . In the darkness You will find no one to listen to Your cries or be touched by Your sufferings. Wash Your tears and mirror Yourself in Your indifference.
Knight: God, You who are somewhere, who *must* be somewhere, have mercy on us.

The knight has forgotten his "one meaningful deed" and is back to the "small and frightened and ignorant" man from the earlier part of the scene at the confessional. Tolstoy found in theism solace and an answer to his questions about the meaningfulness of life, but the knight found only hopelessness and desperation. Jöns's final piece of advice, that the knight at least relish his last remaining moments of freedom as he "can still roll [his] eyes and move [his] toes," falls on deaf ears.

8.4 Embracing Meaninglessness

While the knight is crushed by his acute consciousness of the lack of objective meaning in the world, this response is not a foregone conclusion. Camus writes of a second way out of the dilemma: " 'I conclude that all is well,' . . . and that remark is sacred. It echoes in the wild and limited universe of man. It teaches that all is not, has not been, exhausted. It drives out of this world a god who had come into it with dissatisfaction and a preference for futile suffering. It makes of fate a human matter, which must be settled among men."[6] This response is typical of existentialism. It is both exhilarating (Camus's response) and frightening (Sartre's response) for the freedom it opens up, for within this framework, we must look within ourselves in deciding which way to choose. There is no more holy scripture—there are no more binding rules. According to Sartre, "When we speak of forlornness . . . we mean only that God does not exist and that we have to face all the consequences of this. . . . The existentialist . . . thinks it very distressing that God does not exist, because all possibility of finding values in a heaven of ideas disappears along with Him. . . . That is the very starting point of existentialism. Indeed, everything is permissible if God does not exist, and as a result man is forlorn, because neither within him nor without does he find anything to cling to. He can't start making excuses for himself. . . . We have no excuse behind us, nor justification before us. We are alone, with no excuses."[7]

Sartre's distress at the "death of God" echoes the sentiments of Friedrich Nietzsche (1844–1900), who made famous the exclamation "God is dead!" Without theism as an anchor for values, humanity is adrift in a sea of open possibilities:

"Whither is God" [the madman] cried. "I shall tell you. *We have killed him*—you and I. All of us are his murderers. But how have we done this? How were we able to drink up the sea? Who gave us the sponge to wipe away the entire horizon? What did we do when we unchained this earth from its sun? Whither is it moving now? Whither are we moving now? . . . Backward, sideward, forward, in all directions? Is there any up or down left? Are we not straying as through an infinite nothing? Do we not feel the breath of empty space? Has it not become colder? . . . Do we not smell anything yet of God's decomposition? Gods too decompose. God is dead. God remains dead. And we have killed him. How shall we, the murderers of all murderers, comfort ourselves?"[8]

Is it any wonder that the knight cannot quite manage to throw out theism? He (like Nietzsche and Sartre) understands full well what he would be giving up.

8.5 The Humanistic Response

Despite the knight's reluctance, there is one scene where he tests a possible way out of his absurd dilemma. Shortly after the scene at the confessional, as he enjoys a simple meal with Mia and Jof, this new understanding seems to be taking hold (MM 55:15) as he laments, "Faith is a torment, did you know that? It is like loving someone who is out there in the darkness but never appears, no matter how loudly you call." Mia says that she does not understand what he is saying. Questions about the meaning of life or God's silence just do not crop up in her life of simple needs, simple pleasures, and simple faith. In her company, even the knight's dark brooding starts to fade. He enjoys the simple pleasure of their company, suggesting that his memory of this event will suffice to keep the brooding—the need for objective meaning—from cropping up again. The conversation with Death as the chess game continues in the next scene brings this nascent change in the knight to an abrupt halt.

But, suppose the knight had been able to continue on the path of subjective meaning? Would his life have turned out to be meaningful? How is "meaningfulness" interpreted within this worldview? Certainly it implies more than quiet resignation in the face of objective meaninglessness. In section 8.1 I introduced the concept of subjective meaning in terms of doing something that you care deeply about. Within this framework, one must always keep in mind that an activity or accomplishment has meaning if it is something that the person engaging in that activity or achieving that accomplishment values. Value is generated from within, not from without.

So, was the knight's life meaningful in this sense? I think so. Consider his exchange with Death just after Jof, Mia, and Michael have escaped and the knight is told he is mated at the next move (MM 84:00). Death asks him if he has enjoyed his reprieve. He answers, "Yes, I did." He has succeeded in performing his "one meaningful act" foreshadowed in the scene at the confessional.

Others may adopt the humanistic framework yet come to the conclusion that life is meaningless. One sees this view represented in Professor Levy in *Crimes and Misdemeanors*. He describes quite eloquently one way of fleshing out the humanistic framework (MM 99:30), noting, "It is only we, with our capacity to love, that give meaning to an indifferent universe. And yet, most human beings seem to have the ability to keep trying and find joy from simple things—from their family, their work, and from the hope that future generations might understand more." Indeed, this speech, in voice-over, is the closing commentary to the movie. However, its import strikes us as ironic, given that it is spoken "from the grave" of someone who committed suicide.

Over and above Professor Levy's ultimate dissatisfaction with what subjective meaning has to offer, there is an additional problem with it—a highly counterintuitive implication this worldview shares with other types of subjectivism: if I am the final arbiter of value, then anything goes (so long as my values say it does). Let's return for a moment to the knight and his "one meaningful deed." While we may, along with him, view the saving of three innocent lives as worthwhile, our opinion is irrelevant. It is the knight alone whose valuing of this act makes it (and, as a result, his life) subjectively meaningful. But, does anything go? If I care deeply about exterminating a group of people and devote my life to that activity, is my life meaningful? Consider the lives of the two protagonists in *Leaving Las Vegas*. Ben's suicide, so long as it is done with affirmation and not out of resignation, can give his life meaning. Sera's activities as a prostitute (again, assuming it is a life she really wants) likewise give her life meaning. She says on several occasions that she is satisfied with her life, that she feels she is providing an important service to her customers. We, as external observers, see self-delusion in this, and the interpretation of Sera's remarks as self-deluded is encouraged by their context. When she describes to the off-camera therapist her prostitution as offering an important service (MM 18:50), she is thinking about a group sex act that she facilitated. She saw herself as engaged in some sort of performance art. In the very next scene, as Juri tracks her down in Las Vegas, the audience is given a much grimmer view of her life as a prostitute. Similarly, when Sera says "there'll always be bad times, but my life's good—it's like I want it to be" (MM 34:20), the very next scene shows her (again) with Juri as he threatens her for not bringing in enough money. To say that we, as external viewers, know she is deluding herself is to say that we know what she *really* values (or, what she *should* really value). But this misses the whole point of subjective meaning: *Sera* is the ultimate arbiter of what Sera values—not us, not "decent" society, not traditional morality. Sartre affirms this: "[E]verything is permissible if God does not exist, and as a result man is forlorn, because neither within him nor without does he find anything to cling to." To the extent that we are unwilling to agree with Sera that her life is meaningful because she values her activities, to that extent we reject subjective meaning as a legitimate framework.

8.6 Suicide as a Response to Meaninglessness

What are we to make of Ben's and Professor Levy's suicides? Were they done out of resignation, or were they done with passion, as an act that the character positively wished for? After hearing of Levy's death, Cliff replays a section of a taped interview in which Levy talked about suicide: "[T]he universe is a pretty cold place. It's we who invest it with our feelings. And, under certain conditions, we feel that the thing isn't worth it anymore" (MM 75:00). Assuming he was foretelling his own suicide, it's pretty clear it was done out of resignation. His embrace of the humanistic framework did not allow him to climb out of meaninglessness; thus, he is an example of someone who answered *no* to the question, Is life (subjectively) meaningful?

Recall that, for Tolstoy also, the feeling of objective meaninglessness led him to contemplate suicide. Camus wrote extensively on the topic of suicide; indeed, it is the primary topic in *The Myth of Sisyphus*. Suicide is one possible reaction to the realization that there is no objective meaning to life; as Camus explains, "A world that can be explained even with bad reasons is a familiar world. But, on the other hand, in a universe suddenly divested of illusions and lights, man feels an alien, a stranger. His exile is without remedy since he is deprived of the memory of a lost home or the hope of a promised land. This divorce between man and his life, the actor and his setting, is properly the feeling of absurdity. All healthy men having thought of their own suicide, it can be seen, without further explanation, that there is a direct connection between this feeling and the longing for death."[9] But Camus did not think that suicide was where it had to lead. The absurdity of life could also be affirmed, not merely given in to. One still remains aware of life's ultimate futility, however.

Wouldn't it, though, be a relief for someone to be less aware (or even unaware) of life's futility? Wouldn't that be a blessing? It was not life's futility itself that was the knight's torment, but his *fear of* life's futility. Tolstoy describes in "My Confession" how, prior to his conversion, he was haunted by the image of some malignant superintelligence laughing at his absurd predicament. The cruelty he imputes to his imagined creator was that that creator made him clever enough to see this predicament, but unable to do anything about it. There is indeed something to be said in favor of intellectual stupor.

Ben's choice of a means to kill himself seems significant in this respect. Why did he choose this route? After all, shooting himself in the head would have been a much more efficient method of suicide than drinking himself to death, and, it has the added benefit that his resolve could not possibly be thwarted by some do-gooder (like Sera). The deliberateness of this choice, given its obvious drawbacks, bears discussion.

There are, I think, three relevant differences between the choice in method Ben makes and some other method—say, shooting himself in the head. First, deliberately drinking oneself to death is quite an accomplishment. It requires perseverance, it requires consistency, it requires one to withstand the physical unpleasantness that accompanies it. Were it not for the ultimate goal state, one might even think success at drinking oneself to death is something to be proud of, something to value. But, in Ben's mind, the goal state (his own annihilation) is itself something good. To the extent that he has second thoughts about the value of his nonexistence, the second relevant characteristic about this method of suicide comes to the fore. As he approaches death and his mental faculties grow dimmer from the damaging effects of the alcohol (including his memory of his previous life), he manages to drink himself into unawareness. When Sera asks him why he is killing himself, he responds that he can't remember (MM 47:20). All he knows is that he has one and only one goal in life—to drink himself to death. He has arranged things so that there is at least one thing he will succeed at in the end—his own annihilation. Ben views Sera's request that he seek help for his alcoholism (MM 85:20) as a wrench thrown in the way of this, his last, act. But he finds a way to remove Sera from the picture: the prostitute that he picks up in the casino and brings home that night, knowing that Sera will find the two of them, is the insurance that this potential threat will go away. Ben's single-mindedness and willingness to sacrifice everything and everyone in his pursuit of this goal is quite remarkable.

Finally, Ben's choice of slow death by alcohol is significant, in that this choice constitutes a sort of sneering at fate. While not explicitly stated, we are led to believe that his alcoholism was the origin of his problems. To turn around and consciously use this to achieve his final purpose—his own death—is reminiscent of the attitude adopted by the existentialist hero. This is not the pollyannaish "When life hands you lemons, make lemonade." Ben is not trying to make lemonade. Rather, his choice shows his desire to be master of his fate—at least *he* is the one deciding what will happen to him. This brings up the issue of free will and determinism discussed in chapter 6. Is he really choosing or is he changing what he wants to line up with what is inevitable? If we could give consciousness and the ability to sense the environment to a rock, it may well believe that it was freely choosing its trajectory as it fell to the ground. Ben's "choice" may also be of this sort. His severe addiction to alcohol has forced him onto this path; he is powerless to do anything but acquiesce.

In the final analysis, what are we to make of Ben's suicide? Did he see, in carrying it out, something worthwhile? It is unlike other goals in that, if he succeeds, he won't be around to bask in the feeling of accomplishment. Or was his suicide merely the action of a man who has utterly given up—who has [judged] that "life is not worth living"?[10] Despite what we may see of heroism in his choice of method, for Ben, this may simply have been the path of least resistance. Obviously, *Leaving Las Vegas* is a work of fiction that offers no verifiable answer to this question. Ben's death, though, does leave us with an example to consider in light of the existentialist's argument that the awareness of the meaninglessness of life is something that is positively to be wished for.

Discussion Questions

1. Is the question Is life meaningful? merely a philosopher's question? Have you ever asked yourself this question? If so, what was your answer?
2. What connections do you see between the ultimate harmony defense (against the problem of evil) and the question, Is life meaningful?
3. Does atheism imply "emptiness under the moon"?
4. Do the "poor and downtrodden" have existential crises? Why or why not?
5. What criteria need to be satisfied for a death to count as suicide? Do Ben's actions in *Leaving Las Vegas* constitute suicide? If so, was suicide in his case *rational*?
6. What is the significance of Professor Levy's suicide?
7. What is the significance of Ben's going blind?

Annotated List of Film Titles Relevant to Existentialism

OTHER MOVIES BY INGMAR BERGMAN

There are existentialist themes running through many Bergman films, particularly the early ones. The following list contains some choice titles: *Wild Strawberries* (1957), *The Magician* (1958), *Through a Glass Darkly* (1961), *Winter Light* (1962), *The Silence* (1963), *Persona* (1969), *Shame* (1967), *A Passion* (1969), *Cries and Whispers* (1972), *Face to Face* (1976), *Autumn Sonata* (1978), *From the Life of the Marionettes* (1980), and *Fanny and Alexander* (1982).

FILMS BY OTHER DIRECTORS

Ikiru (1952). Directed by Akira Kurosawa. Starring Takashi Shimura, Nobuo Kaneko, Kyoko Seki.

What would you do if you found out you only had a few months to live? That is the question faced by the protagonist in Akira Kurosawa's masterpiece of existentialist cinema.

American Beauty (1999). Directed by Sam Mendes. Starring Kevin Spacey, Annette Bening, Thora Birch, Wes Bentley.

One of the most recent in a long line of movies about "existential" desperation in modern American suburbia.

Hamlet (1996). Directed by Kenneth Branagh. Starring Kenneth Branagh, Derek Jacobi, Kate Winslet, Julie Christie.

Our protagonist gives voice at one time or another to most of the issues discussed in this chapter.

Fearless (1993). Directed by Peter Weir. Starring Jeff Bridges, Isabella Rossellini.

This film turns the existentialist's dilemma on its head: What would the life of someone be like who was *not* afraid of death?

The Rapture (1991). Directed by Michael Tolkin. Starring Mimi Rogers, David Duchovny.

This focus film from chapter 7 raises questions surrounding the meaning of life in addition to those related to the problem of evil.

Annotated List of Book Titles Relevant to Existentialism

MODERN "CLASSICS" IN THE HISTORY OF EXISTENTIALISM

Fyodor Dostoevsky

Notes from Underground, first published in Russian in 1864. Dostoevsky is considered by many to mark the nascence of existentialism.

Albert Camus
The Myth of Sisyphus, first published in French in 1942. A widely influential collection of essays by Camus.

Jean-Paul Sartre
Existentialism, first published in French in 1946. Sartre attempts to explain and defend his version of existentialism. "The Wall," first published in French in 1939, is widely anthologized in English translation.

Collections of Essays and Short Works in Existentialism

Walter Kaufman, ed., *Existentialism from Dostoevsky to Sartre* (New York: Meridian, 1975). An excellent entry point for a more in-depth reading of existentialist literature.

E. D. Klemke, ed., *The Meaning of Life*, 2nd ed. (Oxford: Oxford University Press, 2000). This book offers a wide array of perspectives.

Leo Tolstoy, *My Confession, My Religion*, trans. Isabel Hapgood (Midland, MI: Avensblume Press, 1994).

Notes

Preface

1. At the time of this writing, the movie *AI: Artificial Intelligence* was only recently in theaters and was not yet available on video.

Chapter 1

1. It may sound strange to refer to the seventeenth century as "modern." The strangeness disappears when one realizes that the periods in contrast are the ancient, the medieval, and the Renaissance.

2. The adjectival form of Descartes's name is "Cartesian" (as in "Cartesian doubt" or "Cartesian coordinate system").

3. René Descartes, *The Philosophical Works of Descartes, Vol. 1*, trans. Elizabeth S. Haldane and G. R. T. Ross (Cambridge: Cambridge University Press, 1911). "Meditation One" is reprinted with the permission of Cambridge University Press.

4. This is a question posed to Neo by Morpheus in the movie *The Matrix*.

5. If you were watching *Total Recall* for the first time, you may not have picked up on this. The scene in question occurs at the 16 minute mark. Ernie, the technician who is loading in the secret agent ego trip prior to implant, remarks, "That's a new one—blue sky on Mars."

6. Henceforth, I shall cite a minute mark as "MM."

7. From "Meditation Six—Concerning the Existence of Material Things, and the Real Distinction of the Mind from the Body," in *Meditations*.

8. See, for example, the third dialogue in *Three Dialogues between Hylas and Philonous*. As we shall see, Berkeley would have rejected the definition given earlier for *genuine*; however, I shall gloss over that point for the time being. Berkeley did talk about real versus imaginary perceptions, and as long as the reader has this general distinction in mind I don't believe there will be any difficulties in understanding.

9. David Hume, *A Treatise of Human Nature*, 2nd ed. (Oxford: Oxford University Press, 1978), 252–53 (book 1, part 4, section vi).

10. Note that the adjective *external* has been left off. This omission is intentional on my part. As we shall see, this whole way of talking and thinking (that is, about *external* objects, as opposed to objects *simpliciter*) is something that Berkeley rejects.

11. This is in the first dialogue in *Three Dialogues between Hylas and Philonous*.

12. George Berkeley, *A Treatise concerning the Principles of Human Knowledge* (London: Bobbs-Merrill, 1970), 248 (part 1, par. 6).

13. The "God response" is usually taken as Berkeley's considered answer. Passages stating outright or implying this route to solving the problem of unperceived objects can be found in both *A Treatise concerning the Principle of Human Knowledge* and the *Three Dialogues between Hylas and Philonous.*

14. Strictly speaking, according to Berkeley, God does not *perceive* (at least not in the same way we do). If anything, God is an active generator of perceptions, not a passive recipient of them. This fine point aside, I don't think anything of substance is lost by referring to God as a perceiver.

15. Immanuel Kant, *Critique of Pure Reason* (London: St. Martin's Press, 1929), Bxl. (Pagination in Kant's *Critique* is somewhat quirky. He made major revisions between the first and second editions, so the standard scholarly translations of the work differentiate between material written in the first edition—denoted by the letter *A* before the page number—and material written in the second edition—denoted by the letter *B* before the page number. Thus, the above quote is from the second edition preface, page xl.)

16. Ibid., Bxvi.

17. David Hume, *An Enquiry concerning Human Understanding* (Indianapolis, IN: Hackett, 1977), 110 (section 12, part 2).

18. For this line of reasoning in Hume, see his *Treatise*, book II, part 3, section iii.

19. Bertrand Russell, "The Value of Philosophy," in *The Problems of Philosophy* (Oxford: Oxford University Press, 1912), 91.

Chapter 2

1. Immanuel Kant, *Critique of Pure Reason* (London: St. Martin's Press, 1929), A51/B75. (As mentioned in Chapter 1, pagination in Kant's *Critique* uses the "A/B" notation to distinguish page numbers in the first versus the second editions of the work. Thus, this quote occurred on page 51 of the first edition and page 75 of the second edition.)

2. In my attempt to keep terminology consistent throughout this chapter, I have used the word *objective* to mean *mind-independent*. Those familiar with Kant will recognize that this usage does not comport with the way *objective* is standardly used in English translations of his *Critique of Pure Reason.*

3. It is cultural anthropological folklore that the part of the Eskimo conceptual scheme dealing with "snow" is markedly different from that of the average Anglo-American. Eskimos can make distinctions between types of snow that are indistinguishable to me. It's not that Eskimo sense organs are any different from mine; rather, the conceptual scheme that the average Eskimo uses is different from mine in some respects. The potential benefit to an Eskimo of this difference should be obvious.

4. This second reason is known as the Sapir-Whorf hypothesis, named after the linguists Edward Sapir (1884–1936) and Benjamin Lee Whorf (1897–1941).

5. Some cognitive relativists hold that pragmatic criteria (for example, the extent to which individuals with a given conceptual scheme thrive in their environment) are useful in judging conceptual schemes.

6. This is the opening sentence from Protagoras's book *On Truth*. It is the only surviving fragment from that work.

7. Taken out of context, it is unclear in this translation whether Protagoras intended "man" to refer to individuals or to humankind collectively. Other sources imply that Protagoras held a subjectivist version of relativism; thus, "man" should be interpreted as referring to an individual.

8. From Alasdair MacIntyre's APA presidential address, "Relativism, Power, and Philosophy," *Proceedings and Addresses of the American Philosophical Association* 49 (September 1985): 5.

9. The only other focus film in this book whose philosophical import is found in its structure is *Memento*.

10. Henceforth, I shall cite a minute mark—the number of minutes that have elapsed in the movie since the opening credits began—as "MM." A plot summary for each of the focus films, along with the minute marks for the important scenes, is given in the appendix.

11. I'm not sure what to make of the final flashback to the day at the beach, as we see for the first time that the person Jackie meets as a young girl is the adult Jackie.

12. The following is a reworking of the argument against relativism in James Rachels, *The Elements of Moral Philosophy*, 3d ed. (New York: McGraw-Hill, 1999).

13. Martin Hollis and Steven Lukes, *Rationality and Relativism* (Cambridge, MA: MIT Press, 1982), 10.

14. Walt Whitman, "Song of Myself," in *Leaves of Grass* (Philadelphia, PA: David McKay, 1891–92), 51.

15. See, for example, Arthur Danto's *Nietzsche as Philosopher* (New York: Columbia University Press, 1965), 97.

16. Friedrich Nietzsche, *Aus dem Nachlass der Achtzigerjahre*, vol. 3 of *Nietzsches Werke in Drei Bände*, Karl Schlechta, ed. (Munich: Carl Hanser Verlag, 1958), 903 and 705, respectively. These passages are as translated by Danto in *Nietzsche as Philosopher*.

17. Danto, *Nietzsche as Philosopher* (New York: Columbia University Press, 1965), 96.

18. Ibid., 80.

19. Friedrich Nietzsche, *Aus dem Nachlass*, 814.

20. Gene Blocker, "The Challenge of Post-Modernism," in *Introduction to Modern Philosophy*, 7th ed., ed. by Alburey Castell, Donald Borchert and Arthur Zucker (Englewood Cliffs, NJ: Prentice Hall, 2001), 554–55.

21. Alison Jaggar, "Love and Knowledge: Emotion in Feminist Epistemology," in Castell, Borchert, and Zucker, eds. *Introduction to Modern Philosophy*, 535.

22. Nietzsche, a postmodernist in all but name, held that a pragmatic criterion for judging adequacy was universally valid.

23. Blocker, "The Challenge of Post-Modernism," 558–59.

24. This series of experiments has been widely discussed. The original research findings were published in Bruner and Postman "On the Perception of Incongruity: A Paradigm," *Journal of Personality* 18 (1949): 206–23.

25. Thomas Kuhn, *The Structure of Scientific Revolutions* (Chicago: University of Chicago Press, 1962), 63.

26. The terms *paradigm* and *paradigm shift* as currently used are recent additions to the Anglo-American lexicon. They were introduced by Kuhn in the early 1960s.

27. Describing others as "living in different worlds" emerged as a locution in the 1920s with the writings of anthropologist and linguist Edward Sapir.

28. The criticism originates with Plato, in his discussion of Protagoras's views in the *Theaetetus*.

Chapter 3

1. This formulation of the meaning of afterlife is based on the one given by John Perry in *A Dialogue on Personal Identity* (Indianapolis, IN: Hackett, 1978).

2. The careful reader will have noticed that this way of talking presupposes some alternative way of determining identity.

3. These examples are updated versions of a thought experiment originally developed in ancient Greece by the philosopher Demetrius, a student of Aristotle. The original did not deal with a car, but rather a ship—the Ship of Theseus.

4. In an interview with *Entertainment Weekly* (June 15, 2001), *Memento*'s director Christopher Nolan suggested viewers don't worry themselves too much about whether the usual symptoms of anterograde amnesia are displayed by Leonard, but that they interpret his situation as "metaphor."

5. Notice that a difficulty has arisen already in how to refer to the lead character portrayed in *Memento* in a non-question-begging way. If I refer to him as "Leonard," I am already making assumptions about his identity. I could refer to him as "the character portrayed by the actor Guy Pearce," but that is rather clumsy. Unfortunately, there is no straightforward non-question-begging way to refer to that character other than by name. Be forewarned, though, that I do not mean to imply anything about his identity by this usage.

6. David Hume, *A Treatise of Human Nature* (Oxford: Oxford University Press, 1978), 252–53 (book 1, part 4, section vi).

7. This aspect of the problem of identity over time as applied to persons is worked out in greater detail in John Perry, *A Dialogue on Personal Identity and Immortality* (Indianapolis, IN: Hackett, 1978). (See the portion of the dialogue that takes place on the second night.)

8. Hereafter I shall cite a minute mark—the number of minutes that have elapsed in the movie since the opening credits began—as "MM."

9. Derek Parfit, *Reasons and Persons* (Oxford: Oxford University Press, 1984), 203.

10. "Cartesian dualism" is named after René Descartes, one of the philosophers whose views we discussed in chapter 1.

11. Parfit, *Reasons and Persons*, 287–88.

12. A good point of entry into this literature is Elizabeth Loftus and Katherine Ketcham, *Witness for the Defense* (New York: St. Martin's Press, 1991).

Chapter 4

1. Bruce Weber, "Swift and Slashing, Computer Topples Kasparov," *New York Times*, May 12, 1997.

2. There is some debate about who should be credited with the production of the first general-purpose programmable computer. Several different inventors working independently each developed prototypes in the early 1940s.

3. The distinction between "artificial" and "fake" is easier to see with another example: an *artificial* diamond is a real diamond made in the lab, whereas a *fake* diamond isn't a diamond at all.

4. IBM describes the evaluation function that Deep Blue (the chess program that unseated Garry Kasparov) uses at <http://www.research.ibm.com/deepblue/meet/html/d.3.2. html>.

5. Deep Blue modifies this brute force technique using a method called "pruning": it does an initial evaluation of the set of legal moves at a level, then prunes most of those moves, only looking into the future for those moves that hold promise according to this initial evaluation. Thus, it can search deeper than seven moves into the future, but can do so only for a small subset of moves.

6. René Descartes, *Discourse on Method*, part V, trans. Laurence Lafleur (New York: Bobbs-Merrill, 1960), 43.

7. See, for example Benjamin Beck, *Animal Tool Behavior: The Use and Manufacture of Tools by Animals* (New York: Garland Press, 1980).

8. See, for example, H. S. Terrace, L. A. Petitto, R. J. Sanders, and T. G. Bever, "Can an Ape Create a Sentence?" *Science* 206 (1979): 891–902.

9. Actually, Turing described this as a test for *intelligence*, not mindedness. Subsequent authors have tended to blur that distinction, and I shall follow their lead. The original description of the Turing test appeared in his "Computing Machinery and Intelligence," *Mind* 59 (1950): 433–60.

10. I've deviated in some places from Turing's original formulation of the test.

11. To compare the linguistic skills of robots depicted in *AI* with the current state-of-the-art computer programs that do natural language processing, an excellent source is the website that describes the Loebner Prize—a contest that puts some money behind the Turing test. The first computer (it's unclear who would "own" the money, the computer or the programmer) to "pass" will get $100,000. The URL for this site is <http://www.loebner.net/Prizef/ loebner-prize.html>.

12. Eliza was developed by Joe Weizenbaum in the 1960s and first described in his "ELIZA—a Computer Program for the Study of Natural Language Communication between Man and Machine," *Communications of the Association of Computing Machinery* 9 (1966): 36–45. Since then, virtually every book on the history of AI has discussed the Eliza program at length.

13. The following analysis of mindedness is borrowed from the discussion of massive adaptability in Copeland, *Artificial Intelligence*, chapter 3.

14. Hereafter I shall cite a minute mark—the number of minutes that have elapsed in the movie since the opening credits began—as "MM."

15. The analysis of consciousness into its three main senses is borrowed from chapter 8 of Copeland, *Artificial Intelligence*.

16. This argument was first described in John Searle's widely anthologized article "Minds, Brains and Programs," *Behavioral and Brain Sciences* 3 (1980): 417–24.

17. P* may be a complex property, that is, it may contain parts, as, for example, the property that defines bachelorhood has parts. An individual is a bachelor if and only if that individual has the property of being male and being human and being adult and being unmarried.

18. This view is closely associated with classical utilitarianism, an ethical theory we shall discuss in chapter 5.

19. For example, plutonium (both from decommissioned nuclear weapons and created as a by-product of civilian nuclear power plants) has a half-life of 25,000 years. It will take well over 25,000 years before this highly dangerous substance no longer poses a threat to humans and the environment.

Chapter 5

1. A variant on the standard version of moral subjectivism described above says that the individual whose moral code is to be used in making moral judgments is the speaker, not the actor. In that case, someone else could (truly) say of me that my eating meat was morally wrong if the speaker believed that eating meat was morally wrong.

2. There is a corresponding variant of cultural moral relativism, according to which moral judgments are true or false based on whether they are in agreement with the *speaker's* culture's moral standards.

3. I owe much of the material presented in this section to the treatment of moral relativism in James Rachels, *The Elements of Moral Philosophy*, 3rd ed. (New York: McGraw-Hill, 1999).

4. For those who know a bit of logic, this is the same as charging the argument with being invalid.

5. Since the argument from cultural norm diversity to cultural moral relativism has the same structural form as the argument discussed in section 2.3 from diversity of opinion to cognitive relativism, the same counterexample can be used to display the argument's invalidity.

6. The careful reader will have noticed that my criticism of the cultural moral relativist's argument assumes that there are objective facts—something that the thoroughgoing *cognitive* relativist denies. Since my purpose here is not to refute cultural moral relativism but only to show that the premises given in the argument do not entail the conclusion, my assumption does not constitute begging the question against relativism.

7. Hereafter I shall cite a minute mark—the number of minutes that have elapsed in the movie since the opening credits began—as "MM."

8. We'll come back a little later to look in detail at the issue of positive benefits arising from Judah's action.

9. John Stuart Mill, *Utilitarianism* (Indianapolis, IN: Hackett, 1979), 7.

10. Ibid., 7.

11. Ibid., 10.

12. A variant of moral egoism judges the moral status of an action based not on how well the *actor* fares, but on how well the *speaker* (i.e., the person making the moral judgment) fares.

13. You may recall that Kant's epistemological theory and its implications were among the topics of chapters 1 and 2, respectively.

14. Immanuel Kant, *Fundamental Principles of the Metaphysic of Morals,* trans. by Thomas Abbott (New York: Prometheus Books, 1987), 58.

15. There is a potential difficulty with squaring divine command theory and moral objectivism as it was defined in section 5.2 as the view that "there are moral facts that do not depend on what anyone . . . happens to think." This apparent inconsistency is dealt with by making a special case for God: God's will *can* ground an objectivist ethical theory.

16. In some respects, moral nihilism doesn't fit within this nice, tidy framework. I've included it as a version of moral relativism for convenience's sake.

17. Kant, *Fundamental Principles*, 17.

18. Kai Nielson, "Why Should I Be Moral?" *American Philosophical Quarterly* 21 (1984): 90.

19. William Lane Craig, "The Absurdity of Life without God." Originally in *Reasoning Faith: Christian Truth and Apologies*, reprinted in *The Meaning of Life*, 2nd edition, edited by E. D. Klemke (Oxford: Oxford University Press, 2000), 43–44.

Chapter 6

1. Pierre Laplace, *A Philosophical Essay on Probabilities*, trans. by Frederick Truscott and Frederick Emory (New York: Dover, 1951), 4.

2. Actually, it is not that the event in question is uncaused, but that it is probabilistic. The exact timing of the event is uncaused. The event is determined to happen eventually. What is uncaused is why it occurs now rather than later.

3. Albert Einstein to Max Born, September 7, 1944, in *The Born-Einstein Letters*, trans. by Irene Born (New York: Macmillan, 1971).

4. While the controversy within physics over the preferred interpretation of quantum mechanics is fascinating, going into more depth would take us too far afield, so I shall simply assert that quantum mechanics implies the falsity of universal determinism.

5. This discussion is drawn from Benjamin Libet "Unconscious Cerebral Initiative and the Role of Conscious Will in Voluntary Action," in *Behavioral and Brain Sciences* 8 (1985): 529–66. Similar findings were reported earlier by L. Deecke, B. Grözinger, and H. Kornhuber in "Voluntary Finger Movement in Man: Cerebral Potentials and Theory," *Biological Cybernetics* 23 (1976): 99–119.

6. You may be familiar with the notion of brain waves. For example, the brains of normal human subjects who are asleep but not dreaming show a characteristic slow wavelike pattern, depending on how deep the sleep is. The pattern of brain activity changes once dreaming begins. These "patterns" are measured with an EEG—an electroencephalograph.

7. Occasionally, this characteristic EEG pattern was not followed by the actual movement. In such instances, the subject reported feeling the urge to perform the action, then consciously vetoing that choice just before the movement would have occurred. So, it is not the case that the brain activity picked up by the EEG is the immediate cause of the movement.

8. Benjamin Libet, "Unconscious Cerebral Initiative," 536.

9. Robert Nozick, *Philosophical Explanations* (Cambridge, MA: Harvard University Press, 1981), 293.

10. Lucretius, *The Nature of the Universe*, book 2, lines 250–55, first published circa 55 B.C.E. This version is from the translation by Ronald Latham (New York: Penguin, 1951).

11. Jean-Paul Sartre, *Being and Nothingness*, trans. by Hazel Barnes (New York: Philosophical Library, 1956), 435.

12. Saul Smilansky, "Can a Determinist Respect Herself?" in *Freedom and Moral Responsibility*, eds. Charles Manekin and Menachem Kellner (College Park, MD: University of Maryland Press, 1997), 92–94.

13. Hereafter I shall cite a minute mark—the number of minutes that have elapsed in the movie since the opening credits began—as "MM."

14. In the United States, laws governing the use of the insanity defense differ from one state to another. I describe here the most common version.

15. For a very illuminating and in-depth treatment of this topic, see chapter 6 in Dirk Pereboom, *Living without Free Will* (Cambridge: Cambridge University Press, 2001).

16. Daniel Dennett, *Elbow Room* (Cambridge, MA: MIT Press, 1984), 14.

17. It is part of folklore surrounding early attempts at thoracic surgery that curare was used on a few human subjects based on the misconception that it caused unconsciousness; however, I can find no scholarly source to corroborate this claim. A synthetic form of curare does find use in modern surgery in conjunction with local or general anesthesia.

18. In section 3.13 of *Nichomachean Ethics*, Aristotle gives a similar example and argues that an action done under duress in not necessarily involuntary.

19. Frankfurt's view has shifted over the years. The view I attribute to him here is the view he espoused in his 1971 paper "Freedom of the Will and the Concept of a Person," included in *Free Will*, ed. Gary Watson (Oxford: Oxford University Press, 1982).

20. For a discussion of where Frankfurt's hierarchical approach goes wrong, see chapter 3 in Laura Ekstrom, *Free Will* (Boulder: Westview Press, 2000).

Chapter 7

1. Epicurus (341–270 B.C.E.) writes, "Is he [God] willing to prevent evil, but not able? Then he is impotent. Is he able, but not willing? Then he is malevolent. Is he both able and willing? Whence then is evil?"

2. This argument is most closely associated with Thomas Aquinas (1225–1274). It is one from a cluster of arguments for theism referred as the "cosmological argument."

3. This argument is most closely associated with William Paley (1743–1805), who gave it its most famous formulation, and David Hume (1711–1776), who attacked it. It is also known as the "teleological argument."

4. Bertrand Russell, "The Essence of Religion" in *The Basic Writings of Bertrand Russell* (New York: Touchstone, 1963), 569.

5. Rev. 8:1–9:6, Revised Standard Version.

6. Rev. 21:1–4, Revised Standard Version.

7. Hereafter I shall cite a minute mark—the number of minutes that have elapsed in the movie since the opening credits began—as "MM."

8. That God knew this would happen—it was all a part of God's plan, right from the beginning—is implied by a later passage: "and the dwellers on earth whose names have not been written in the book of life from the foundation of the world . . ." (Rev. 17:8). For reference to God's foreknowledge of who would be saved and who would not, see also Rom. 8:29, and Eph. 1:4. There is considerable debate among philosophers of religion concerning whether human free will rules out God's foreknowledge.

9. This is how Bergman described this image in his original screenplay for *The Seventh Seal*. Quoted in Bergman, *Four Screenplays*, trans. Lars Malmstrom and David Kushner (New York: Simon and Schuster, 1960).

10. The view that reason in inapplicable to issues of religious faith is called *fideism*. One of its most ardent supporters is the nineteenth-century Danish philosopher Søren Kierkegaard.

11. Arthur Gibson, *The Silence of God* (New York: Harper and Row, 1969), 30.

12. The initial formulation of the free will defense is attributed to Saint Augustine (354–430 C.E.). Whether he is its actual originator is debatable. Clearly, though, it was his influence as an early church leader that brought about its acceptance as orthodoxy within Christianity. The way the free will defense is presented in this section is based on J. L. Mackie, "Evil and Omnipotence," *Mind* 64, no. 254 (1955): 200–12.

13. Edward Madden, "The Many Faces of Evil," in *Philosophical Issues*, eds. James Rachels and Frank Tillman (New York: Harper and Row, 1972), 472.

14. This is a paraphrase of Ivan's speech from Dostoevsky's *The Brothers Karamazov*, quoted in Madden, "The Many Faces of Evil," 473.

15. Mark 10:15, Revised Standard Version.

16. Much of this section draws from Madden's "The Many Faces of Evil."

17. As mentioned previously, there is some debate among philosophers of religion concerning whether human free will makes this sort of foreknowledge on God's part impossible. Unfortunately, the scope of this chapter precludes addressing this topic at length.

Chapter 8

1. Leo Tolstoy, "My Confession," in *My Confession, My Religion*, trans. Isabel Hapgood (Midland, MI: Avensblume Press, 1994), 16.

2. Albert Camus, *The Myth of Sisyphus*, trans. Justin O'Brien (New York: Alfred A. Knopf, 1955), 3.

3. Thomas Nagel, *What Does It All Mean? A Very Short Introduction to Philosophy* (Oxford: Oxford University Press, 1987), 99–100.

4. Hereafter I shall cite a minute mark—the number of minutes that have elapsed in the movie since the opening credits began—as "MM."

5. Albert Camus, "An Absurd Reasoning," in *The Myth of Sisyphus*, 21.

6. Albert Camus, "The Myth of Sisyphus," in *The Myth of Sisyphus*, 122.

7. Jean-Paul Sartre, *Existentialism*, trans. Bernard Frechtman (New York: Philosophical Library, 1947), 25–27.

8. Friedrich Nietzsche, *The Gay Science*, in *The Portable Nietzsche*, ed. and trans. Walter Kaufmann (New York: Penguin, 1976), 95.

9. Albert Camus, "An Absurd Reasoning," in *The Myth of Sisyphus*, 6.

10. Albert Camus, introduction to *The Myth of Sisyphus*, 4.

Appendix

Story Lines of Films by Elapsed Time

Total Recall (total running time: 113 minutes)

Minute Mark	Story Item
0:00	Credits begin.
2:20	Opening scene—on Mars.
3:15	Quaid awakens.
5:20	Quaid watches TV—breakfast-time newscast about rebel attack on Mars.
6:20	Quaid asks Lori (wife) about moving to Mars.
8:15	**Quaid:** I want more than this. . . . I want to be somebody.
9:10	Quaid sees ad for Rekall on subway. Rekall's motto: "For the memory of a lifetime."
11:30	Quaid goes to Rekall.
13:00	**Salesman (Bob)** (describing memory package): As real as any memory in your head. . . . Guaranteed, or your money back.
14:30	Quaid picks out secret agent ego trip.
16:00	**Ernie (the technician):** That's a new one—blue sky on Mars.
17:10	Picture of Melina flashes on monitor as woman that will be in ego trip.
17:40	"Schizoid embolism"—Quaid goes berserk.
20:00	Quaid regains consciousness in taxi.
21:00	Quaid is attacked by coworker and others.
23:00	Quaid returns home.
24:00	Quaid is attacked by Lori.
26:00	Lori explains, "Our marriage was just an implant." The implant was performed six weeks ago.
26:30	**Lori:** Sorry, Quaid, your whole life is just a dream.
31:00	Quaid escapes in subway.
33:40	Quaid receives call from man with suitcase.
37:30	Quaid opens suitcase.
43:00	Quaid arrives on Mars in disguise.

50:00	Quaid arrives at hotel on Mars—looks at contents of safety deposit box.
52:00	Quaid meets taxi driver (Benny)—they go to Venusville.
55:30	Quaid meets Melina.
57:40	**Melina** (on hearing of switched identities): This is too weird!
59:30	Dr. Edgemar from Rekall knocks at hotel door.

Edgemar: You're not really standing here right now. . . . You're not here, and neither am I. You're strapped into the implant chair at Rekall.

Quaid (reaching out and touching Edgemar): That's amazing!

Edgemar: Think about it. Your dream started in the middle of the implant procedure. Everything after that . . . are all elements of your Rekall secret agent ego trip. You paid to be a secret agent. . . . And what about the girl? Brunette, athletic, sleazy, and demure. Is she coincidence?

62:00	Lori enters.
65:00	Quaid kills Edgemar.
66:00	Melina saves Quaid.
67:30	Quaid kills Lori.
69:40	Melina and Quaid get ride with Benny (same taxi driver) back to Venusville.
78:00	Quato appears.
79:00	**Quato:** You are what you do.
82:30	Quato is shot by Benny.
83:45	Quaid and Cohaagen meet. Quaid-the-perfect-mole plan is explained to Quaid.
85:40	Cohaagen plays tape of Hauser.
86:40	**Hauser:** Maybe we'll meet in our dreams. You never know!
89:30	Quaid gets loose. He and Melina escape.
92:30	Benny tries to kill Quaid and Melina.
94:30	Quaid kills Benny. He and Melina find reactor.
99:45	Quaid and Cohaagen meet again at reactor switch—Quaid turns on reactor.
103:30	Reactor starts creating Martian atmosphere.
106:30	Blue sky appears on Mars.
108:10	Final scene—conversation as Melina and Quaid look out over Mars:

Melina: I can't believe it, it's like a dream. What's wrong?

Quaid: I just had a terrible thought. What if this *is* a dream?

Melina: Then kiss me before you wake up.

108:40	Fade to white. Credits roll.

The Matrix (total running time: 136 minutes)

Minute Mark	*Story Item*
0:00	Warner Brothers logo.
1:50	Police enter room with Trinity.
2:15	Agents arrive.
5:45	Trinity gets to phone booth just as it is run over by truck.
6:45	Neo asleep on couch. He awakens.
7:10	Message on screen: "Wake up, Neo."
7:40	Knock at Neo's door.
9:00	**Neo:** Ever had that feeling where you're not sure if you're awake or still dreaming?
9:40	Neo and others at party.
10:00	Trinity greets Neo.
12:00	Neo wakes, goes to work.
13:00	Neo (Thomas Anderson) at work in cubicle—receives FedEx package containing cell phone.
13:30	Cell phone rings—call from Morpheus warning of agents.
14:00	Morpheus guides Neo out.
16:45	Neo taken into custody.
20:30	Interrogation scene.
21:30	Neo awakens.
21:45	Phone rings; it's Morpheus.
22:45	Neo picked up by Trinity.
24:30	Removal of bug.
25:40	Neo and Morpheus meet face-to-face.
26:30	**Morpheus:** You have the look of a man who accepts what he sees, because he is expecting to wake up. Ironically, this is not far from the truth.
28:00	**Morpheus:** It [the matrix] is the world that has been pulled over your eyes to blind you from the truth.
29:30	Neo chooses red pill.
31:30	**Morpheus:** Have you ever had a dream, Neo, that you were so sure was real? What if you were unable to wake from that dream? How would you know the difference between the dream world and the real one?

32:20	The "real" Neo awakens in the vat. Neo looks around and sees huge number of other, similar vats.
34:20	Neo "flushed."
35:00	Neo is aboard Morpheus's ship.
35:15	**Morpheus:** Welcome to the real world.
37:00	Neo awakes, still aboard ship. Morpheus explains that it is approximately 2199.
39:15	Neo enters construct.
40:00	**Neo** (feeling sofa): This isn't real?
41:30	Morpheus explains history and current condition of human species.
43:00	**Morpheus:** The matrix is a computer-generated dream world. **Neo:** No, it's not possible. Neo exits from construct and becomes sick.
46:00	Morpheus says he believes Neo is "the One."
48:20	Neo begins training.
49:00	Morpheus and Neo meet in sparring program.
54:00	Morpheus and Neo switch to jump program. **Morpheus:** You have to let it all go, Neo—fear, doubt, disbelief.
57:00	Morpheus and Neo enter training program similar to matrix. Morpheus explains role of agents within matrix.
59:00	The ship is attacked by sentinels.
63:30	Dinner conversation between agent and Cipher.
65:00	Breakfast onboard.
65:30	Conversation about switched perceptions.
67:30	Neo reenters matrix.
68:00	Neo looks out car window as they are driving through familiar area. **Neo:** I have all these memories from my life. None of them happened.
73:00	Neo meets the oracle.
78:30	Neo sees double black cat.
79:00	They are trapped in building.
81:00	They hide inside wall.
84:45	Agents capture Morpheus.
86:00	Cipher shoots Tank and Dozer.
90:45	Tank kills Cipher.
92:00	Agent interrogates Morpheus.
98:40	Neo and Trinity reenter matrix to free Morpheus.
101:30	Neo and Trinity begin break-in.
109:40	Helicopter rescue of Morpheus.
113:00	Morpheus gets back to ship.
114:00	Trinity gets back. Fight between agent and Neo begins.

121:20	Sentinels attack ship.
122:30	Agent shoots Neo.
127:30	Neo comes to on ship.
128:00	Computer and Neo's voice. SYSTEM FAILURE message.
128:30	Neo hangs up phone, back in 1999 world.
129:00	Credits roll.

Hilary and Jackie (total running time: 124 minutes)

Minute Mark	Story Item
0:00	October Films logo.
1:20	Scene at seashore with the young Hilary and Jackie.
2:30	Children see woman in distance. Jackie walks over to her.
3:30	Words "Hilary and Jackie" flash on screen.
3:40	Mother writes "Holiday Song."
4:30	Jackie awakens to find score; the girls play it.
5:50	Mother at piano. Children "dancing."
6:30	Mother reads letter from BBC asking her to conduct and Hilary to play.
7:10	Recording of Haydn's "Toy Symphony."
8:20	**Mother** (scolding, to Jackie): If you want to play with Hilary, you've got to play as good as Hilary.
8:30	Jackie applies herself to practicing.
9:15	Hilary and Jackie play (together) at competition.
10:30	Hilary and Jackie play (separately) at competition.
12:15	Jackie wins, to standing ovation. Hilary also wins.
13:30	Hilary storms out of auditorium and hides.
14:00	Photographer and Jackie.
15:00	Jackie has first private lesson. Hilary outside, dejected looking.
17:40	Jackie (now played by Emily Watson) has cello lesson at home. Hilary (now played by Rachel Griffiths) dejected-looking on stairs.
18:30	Jackie's cello teacher to arrange first public performance.
19:00	Jackie gives concert, to standing ovation.
20:30	Reception after the concert. Jackie presented with cello.
21:00	**Cello Teacher** (on presenting the cello to Jackie): It will give you the world, Jackie, but you must give it yourself.
21:30	Sisters dancing at wedding reception.
22:40	Sisters in bed, drinking afterward.
23:20	Word "Hilary" flashes on screen.

23:40   Hilary wakes up the next morning. Jackie is gone.

24:10   Hilary at Royal Academy of Music audition. Teacher discouraging.

27:00   Hilary very excited when parcel from Jackie arrives. Excitement turns to disappointment (especially for Hilary) when contents turn out to be laundry.

27:50   Hilary meets Kiffer.

28:30   Hilary fails exam miserably.

29:15   Hilary sits outside house in rain.

30:55   Kiffer barges in.

31:20   Jackie meets Kiffer.

32:15   Nighttime conversation between sisters.

33:20   Hilary performs, Kiffer conducts.

35:20   Second nighttime conversation. Hilary comes in late and announces her engagement to Kiffer.

38:20   Hilary and Kiffer marry.

39:15   Jackie brings Danny home. Jackie acts differently.

40:00   Jackie announces they plan to get married and that she plans to convert to Judaism.

41:15   News coverage of Jackie and Danny, including their marriage.

42:40   Several years later. Hilary (now living in farmhouse with Kiffer and two children) pastes news clippings in scrapbook.

43:20   Hilary and Kiffer start to have sex in back of car.

44:40   Jackie arrives at farmhouse alone.

45:40   Everyone is quite drunk that evening. Tapping music on wine glasses.

46:20   Conversation: Jackie tells Hilary she wants to sleep with Kiffer.

47:45   Jackie comes into Hilary and Kiffer's bedroom.

48:30   Outside of house the next morning—who is going to get the cheese?

50:30   Hilary finds Jackie hysterical.

50:50   **Jackie** (screaming): Get away from me. You don't love me. Nobody loves me. All I want is a fuck.

51:20   Hilary asks Kiffer if he will have sex with Jackie.

52:00   Danny arrives.

54:00   Danny offers to buy house nearby. Jackie responds with raspberry sound. Danny leaves.

55:20   Kiffer has sex with Jackie. Hilary hears creaking bed—goes to sleep with daughter.

56:00   Morning after, in kitchen.

57:00   Jackie thanks Hilary.

57:45   Beginning of home movies. Mother visiting. Jackie looking more like the wife and mother. (Unclear where home movies ends and "real life" picks up again.)

59:00   Kiffer throws ball, hits Hilary. Hilary walks away.

60:00   Kiffer has sex with Hilary.

61:00   Jackie plays cello. Hilary tries to talk to her.

62:30   Jackie leaves. Jackie remembers previous events—the two of them at the seashore as children, dancing at the wedding in Italy, night of drinking.

63:30   Word "Jackie" flashes on screen.

64:10   Jackie awoken morning after wedding to catch train.

65:00   Backstage. Jackie gives performance in "German."

66:00   Jackie tries unsuccessfully to call home.

67:00   Jackie kicks cello.

68:00   Jackie tries to get clothes washed.

68:30   Jackie leaves cello in direct sunlight.

69:10   Jackie studies cello in Moscow.

69:45   Jackie says she doesn't really want to play the cello.

71:00   Jackie gets package—cleaned clothes. She is overjoyed.

71:30   Jackie leaves cello outside in snow and lays on bed, surrounded by clothes.

72:30   Cello back inside.

72:50   Jackie back home. Kiffer barges in and announces, "I'm in love with Hilary."
         Beginning of voice-over of "same" nighttime conversation between Hilary and Jackie, when Hilary announces her engagement.

74:00   Jackie "forgets" cello in back of taxi on way to party, where she meets Danny for the first time.

76:30   Jackie starts to play. Danny stays.

77:20   Jackie and Danny in bed together.

78:40   Jackie thanks, and apologizes, to cello.

79:00   Jackie and Danny at recording session.

80:20   Jackie has cold hands. (First symptoms?)

81:50   Jackie, with perception somewhat altered, drops bow.

82:40   Jackie's hand shaking noticeably.

83:20   Conversation in hotel room as they are packing up to leave.

84:20   Danny walks out of room to find that Jackie has disappeared.
         Jackie arrives at Kiffer and Hilary's farmhouse.

85:00   Jackie, dejected-looking, curled up on bed.
         Kiffer comes in and comforts her.
         Home movies.
         Jackie leaves.

85:50   Jackie urinates on herself. She is very frightened.

87:00   Jackie in concert. Perception very altered.

88:40   Jackie can't get up at end of concert.

89:20	Jackie in hospital, announces she has MS.
90:00*	Hilary visits Jackie in hospital. Jackie insults her.
92:00	Hilary and parents in hospital waiting room.
92:40*	Jackie and Danny playing together.
	Danny helps Jackie with physical therapy.
93:00	Danny tells her of job offer in Paris.
96:00	Parents visit Jackie.
97:00	Jackie tries to play cello, but can't.
97:15	Jackie plays drum in concert of Haydn's "Toy Symphony"—even more altered perception.
	Jackie reports she is losing her hearing.
100:20*	Family conversation in car.
101:30*	Jackie answers phone. It's Danny. Sound of baby crying.
103:30	Jackie shaking badly, can barely talk. Mother visits.
104:20	Jackie plays record of her performing Elgar's cello concerto.
106:20	Violent storm. Jackie shaking in bed. Danny comforts her. Jackie screams.
107:00*	Hilary wakes with a start.
	Hilary and younger brother Piers arrive.
107:40	Hilary goes back in with Jackie. Danny leaves.
110:30	Hilary reminds Jackie of day on beach, when there were children.
111:40	Car ride back. Jackie's death announced on radio.
	Hilary asks Piers to stop the car.
	Flashback through several ages to day at beach.
113:40	Young Jackie walks over to adult Jackie.
115:00	Credits roll.

(* denotes a clear change of perspective in narrative)

Being John Malkovich (total running time: 112 minutes)

Minute Mark	*Story Item*
0:00	Credits begin.
0:50	Curtains open on puppet show.
3:00	Craig wakes up.
4:45	Craig on street doing puppet show.
8:45	Craig arrives for interview on 7½ floor.
12:45	Craig arrives for orientation.
20:50	Craig meets Dr. Lester at juice bar.
21:45	Craig meets Maxine at bar.
25:00	Craig explains why he likes puppeteering: to be inside someone else— seeing what they see, feeling what they feel.

27:30	Craig pulls away filing cabinet revealing door.
29:30	Craig "becomes" John Malkovich.
32:00	Craig is spit out.
33:30	**Craig:** It raises all sorts of philosophical-type questions, you know, about the nature of the self, about the existence of a soul. Am I me? Is Malkovich Malkovich? . . . Do you see what a metaphysical can of worms this portal is?
34:40	Maxine calls with business proposition.
37:15	Lotte "becomes" John Malkovich (JM).
41:50	Lotte comes to work and meets Maxine.
44:30	Lotte becomes JM for the second time.
45:00	Maxine calls JM.
46:00	Lotte feels herself (at least partially) "in control."
47:15	Maxine and JM (with Lotte inside) meet at restaurant. On being asked why he came, JM reports feeling "oddly compelled."
49:30	JM, Inc., gets its first paying customer.
51:20	Maxine comes over for dinner at Craig and Lotte's.
54:10	Business at JM, Inc., is brisk.
55:15	Maxine arrives at JM's house (with Lotte inside).
60:00	Craig attacks Lotte and makes her call Maxine.
62:20	Maxine arrives at rehearsal.
63:30	JM feels forced to be puppet.
64:20	JM explains experience of being puppet.
66:20	JM tails Maxine and learns of JM, Inc.
67:30	**JM:** What type of service does this company provide? **Customer:** You get to be John Malkovich for fifteen minutes for two hundred clams.
69:15	JM enters the portal.
75:00	Elijah (the chimp) has flashback to his capture.
76:30	**Maxine:** This is a very confusing situation.
77:50	Maxine meets JM (with Craig inside).
79:00	Lotte goes to visit Dr. Lester.
81:40	Craig has absolute control over JM's body.
88:20	"Eight months later" flashes on screen.
96:00	Lester calls JM/Craig.
98:00	Lotte and Maxine arrive in JM's subconscious.
99:15	Lotte and Maxine are spit out of portal.
101:50	Craig leaves JM.
102:00	The others enter portal.
104:10	"Seven years later."
106:40	Credits roll.

Memento (total running time: 116 minutes)

Memento can be a very disorienting movie the first time you see it. In the summary below, I have indicated which scenes "match up" by listing them in **boldface** and giving the minute mark (MM) of the other occurrence of the scene. Since the scenes shot in black and white are important for marking off the backward-progressing scenes, they have also been identified, with ****(B/W)**.

Minute Mark	*Story Item*
0:00	Credits begin (Newmarket logo).
0:45	Leonard holds photo while it undevelops.
2:00	Leonard takes photo.
2:30	**Leonard shoots Teddy** (see scene at 6:20 MM—same scene).
2:30	****(B/W)**—Leonard in motel room with voice-over.
3:00	**Teddy meets Leonard in motel lobby** (see 10:00 MM).
4:00	Teddy and Leonard drive to abandoned warehouse.
5:30	Leonard looks at back of Teddy's picture.
6:20	**Leonard shoots Teddy** (see 2:30 MM).
6:21	****(B/W)** more voice-over in motel room
7:00	**Leonard writes on back of Teddy's picture "KILL HIM"** (see 16:00 MM).
8:30	Leonard explains his condition to man at motel desk.
10:00	**Teddy meets Leonard in motel lobby** (see 3:00 MM).
10:01	****(B/W)** more voice-over in motel room.
11:00	**Leonard in washroom—tries to wash off tattoo** (see 22:00 MM).
12:45	Leonard looks through envelope contents—sees driver's license record for Teddy (John Gammell). Leonard calls Teddy.
15:00	Leonard writes "HE'S THE ONE" on back of Teddy's picture.
16:00	**Leonard writes on back of Teddy's picture "KILL HIM"** (see 7:00 MM).
16:10	****(B/W)** Leonard is talking on the phone about Sammy Jankis.
17:30	**Leonard meets Natalie at diner** (see 26:30 MM).
20:00	Natalie asks Leonard to describe his wife.
21:00	Natalie suggests Leonard "handle" John G. at location—she gives him address. Natalie returns Leonard's motel room key.
22:00	**Leonard in washroom—tries to wash off tattoo** (see 11:00 MM).
22:01	****(B/W)** Leonard is talking on the phone about Sammy Jankis. (Leonard also describes his job as insurance claim investigator.)

23:00	**Leonard meets Teddy outside house** (see 31:45 MM). Teddy and Leonard eat lunch together. Leonard explains why he trusts his notes, not memory.
25:30	Motel clerk explains about two rooms.
26:30	**Leonard meets Natalie at diner** (see 17:30 MM).
26:31	****(B/W)** Leonard is talking on the phone about Sammy Jankis, with long flashback.
28:30	Leonard wakes up in bed with Natalie. Natalie says she knows someone who can get driver's license record; she sets up appointment for that afternoon with Leonard.
31:45	**Leonard meets Teddy outside house** (see 23:00 MM).
31:50	****(B/W)** Leonard is talking on the phone.
32:30	**Leonard arrives at Natalie's—asks about Dodd** (see 44:50 MM). **Leonard:** Something doesn't feel right. I think someone's fucking with me—trying to get me to kill the wrong guy.
36:00	Natalie and Leonard at Natalie's, talking. Natalie shows picture of her and Jimmy.
38:30	Later that night, Leonard gets up and writes on back of Natalie's picture "SHE HAS ALSO LOST SOMEONE. SHE WILL HELP YOU OUT OF PITY." He then gets back into bed with her.
39:20	****(B/W)** Leonard is talking on the phone; has flashback to crime.
40:00	**Leonard lying on motel room bed, asleep** (see 48:50 MM).
41:00	Leonard discovers Dodd bound and gagged, just as Teddy arrives.
43:30	Teddy helps Leonard "deal with" Dodd.
44:20	Dodd is let out of car.
44:50	**Leonard arrives at Natalie's—asks about Dodd** (see 32:30 MM).
44:51	****(B/W)** Leonard is talking on the phone; he takes out a needle.
46:00	**Leonard sitting on toilet seat, holding bottle** (see 52:00 MM). Leonard takes shower, then hears someone come in.
47:00	Leonard attacks Dodd, takes his picture, then leaves message on Teddy's answering machine asking for help.
48:40	Leonard lies down on bed.
48:50	**Leonard lying on motel room bed, asleep** (see 40:00 MM).
48:51	****(B/W)** Leonard is talking on the phone. The person he's talking to hangs up; Leonard starts preparing to apply tattoo.
49:30	**Leonard is running** (see 52:30 MM).
49:40	Leonard is being chased by Dodd.
50:00	Leonard goes to Dodd's motel room.
52:00	**Leonard sitting on toilet seat, holding bottle** (see 46:00 MM).
52:01	****(B/W)** Leonard is preparing to apply tattoo.

52:15   **Leonard is in deserted area (early morning). He stamps out fire** (see 56:30 MM).

52:20   Leonard is driving a Jaguar. Dodd begins attack.

52:30   **Leonard is running** (see 49:30 MM).

52:31   ****(B/W)** Leonard is preparing to apply tattoo when the phone rings.

54:00   **Leonard goes to car with bag of belongings** (see 59:00 MM). He drives to deserted area and burns them.

56:30   **Leonard is in deserted area (early morning). He stamps out fire** (see 52:15 MM).

56:31   ****(B/W)** Leonard talks on phone—gets evidence related to crime.

57:45   **Leonard is asleep. Wakes to sound of door shutting** (see 62:30 MM).

58:50   Leonard tells prostitute to leave.

59:00   **Leonard goes to car with bag of belongings** (see 54:00 MM).

59:01   ****(B/W)** Leonard talks on phone—more leads. Changes "Fact 5."

60:00   **Leonard takes picture of motel sign** (see 68:30 MM).

61:00   Leonard calls up escort service. Prostitute arrives.

61:30   Leonard explains what he wants.

62:30   **Leonard is asleep. Wakes to sound of door shutting** (see 57:45 MM).

62:31   ****(B/W)** Leonard tattoos "FACT 5"; talks about Sammy Jankis's "test."

65:00   **Leonard gets into his car. Teddy is already in it** (see 73:00 MM). Teddy gives him name of motel. Teddy and Leonard talk about Natalie and Leonard's weirdness.

68:30   **Leonard takes picture of motel sign** (see 60:00 MM).

68:40   ****(B/W)** Leonard talking. Unbandages tattoo "NEVER ANSWER THE PHONE."

69:00   **Leonard is at Natalie's as Natalie comes in.** (see 76:40 MM). Natalie comes in. (She's been beaten.) She says Dodd did it. Leonard offers to help. Natalie writes Dodd's address and description. Leonard leaves Natalie's.

73:00   **Leonard gets into his car. Teddy is already in it** (see 65:00 MM).

73:01   ****(B/W)** Leonard doesn't answer ringing phone.

73:30   **Natalie arrives at her house. Leonard is inside** (see 81:00 MM). Natalie is busy removing all the writing implements.

75:00   Natalie provokes Leonard into striking her. She leaves.

76:30   Leonard is frantically searching for a pen.

76:40   **Leonard is at Natalie's as Natalie comes in** (see 69:00 MM).

77:10   ****(B/W)** Leonard is straining to hear. Motel clerk comes—announces cop is trying to call Leonard.

78:00	Leonard is at Natalie's, talking about his wife.
80:00	Leonard takes Natalie's picture as she is leaving.
81:00	**Natalie arrives at her house. Leonard is inside** (see 73:30 MM).
81:40	****(B/W)** Leonard is in motel room. Envelope appears under door. Picture of triumphant Leonard inside.
82:30	**Leonard drinks beer** (see 85:30 MM).
83:00	****(B/W)** Leonard excitedly talking on phone.
83:40	**Leonard looks at coaster with note on back** (see 93:40 MM). Leonard goes into bar.
	Natalie: You're that memory guy.
	Natalie tests him with beer.
85:30	**Leonard drinks beer** (see 82:30 MM).
86:30	****(B/W)** Leonard talking on phone. Tells what happened to Sammy Jankis. Flashback with picture in institution.
90:00	**Leonard is in tattoo parlor** (see 110:00 MM).
	Teddy arrives—suggests Leonard leave town. **Teddy:** Your business here is done.
92:00	Teddy says phone calls coming from "bad cop."
	Leonard exits parlor via washroom window.
93:30	Leonard arrives outside bar. Natalie mistakes him for Jimmy.
93:40	**Leonard looks at coaster with note on back** (see 83:40 MM).
93:50	****(B/W) from here until minute mark 100:00.**
	Leonard talking on phone. Leonard meets Teddy in lobby: "Officer Gammell?" Leonard takes Teddy's picture. Teddy gives Leonard information on Jimmy. Leonard leaves in his pickup truck. Leonard arrives at deserted warehouse. Enters building.
97:15	Jimmy arrives and enters warehouse. Leonard confronts Jimmy. Jimmy was expecting Teddy.
99:00	Leonard kills Jimmy by strangulation, then takes his picture. Leonard puts Jimmy's clothes on.
100:00	**Switchover to color.** Teddy arrives, flashes badge.
102:00	Teddy tells Leonard *he* is really Sammy Jankis.
104:00	Teddy tells Leonard he has already killed wife's rapist.
105:45	Leonard looks through his pocket of photos. Sees picture of himself triumphant.
107:00	**Leonard:** I should kill you. Leonard throws Teddy's keys in bushes. Leonard writes "Don't believe his lies" on back of Teddy's picture. Leonard burns pictures (of Jimmy, and himself, triumphant), writes down Teddy's car's license number.
108:00	**Leonard:** You can be my John G.

Leonard takes Jaguar.

110:00   Flashback of Leonard (with tattoos+) and wife. Leonard drives to tattoo parlor.

110:10   **Leonard is in tattoo parlor** (see 90:00 MM).

110:20   Credits roll.

AI: Artificial Intelligence (total running time: 145 minutes)

Minute Mark	*Story Item*
0:00	Warner Brothers logo.
1:00	Explanation of recent history in voice-over.
2:00	Professor Hobby's presentation describing David.
7:00	Twenty months later—Henry and Monica visit Martin in cryo-vat.
9:00	Physician and Henry discuss Martin's prognosis and Monica.
9:30	Professor Hobby and others discuss who is to "adopt" David.
10:00	Henry presents Monica with David.
13:00	Henry explains about imprinting procedure.
18:00	The family at the dinner table.
19:45	David "laughs" at spaghetti.
21:45	Monica starts imprinting protocol.
23:40	Protocol imprinting works.
29:40	Martin recovers.
34:00	Martin suggests Monica read *Pinocchio*.
36:30	David eats spinach.
39:00	Martin dares David to cut lock of Monica's hair. Henry wants to return David.
42:30	Pool party incident.
46:00	Monica sees David's letters to her.
47:15	Monica and David "go for a ride in the country."
50:00	Monica abandons David in the woods near Cybertronics.
52:30	Fade in on Gigolo Joe and trick.
56:30	Joe enters on murder scene.
58:00	David and Teddy in woods—they come upon mecha parts dump.
60:00	Hunters for Flesh Fair.
64:30	David and the others are caught.
65:40	At the Flesh Fair.
77:00	The crowd turns against emcee—David and Joe escape.
83:00	David and Joe get ride to Rouge City.

85:30	Visit to Dr. Know.
92:00	Joe explains relationship between humans and robots.
94:30	David and Joe steal helicopter and travel to Manhattan.
98:00	David and Joe arrive at Cybertronics.
99:00	David meets another David and destroys him.
102:00	Professor Hobby explains his experiment to David.
104:00	David sees room full of robots.
107:10	David jumps off building into water.
112:00	David finds the Blue Fairy, then is trapped by falling Ferris wheel.
115:20	2,000 years later—David and Teddy are rescued.
121:30	David awakens in his old house.
131:30	Monica is re-created for one day only.
138:20	Credits roll.

Crimes and Misdemeanors (total running time: 104 minutes)

Minute Mark	Story Item
0:00	Orion logo—opening credits roll.
1:15	Judah introduced at banquet.
2:15	Flashback to earlier in day, as Judah reads Delores's letter.
4:00	Judah throws Delores's letter in fire.
4:40	**Judah:** The eyes of God are watching you.
5:30	Judah confronts Delores in her apartment.
7:15	Cliff and Jenny (niece) at the movies.
9:40	Lester's party.
12:50	Judah, driving in car, has flashback to initial meeting with Delores.
13:50	Conversation between Ben and Judah.
17:40	Delores has flashback to jogging on beach with Judah.
18:45	Judah arrives at Delores's apartment.
21:20	Delores threatens to expose their affair and Judah's embezzlement.
22:30	"Interview" with Lester.
25:50	Halley and Cliff watch tape of Professor Levy.
28:20	Barbara (Cliff's sister) tells of "date."
32:20	Conversation between Judah and Jack.
38:30	Delores calls, threatening to come over.
40:50	Imagined conversation with Ben.
43:00	Judah calls Jack.
44:45	Second taped interview with Levy.

49:50	Hit man parks car.
52:35	**Jack** (to Judah): It's over and done with.
56:40	Judah goes back to Delores's apartment.
58:15	Judah has flashback.
65:00	Conversation between Cliff and Jenny.
66:30	Second conversation between Judah and Ben.
68:50	Judah visits his old family home.
69:50	Flashback to Passover seder.
75:00	Professor Levy committed suicide—tape of Levy talking. Halley arrives and she and Cliff discuss Levy's suicide.
75:40	Levy's third taped interview.
78:20	Judah interviewed by police officer.
80:00	Judah tells Jack he can't stand it anymore—he wants to confess.
86:40	"Four months later" flashes on screen. Wedding reception for Ben's daughter.
88:20	Judah is feeling chipper.
89:00	Halley and Lester engaged.
91:20	Halley and Cliff talk.
93:30	Judah and Cliff talk.
99:30	Voice-over of Professor Levy.
100:45	Credits roll.

Gattaca (total running time: 107 minutes)

In order to distinguish the character played by Ethan Hawke from the character played by Jude Law, I am calling the former "Vincent" and the latter "Jerome."

Minute
Mark   *Story Item*

0:00	Credits begin (Columbia logo). Vincent prepares himself under credits.
4:20	"Not too distant future" flashes on screen. Vincent arrives at Gattaca, followed by Irene.
5:30	**Supervisor** (to Vincent): You leave in a week.
6:45	Vincent gives urine sample.
8:30	Vincent tells his true story and explains role genetic information plays in society.
9:40	Vincent is born. His story told in voice-over.
17:40	Anton nearly dies in swimming challenge.
	Vincent leaves home, gets job as janitor at Gattaca.

22:30	Vincent arranges for switch in identity. Jerome's story is told.
24:20	Jerome and Vincent meet. Jerome is in wheelchair.
29:40	Jerome and Vincent watch rocket take off.
31:30	Jerome's urine sample passes the test.
34:00	Mission director found murdered.
36:00	Jerome and Vincent discuss the murder and Vincent's mission.
37:00	Jerome and Vincent go out to celebrate.
37:50	Irene gives Vincent's (actually Jerome's) hair to sequencing service.
39:00	Jerome and Vincent discuss Jerome's plans.
42:10	Jerome admits "accident" was intentional.
42:40	Vincent's picture comes up in crime lab.
43:40	Vincent gets recording of Jerome's heart and uses it on treadmill.
44:30	Police discuss identity of murder suspect (Vincent).
47:50	Vincent breaks off treadmill test.
48:10	Policeman questions Irene.
48:50	Vincent and Irene talk.
52:20	Vincent tells Jerome he is murder suspect—wants to quit; Jerome talks him out of it.
55:40	Irene and Vincent go to piano recital. Afterward, they are stopped at checkpoint.
64:20	Police identify murder suspect again, using cup.
66:30	Vincent passes blood test.
68:30	Jerome stocking up on samples.
69:00	Vincent and Irene on date, cut short as police do sweep of club.
74:00	Irene and Vincent have sex.
76:00	Irene and Vincent talk the next morning.
79:20	Vincent phones Jerome to warn him.
81:30	Policeman and Irene enter Jerome's apartment; Jerome pretends to know Irene.
83:30	Policeman takes blood sample from Jerome.
85:00	Just after policeman leaves, Vincent appears.
87:00	Policemen find true culprit, who, according to his genetic profile, "didn't have a violent bone in his body."
88:30	Vincent meets policeman—it is his brother, Anton.
90:40	Anton and Vincent go swimming. Again, Vincent saves Anton.
95:00	Vincent back with Irene.
96:30	Jerome shows Vincent stash of samples.
97:30	Vincent back at Gattaca. Surprise urine test.
99:00	Vincent's mission intercut with Jerome's suicide.
102:40	Credits roll.

The Seventh Seal (total running time: 96 minutes)

Minute Mark	Story Item
0:00	Credits begin (Svensk Filmindustri logo).
1:20	Opening scene along beach (voice-over from Book of Revelation).
2:00	Knight is asleep on beach next to chess board.
3:40	Death appears.
5:00	Knight and Death begin playing chess.
7:20	Knight and Jöns come upon dead man.
10:10	Jof has vision of Mary and baby Jesus.
16:00	Jöns and Knight arrive at church, where Jöns has conversation with painter.
18:30	Knight prays before the crucifix.
19:00	Knight goes over to confessional booth—conversation with Death.
23:30	Jöns and the painter in the church drink and talk.
25:20	Knight and Jöns pass by Tyan the witch, who has been put in the stocks.
27:20	Knight and Jöns come upon cluster of farm buildings.
30:45	Jöns saves young woman and threatens Raval.
32:00	Young woman follows Jöns.
32:10	Jof, Mia, and Skat perform.
36:30	Flagellants pass through the town.
38:00	One among group (monk) gives speech reproaching those present.
42:40	Jof is eating at a tavern.
46:50	Raval and Plog force Jof to dance like a bear.
48:20	Jöns cuts Raval's face.
48:40	Knight joins Mia and Michael.
50:15	Jof joins Mia and Knight.
53:00	Mia offers Knight a simple meal.
55:15	Knight explains to Mia why he is so solemn.
57:00	Death reappears; he and Knight resume chess game.
58:30	Jöns and Plog talk. Plog decides to join them.
61:40	The group heads off into the forest.
62:20	They come across Skat and Lisa (Plog's wife).
66:20	Skat pretends to kill himself.
69:20	Death kills him for real.
70:45	Cart taking Tyan the witch to execution area gets stuck in stream.
72:15	They all arrive at execution area.
73:00	Knight and Tyan talk.
75:00	Knight sees that Death is the monk escorting Tyan.

75:10	Tyan is tied to the stake and hoisted onto nearby tree.
76:50	Conversation between Knight and Jöns on Tyan, as she looks terrified.
79:40	Raval, now dying of the plague, asks for help.
81:40	Jof sees Knight and Death playing chess.
83:10	Knight pretends to knock over chess pieces as Jof and Mia escape.
84:00	Checkmate.
86:00	The group arrives at Knight's castle.
87:15	They are greeting by Karin, the Knight's wife.
89:20	As they eat, Karin reads from the Book of Revelation.
91:00	Death has entered room. They all introduce themselves.
92:20	Knight tries to pray, Jöns reproaches him.
94:30	Jof describes the Dance of Death.
95:50	End.

The Rapture (total running time: 100 minutes)

Minute Mark	Story Item
0:00	Fineline logo. Title appears.
1:00	A room with telephone operators.
3:55	Sharon and Vic out cruising.
5:00	Sharon and Vic join other couple (including Randy).
6:15	The foursome go back to Vic's.
9:15	Sharon back at work.
10:00	During break, Sharon overhears colleagues.
10:55	Sharon in bed with Randy, who tells of his past.
13:45	**Sharon:** Everything just seems so empty. **Randy:** I think you're depressed and I think you should see a therapist.
14:35	Mormon-like evangelists appear at Sharon's door.
18:30	Another foursome date, this time with the tattoo woman.
20:10	Sharon very uninterested in sex with her partner, more interesting in hearing about significance of tattoo.
22:10	Sharon tries to talk to colleagues about dreams; becomes defensive.
23:20	Sharon arrives back at her apartment to find Vic and another woman.
23:40	**Sharon** (making Randy get up): This bed is unclean. . . . There is a God and I'll meet him. . . . I want my salvation. Sharon and Randy have conversation about God.
28:20	**Sharon** (telling Randy to leave): There's got to be something more. . . . I'm tired of the emptiness in my life. Randy leaves.

30:00	**Sharon** (praying): Please help me. God, I'm lost.
30:35	Sharon picks up talkative hitchhiker from Vermont (Tommy).
33:00	Sharon and Tommy go to motel room. Sharon takes his gun.
34:30	Sharon tries to kill herself, but is unable.
35:50	Sharon has dream about the pearl.
36:50	Vic appears. Sharon tells him about her new religion.
40:20	**Sharon** (back at work): Have you met Jesus?
41:00	Sharon called into supervisor's office.
44:20	Sharon goes to church service.
45:45	Sharon visits Randy in workshop.
47:30	"Six years later" flashes on screen. Randy, Sharon, and Mary at church.
48:10	**Boy:** The end is coming soon—this year.
49:20	Sharon and sister (Paula) have conversation at pool.
50:10	Randy fires employee.
51:50	Disgruntled employee returns, kills Randy.
53:00	The funeral. Paula says that at times like this she would find faith a comfort.
55:40	Sharon sees "sign"—the photos.
56:00	Sharon back at church—asks about significance of "sign."
	Boy: Don't ask God to meet you halfway.
56:30	Sharon and Paula talk—Paula gives Sharon a gun.
59:15	Sharon and Mary arrive in desert.
62:50	Car alarm goes off—Mary starts to complain: "I want to die."
	Sharon suggests they give God one more chance.
65:00	Policeman (Foster) arrives—they've been in desert waiting two weeks.
70:00	Mary asks again to die.
	Sharon: Let's give God one more chance.
70:30	Foster stops by at night.
72:10	**Mary** (in nightmare, screaming): Don't make God meet you half way.
	Mary says in dream she was in heaven and Sharon was, "sort of."
73:25	Sharon steals food at drive-thru restaurant.
76:50	Sharon shoots Mary. Tries to shoot self, but is unable.
78:00	Sharon is being chased by the horseman as she drives in her car. Foster pulls her over.
80:50	Sharon tells Foster she killed Mary.
	Sharon: He [God] let me kill my little girl and He expects me to love Him?
84:45	Sharon put in same jail cell as tattoo woman.
	Sharon: Who forgives God?
86:30	Mary (and two others) appear to Sharon at jail.
87:30	The rapture begins.
89:30	Jail is emptied; Sharon leaves with Foster.

93:00	Sharon and Foster arrive at entrance to heaven; Mary greets them.
94:00	Foster goes to heaven.
	Sharon: Why should I thank Him for a life with so much suffering?
	Sharon refuses. Heaven becomes visible. Mary pleads one last time.
96:00	Mary disappears; Sharon is left alone.
96:40	Credits roll.

Leaving Las Vegas (total running time: 111 minutes)

Minute Mark	*Story Item*
0:00	Credits begin (United Artists logo).
0:50	Ben fills up shopping cart with liquor.
1:50	Ben interrupts friend (Peter) at restaurant.
3:20	Ben borrows money from Peter.
3:45	Ben at bar with woman.
6:50	Ben at strip joint.
7:45	Ben picks up hooker.
9:00	Ben wakes up next morning on floor.
9:30	Ben notices wedding ring is gone.
9:40	Ben unable to sign check at bank.
10:30	Ben at bar. Bartender gives advice.
11:50	Ben back at bank.
14:50	Ben gets fired from job.
15:30	Ben announces intention to move to Las Vegas.
16:00	Juri introduces himself and Sera to customers.
18:50	Sera talking to off-camera therapist. She describes herself as a "service."
19:30	Sera and Juri eating. Sera obviously uncomfortable.
20:10	Juri and Sera have sex.
20:35	Ben buying supplies and setting fire to/throwing out possessions.
21:25	Ben sets off for Las Vegas.
23:00	Arrival in Las Vegas.
23:15	Ben nearly runs over Sera.
24:00	Ben checks into Whole Year Inn (Hole You're In).
24:50	Sera describes bad trick to therapist.
26:40	Ben picks up Sera.
28:15	They arrive at Ben's motel room.
32:00	**Sera:** So, Ben, . . . what brings you to Las Vegas?
	Ben: I came here to drink myself to death.

Sera: How long's it gonna take to drink yourself to death?

Ben: Oh, I don't know. About four weeks.

34:20   **Sera:** There'll always be bad times, but my life's good. It's like I want it to be.

34:40   Sera arrives back at her place that morning.

35:00   Sera gives money to Juri, who is mad at the small amount.

36:30   Sera talks to therapist about Juri.

37:20   Juri at pawn shop, trying to sell jewelry.

37:50   Ben sells watch.

38:10   Sera tries to pick up conventioneer.

39:50   Sera tells therapist about Ben and her strange attraction to him.

40:45   Sera meets up with Ben on street.

41:30   Ben asks Sera out for dinner. Sera declines then leaves.

42:40   Sera arrives at Juri's room—he is paranoid. She gives him money, then he tells her to leave and never come back.

45:00   Hit men arrive just after Sera leaves.

45:20   Sera knocks at Ben's motel door, invites him to dinner.

46:00   Ben and Sera at restaurant.

47:20   **Sera:** Why are you killing yourself?

Ben: I don't remember.

48:30   Sera invites Ben to stay at her apartment.

50:30   Sera at therapist talking about Ben.

51:50   Sera suggests Ben move in permanently.

53:50   Ben accepts, but only on condition Sera never ask him to stop drinking.

54:30   Ben packs up his stuff from motel.

55:10   Sera arrives at her apartment building to find Ben passed out in front.

60:00   Sera presents Ben with flask as gift.

61:00   Ben and Sera go to casino.

62:50   Ben goes berserk.

66:50   **Sera:** I'm just using you. I need you.

68:00   Ben at bar. Has run-in involving bitter couple.

72:00   Ben and Sera go out shopping. Ben gives her earrings.

76:20   Motel in desert.

80:50   Ben breaks table. They get kicked out.

83:00   Back in Las Vegas.

85:20   Sera renegs on earlier agreement.

Sera: I want you to see a doctor.

Ben: Maybe it's time I moved to a motel.

Sera: And do what? Rot away in a room?

87:20   Sera goes to work. Ben goes to casino.

88:45	Sera returns to find Ben with prostitute.
90:00	Sera kicks Ben out.
91:00	Sera is picked up by three football players.
95:50	Sera gets evicted.
97:20	Sera tries to locate Ben.
99:50	Sera gets call from Ben.
100:30	Sera arrives at Ben's room.
103:40	Sera mounts Ben.
105:40	Ben dies.
106:00	Voice-over as Sera talks to therapist.
107:30	Credits roll.

Index